MAKE THE SHIFT

ADJUSTING OUR HEARTS TO RECEIVE GOD'S BEST

Torn Curtain Publishing
Wellington, New Zealand
www.torncurtainpublishing.com

ISBN Softcover (Premium) 978-0-473-55569-6
ISBN Softcover (Standard) 978-0-473-55218-3

All text in bold or in parentheses are the author's own.

Cover and internal design by Ella Paramore
Photographs © Copyright 2021 Ella Paramore. Used by permission.

Cataloguing in Publishing Data
Title: Make the Shift
Author: Helen Monk
Subjects: Devotions, Christian life, Spirituality

A copy of this title is held at the National Library of New Zealand.

author's note

This book gives expression to heart adjustments I personally have made in response to the prompting of the Holy Spirit, enabling me to position myself to more fully apprehend and understand the love of God toward me. This 'devotional' testifies strongly to the power of the Word of God in this process, to lead, guide and transform. As Psalm18:28 (TPT) declares,

"God, all at once You turned on a floodlight for me! You are the revelation-light in my darkness, and in Your brightness I can see the path ahead."

I would like to firstly express my gratitude to God for His gracious work in my life, being eternally thankful for the 'shifts' in the deepest spaces of my heart. Thanks also to my beloved husband, Bruce, who has always fully believed in me and championed me to be all God has called me to be; to our beautiful granddaughter, Ella Paramore, who has lovingly devoted many long hours to make this Classic version of the devotional 'come alive,' the illustrations paying tribute to precious memories shared as a family over the years. There is a richness and blessing in family God has ordained which Bruce and I wholeheartedly love and enjoy. So, to our family we express our gratitude to God for each one of you for being who you are, doing what you do and for bringing great joy into our lives. Praying God's richest blessings over you, Rebecca, Ella, Jamin, Elijah and Levi, Hamish, Nicola, Theo, Chloe and Callum, Samuel, Kathy, Mikayla, Ruby and Sophia, James, Olivia, Joel and Greer, as you and generations to come read the pages of this book.

Thanks also to my publisher, Anya McKee, who has kindly and skilfully guided the whole process of bringing this book to completion.

Thank you all.

anya mckee

Every now and then God brings someone alongside to impart strength, offer wisdom and call us higher in our walk with God. Helen Monk is such a woman. These heart-warming devotions are a gift to our generation; they are the accumulation of decades of faith-filled living, of breaking ground for the Kingdom, and of deep personal intimacy with God.

It has been an immense privilege to work with Ps. Helen on the publication of this book. I firmly believe her words have the power to transform us at the deepest level of our being and will equip us to partner with God for breakthrough in our families, communities and nations.

Most significantly, these devotions encourage and empower us to lift our gaze beyond this world—to step with confidence into the fullness of our authority and gifting in Christ. Whether you are young in the faith or have walked the journey for many years, 'Make the Shift' is a book that will enrich your discipleship journey and take you further into spiritual maturity. Be blessed as you read!

Anya McKee
Torn Curtain Publishing

ella paramore

Ever since I was a little girl, my "Mammie" has been my hero. My favourite colour was yellow, just like her. I dreamed of traveling to faraway places, just like her. My fashion icon was (and still is) her!

After 24 years of watching the beautiful life my grandmother leads, I still want to be just like her. I want to learn to love others as hard as she does and be as kind and hospitable as she is. I want to be bold and confident as I learn to walk in alignment with God's calling on my life, just as she does. I want to be as strong, spiritually sharp and full of faith as she is.

My grandmother carries herself with a grace that extends into all aspects of her existence. She is bold, fearless and confident in who she is and what she's called to do while being one of the most loving, generous and merciful people you'll ever meet.

She doesn't just have grace but grit too. She's not afraid to roll up her sleeves and get amongst the action. She lives a fuller life than many, has an enviable amount of energy and an incredible capacity to love and serve others.

To live in her legacy is an honour I never want to take for granted. I am overwhelmingly grateful for my Mammie and the role she plays in my life - not just as a loving grandma but as a mentor and dear friend.

It has been an absolute honour to compile the images for this book. Embedded in these pages are family memories and visual depictions of the analogies my grandma brilliantly uses to communicate biblical concepts. I know you'll be blessed by the wisdom and life lessons in this book.

Ella Paramore
Helen's Grandaughter

6

Contents

part one:

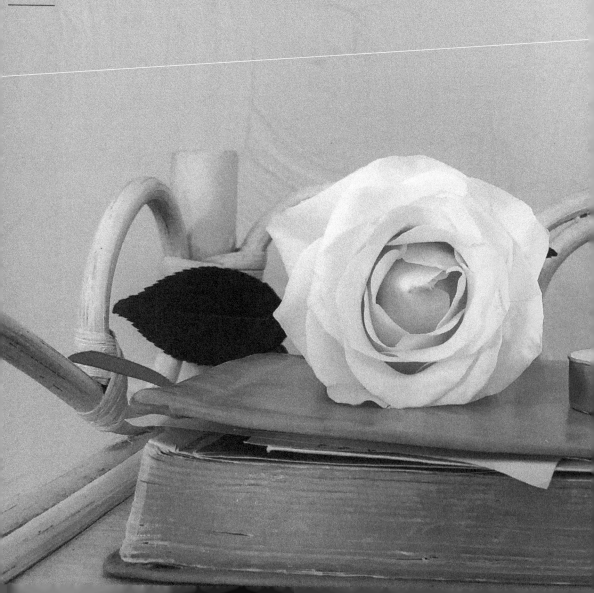

peace

the gift of peace

*And suddenly there was with the angel a multitude of the
heavenly host praising God and saying, "Glory to God in the
highest. And on earth, peace, goodwill toward man."*
Matthew 2:13

The world is crying out for peace—we see this desire expressed globally in peace marches, peace protests and legislation. Ironically, many who begin passionately about seeking peace for a cause turn bitter in the battle, with anger embedded in their spirit and strain etched upon their faces. Human battles never result in godly peace!

Where are we looking today for our peace? People think of peace as a place of escape, such as a holiday—which may at times prove to be helpful! Certainly no one is going to object to a week's rest on a tropical island with no responsibility except to enjoy the sea, the sand and the food! But do you know, we could even be in such a place of beauty and relaxation and still not have the peace that we are searching for? Internally, we could still be anxious about situations, relationships, finances and health; fearful of scenarios, potential outcomes and reactions. These scenes could still be playing out in our minds even in the most tranquil of settings!

For others, peace may be the absence of noise—when the TV is turned off, bringing instant relief from the sound of a program that has dominated the lounge space, or when smaller children are in bed and have finally fallen asleep, giving parents some emotional and mental space. We may be able to quieten atmospheres naturally, yet even then we can find ourselves unable to quieten the inner conversations of guilt, fear and condemnation.

Where do we find peace then? For believers, peace is the presence of a Person—Jesus! God has given us the gift of peace in His Son, Jesus, who is able, through His death on the cross, to take from us every weight, anxiety and condemnation.

> For unto us a Child is born, unto us a Son is given;
> And the government will be upon His shoulder. And His
> name will be called Wonderful, Counsellor, Mighty God,
> Everlasting Father, **Prince of Peace**. And of the increase of
> His government and **peace** there will be no end.
> Isaiah 9:6-7

What a promise! When we receive Jesus and His gift of salvation, we welcome Him to set up His rule in our hearts as the Prince of Peace. This is something the world cannot offer! This is beyond an 'earthly peace'— it is what the Bible calls a peace that "surpasses all understanding" (Philippians 4:7). Jesus responds to our surrender by taking the government of our lives upon His shoulders, protecting, guiding, reassuring and releasing us from all destructive pressure that could steal our joy and peace. Know Jesus, know peace!

Is it time to let God take over—to welcome Jesus, the Gift of Peace, into the space of your heart and life? Today, fully place your affairs in Jesus' hands through prayer and thanksgiving. If you do not place your concerns in God's hands, then whose hands do they remain in? Today, welcome God's peace as you surrender your life afresh to Him!

the greeting of peace

*The same day at evening, being the first day of the week, when the doors were shut where the disciples were assembled for fear of the Jews, Jesus came and stood in the midst and said to them, **"Peace be with you."** When He had said this, He showed them His hands and His side. Then the disciples were glad when they saw the Lord.*
John 20:19-20

Jesus addressed the disciples with a greeting of peace! The disciples were in 'lock down.' They had walked openly with Jesus, witnessed His miracles and seen His great power, but now they were hiding from the Jews. Fear filled their hearts following the crucifixion of their beloved Jesus, leaving them wondering if they, as His followers, would become the next victims. The future was looking pretty grim!

Do we go into 'lock down' from time to time? When God's promises seem slow in coming according to the timeframe we have set, or when outcomes seem contrary to what we have believed, do we retreat into a state of 'lock down,' hiding to protect ourselves from the fear of future disappointment? Have we become hard for Jesus to reach?

Notice that Jesus did not just greet His disciples once—He continued to greet the disciples! He needed to repeat His greeting of peace, as they had failed to comprehend the magnitude and full effect of His resurrection because of the overwhelming fear in their heart.

*Jesus said to them again, **"Peace to you.** As the Father has sent Me, I also send you." And when He said this, He breathed on them and said to them "Receive the Holy Spirit."*
John 20:21,22

Jesus was reassuring the disciples that He had succeeded in His mission and was now sending them forth to bring peace to a troubled world, to troubled hearts, to troubled minds and to troubled circumstances. They were to be His answer to the world's cry for peace, and they needed His presence with them to impart peace to others. He breathed on them!

Where are you today? Living free, or in lockdown? Are you 'locked down' by the fear of potential mishaps, danger or persecution? Have you placed walls of protection around your heart, and in doing so, become hard for

Jesus to reach? Today Jesus wants to reveal Himself to you again; to greet you with the peace that only He can impart.

Could it be that you have only viewed Jesus through the anguish of the crucifixion and not through the glory of the resurrection and the wonderful victory that resulted? Maybe you are fearing something that Jesus has already overcome for you? Today Jesus wants to interrupt you, reassure you, restore peace in your heart, and breathe His Holy Spirit on you. Jesus is able to reach you wherever you are! Just like He broke through the natural wall that day to reach the disciples, He can break through any wall in your heart to release you from any fear or apprehension, filling you instead with boldness and courage!

Today, receive Jesus's greeting: **Peace be with you.** *Receive His empowerment, the breath of the Holy Spirit. Today bring a greeting of peace wherever you go, reaching through walls and barriers to bring the gospel of peace to hurting and anxious hearts.*

in the storm

God is our refuge and strength, a very present help in trouble. Therefore, we will not fear even though the earth be removed, and though the mountains be carried into the midst of the sea; though its waters roar and be troubled, though the mountains shake with its swelling.
Psalm 46:1-3

Life is not always as the saying suggests, 'a bed of roses.' As well as being great and exciting, life can also be challenging, and at times, terrifying, as unpleasant and unexplainable situations arise. Nature, with all its beauty, has the ability to change from a state of tranquillity into a fierce storm in a moment, leaving us reeling and overwhelmed. The worst storms are the ones we didn't anticipate and had no time to prepare for; if we had known in advance a storm was pending, we may have had time to build shelters, batten down hatches, collect supplies, or even evacuate the danger area!

Just as the elements of nature can rise with fury and cause devastation by their sheer force, so our wellbeing can be suddenly threatened by relational storms, financial storms, health storms and other storms of life that lift their head in an unpleasant and unwelcome manner. These sudden, unexpected storms have the potential to knock us off balance and make us feel like a small cork being tossed around in a heaving ocean, a vast and relentless sea!

At the end of Psalm 46, the writer exhorts us, saying, "Be still, and know that I am God; I will be exalted among the nations, I will be exalted in the earth" (v. 10). God always has the last say, and His authority *will* triumph in and over the storms. His word and His ways will calm every dispute, annul any danger and silence any opposing force.

The last say! Are you the person, in the argument with another, who always has to have the last say? Could you be the person who is the loudest and talks the fastest? Maybe you even enter into similar arguments with God, reserving the right to make your own decisions, closing down dialogue because you insist on having everything your own way. In relationships, that force of opinion often leaves others reeling, like they have been battered by a huge wave and have no voice in the situation. In the storms of life, we need to quieten down and hear God's voice, knowing that He is in control and He will bring resolution to the storm.

What does stillness look like? It is taking time to breathe, to quiet the panic and irrational thoughts within, and transfer trust to the One who holds all things in His hand—even the earthly elements. We cannot be ignorant of the wind and the torrential rain, the rising water levels, the earthquakes, and the sheer noise of life's storms, but we *can* shift our focus to God, our strength, our shelter and our very present help in trouble, the One who has all authority and *the ultimate say* in every situation. In the natural, the storm has the authority and the potential to destroy everything in its wake. But in the spirit realm, God has the authority to quieten and calm the storm. The key is to 'be still and know' who He is and the authority He holds!

What is God speaking to us in our storm? There is no need to fear when He is in control! But that is a decision we need to make. Will we trust Him, or attempt to battle the storm ourselves? Unsettledness and angst are things we can feel when life seems to be in turmoil. As we exalt God, however, He is able to speak into our situation. In a dilemma I once faced, I heard God clearly speak to me, exhorting me to let go of any related anxiety. He simply said, "Watch me, Helen. Watch how I do it." God wants to show His power in complex situations, and we just need to be the ones who observe and witness significant shifts in circumstances.

Are you in the midst of a storm which has raised its voice in a threatening manner? Remember that God has the ultimate authority over every storm of life. He will have the last say! Transfer your trust to Him today, and experience His supernatural peace as He intervenes on your behalf.

the protection of peace

*Be anxious for nothing, but in everything by prayer and supplication, with thanksgiving, let your requests be made known to God; and the **peace of God,** which surpasses all understanding, will **guard** your hearts and minds through Christ Jesus.*
Philippians 4:6-7

Peace is an inner settledness that comes from a strong conviction of what is right and essential for life and health, establishing a platform of internal security from which one can operate. Many adverse situations may come in life to unsettle and challenge us, but the peace of God within will hold us, keeping us steady, internally free, and operating with soundness of mind.

Peace protects us. Have you ever seen the guards at London's Buckingham Palace? These sentries stand guard day and night, protecting the monarch and the royal household from intruders that may attempt to threaten their peace and safety. These guards stand at attention, perfectly still for the majority of their shift, not flinching, not distracted, but with their eyes trained and focused ahead. Likewise, the peace of God stands as a guard at the door of our heart, at attention, eyes trained to detect any disturbance or negative advance. God's peace standing tall in our heart makes us feel safe! Just as the guards at Buckingham Palace blow a whistle to alert a highly-qualified security team to apprehend any trespassers, God's peace, like an internal guard, will blow the whistle to warn us of any contrary advance of the enemy.

Peace protects us by setting up a *covering* over our life, a standard under which we can express ourselves freely and without fear. Have you ever wondered why some environments feel more peaceful than others? Maybe it's because *peace* has intentionally been stationed as a guard over that environment through powerful prayer and intercession. It's like an 'umbrella of peace' has been raised that releases a liberty in the Spirit of God.

Peace pays a price. Jesus paid a huge price on the Cross for our salvation and freedom from sin, and at times we need to contend for the peace Jesus purchased for us! Could there be anything disturbing our peace, our household, our workplace or our communities that we need to call time on? Where may we need to reinstate the authority of *peace* as captain over our affairs?

In the Old Testament, we read of a man who took action against the disruption of peace over Israel, dealing with those who had brought a curse on the nation through their sinful ways. Phinehas made a stand for righteousness, put a javelin through the perpetrators, and stopped a plague which had already killed twenty-four thousand people.

In Numbers 25: 10-13 we read,

> *Then the Lord spoke to Moses, saying; "Phinehas the son of Eleazar the son of Aaron the priest, has turned back My wrath from the children of Israel, because he was zealous . . . so that I did not consume the children of Israel in My zeal. Therefore say, 'Behold I give him my* **covenant of peace**; *and it shall be to him and his descendants after him a covenant of an everlasting priesthood, because he was zealous for his God and made atonement (covering) for the children of Israel.'"*

Phinehas received commendation from God, and was granted *His covenant of peace.* When we take responsibility for the welfare and well-being of others, we too can reverse any curse through authoritative prayer, reinstating God's peace. Perhaps there are some 'set prayers' we could station as guards to protect the peace and atmosphere of our dwelling.

What worry or anxiety has infiltrated your heart and robbed you of your peace? Have you stationed peace as a guard over your heart, listening to the alerts and warnings of the Holy Spirit? Set up a covering today, an umbrella of peace over your environments to safeguard freedom for you and for those you love. Then enjoy the peace of God that protects you, covers you and keeps you safe!

sweep the house

*Or what woman, having ten silver coins, if she loses one coin,
does not light a lamp, **sweep the house**, and search carefully
until she finds it? And when she has found it, she calls her
friends and neighbors together, saying, "Rejoice with me,
for I have found the piece, which I lost!"*
Luke 15:8-9

I am sure everyone has experienced the feeling of relief that comes once the house is swept, the carpet vacuumed and anything lying on the floor put away in its rightful place. It's quite satisfying, as we look forward to enjoying a space of uninterrupted peace for the duration the orderliness exists! In the book of Luke, Jesus tells His disciples three parables relating to lost things. One of these is the parable of a woman who had ten coins. Having lost one of them, she engages in a full-on search for her missing coin. It mattered to her that she retained the complete set in her possession.

We too, need to go searching for the things that matter, the things which may have gone missing or even been stolen from us! Scripture tells us that the enemy comes only to "steal, kill and destroy" (John 10:10). Sometimes we have just accepted our lot, resigning ourselves to the loss instead of mounting a 'full-on search' to recover the missing items! The enemy is after our peace, which is the supernatural, stabilising quality Jesus brings to our lives; the "peace that passes all understanding" (Philippians 4:7). This is a peace that really shouldn't exist in some given situations, but is present because of the grace of God. Without God's peace in our heart, anxiety could potentially overwhelm us, blinding us to the ability we have in God to recover what has been taken!

On a personal level, the presence of God's peace in my life is of extremely high value! It matters to me, and when peace is lost, I mount a 'full-on search' and *sweep the house of my heart!*

Has anxiety replaced your peace, or negativity replaced the faith which generates peace? In the natural, we have all experienced turning our house 'upside down' to find something important that has gone missing— the car keys, or maybe wedding rings? To find these articles, there is a need to retrace our footsteps, going over territory where they may have slipped out of our hands. In a similar manner, we need to retrace our *thoughts* until we find the point where our inner peace was lost, asking ourselves the questions: *What concerns have I been thinking about? What lies of the enemy have I been entertaining? What criticism have I sunk under? What heavy situation have I personally taken on board?* Like the lady who lit a lamp to search all the dark corners of her house, we need to hold up the Word of God to enlighten the darkness and reveal where the missing item is, so we can fully reclaim what is rightfully ours.

On one occasion, when I realised peace had slipped from my heart because many things in my life were changing all at once, I recovered peace once again by holding up the lamp of God's word, and sweeping anxiety and uncertainty from the corners of my heart. The scripture that God used for me to locate peace again was Hebrews 13:8, "Jesus Christ is the same yesterday, today and forever." The truth was, though things may have been changing all around me (which is the nature of the world we live in), the one thing that remained constant was *Jesus,* and He is the Truth! You see, peace is directly linked to truth! No wonder the Word of God tells us that the "truth will set us free" (John 8:32). We may have lost peace in a moment, or perhaps our peace has been eroding over a period of time and we have only just noticed? Friend, don't live without God's peace in your heart; it matters and is of extreme value to your wellbeing!

 *Have you lost peace? Has that 'completeness' in Christ slipped from your possession? Today, retrace your thoughts. Has your mind wandered toward anxiety and loss? What is out of place in your heart? Sweep the house of your heart and mind today and recover God's abiding peace by holding up the Word of God. Experience the joy that comes with finding what was missing. Find Jesus, find peace!*

part two:

mission

the mission dream

*Prepare your outside work, make it fit for yourself
in the field; and afterward build your house.*
Proverbs 24:27

God has placed a dream in all of our hearts to live a much bigger, more meaningful life than just the life we see. He awakens our hearts to *mission*, revealing possibilities of different and better futures by writing scripts on our hearts, giving us a general sense of direction, prompting us internally to take action externally!

Many people intuitively know the script for their life at the time of their salvation. My husband, Bruce, for example, knew from the moment of his conversion that God had designed him as a church-planter, a master-builder, and he stepped immediately into fulfilling that assignment. My own *mission-dream* unfolded more gradually as I personally experienced Christ's love and deliverance and a passion awakened within me for others to experience the same freedom. You see, we all dream of making a difference, but we apprehend our own particular 'God-dream' in different ways. Many of us have a clear picture from the start, while for others, the revelation of their mission dawns clearer over time.

When we begin to recognise and identify God's bigger picture, or 'mission,' for our lives, this proverb encourages us to prepare for it by prioritising accordingly. *What comes first?* We can so want our own 'house' and our own lives to be firmly established before even considering mission; however, in focusing too much attention on our own needs and desires (and perhaps even our own apprehensions), we can delay and even indefinitely forfeit the satisfaction of fulfilling the amazing purpose God has designed for our life. When we prioritise God's mission, however, He is faithful to build our house as well—as a result of our eternal investment.

*Jesus said to them, "My food is to do the will of
Him who sent Me and to finish His work."*
John 4:34

It was doing God's will that kept Jesus sustained, on course, on mission and triumphant as He went about the task of accomplishing God's purpose to save and reconcile mankind to Himself.

What can ruin the mission-dream? Becoming focused primarily on our own needs! So let's not make ourselves the mission. Let's not allow *self* to take the platform by demanding its own way and in doing so, deny ourselves the satisfaction of God's best. Sure, self-help programs have their place and can benefit us, but they also can become self-defeating when they become the driving focus in our life. It is the will of God, outworked in our life, that will ultimately help us as His people to be better, do better, get better and feel better—and to glorify God in the process.

All of us want to 'make it' in our life, our marriage and relationships, and in our career. Who wouldn't? In every Christian, God has placed the potential to 'make it' as we follow the mission-dream He has placed in our heart. That's why 'making it' is ultimately fulfilling the will of God for our life!

Can you recognise any area of dissatisfaction—a place where you may be missing God's mark for your life? Take the time to identify where in life you desire to make a difference. Thank God today for the mission-dream He has placed in your heart, and begin making preparations to prioritise that mission. Then, watch as God helps you make it!

pure delight

I delight to do Your will, O my God,
and Your law is within my heart.
Psalm 40:8

Like the Psalmist, we are all 'on mission' to fulfil the will of God. In the heart of every born-again Christian is a deep desire to be pleasing and fruitful for the glory of God. But although our hearts may be stirred in moments of conviction, it takes a lifetime to continuously and steadfastly outwork God's will in our lives.

When we hear the word 'mission' it may provoke either positive or negative feelings within. To some people, mission represents privilege, opportunity and service, while to others it may conjure up thoughts of hardship and enormous personal cost.

Have you ever described an event in your day as 'a mission'? Maybe you lost the car keys, ended up being late for an important event or left your purchase at the shop, wasting valuable time and energy. Maybe a crucial part was missing when you were trying to assemble an object. Whatever it was, the day just seemed more difficult and wearisome than normal, sapping the life out of you. In others words, it was just plain frustrating!

Sometimes we can project that sort of negativity and expectation onto God's mission! *What if it saps our energy and drains our resources?*

But nothing could be further from the truth! Yes, it's true that the word 'mission' means "an assignment or commission, an expedition, errand, undertaking, operation, pursuit, aim or quest." There can be no conquest without a quest. A struggle. A battle. We need to fight for the will of God to be paramount in our lives, not allowing it to become subservient to our own selfish or fearful thinking. We are called as God's agents to fight for freedom and make a mark on this world for eternity.

God's mission will require effort, perseverance and sometimes just plain hard work! There will be times of frustration as our faith grapples with contradictions, delays and obstacles. And yet, God's will remains the most satisfying, *heart-delighting,* spirit-energising activity we could ever be involved in as we experience His presence with us, His pleasure toward us and His supernatural power, enabling us to bring heaven to earth.

Living on-mission comes with a cost, the cost of our own will as we surrender to the unfolding will of God in our lives. But who wouldn't want our limited perspective and ability to be superseded by the amazing and outstanding will of God? It will literally 'out-do' and 'out-stand' all human endeavours!

The way we approach God's mission will determine whether we are *empowered* or *disempowered* in our service to God. So how are we going to view God's mission? Through our own natural resources or lack thereof, or through the eyes of faith, focused on God, knowing He will fully back us and resource us on mission?

Where may you need to adjust your thinking or your approach to God's mission? Take a moment today to identify the mission God has called you to be engaged in, and give thanks for God's empowerment and provision for the journey. Declare your delight in doing God's will today!

time to spring clean

Then the priests went into the inner part of the house of the Lord to
cleanse it, *and **brought out all the debris** that they found in the*
temple of the Lord to the court of the house of the Lord. And
the Levites took it out and carried it to the Brook Kidron.
2 Chronicles 29:16

Just as it is in the natural, so it is in the spiritual—we need to 'spring-clean' at times, to make space for new shoots of initiatives to sprout, to clear the way for mature plants of mission to develop even further. In the book of Second Chronicles, the children of Israel had just come through a winter season. During that time, the house of the Lord had fallen into disrepair as a result of neglect. But Hezekiah, the new king of Israel, anticipated the season ahead and began to repair, to 'spring-clean,' the house of God. He had a vision in his heart to restore true worship to Israel. But before that could come about, the rubbish that had accumulated within the temple had to be removed. The call of God was to *clean the house* so worship could be restored.

What had previous generations invited into the temple that had caused it to be in such disrepair? What was in the house that needed to be thrown out? Well, we read that prior to Hezekiah's reign, King Ahaz hadn't followed the ways of God; he didn't do what was right in the sight of God but had entertained idols and sacrificed to other gods. Ahaz not only decimated the house of God with his disobedience and idolatrous heart, he literally *shut the door,* destroying true worship.

So Ahaz gathered the articles of the house of God, cut in pieces
*the articles of the house of God, **shut up the doors** of the house of*
the Lord, and made for himself altars in every corner of Jerusalem.
2 Chronicles 28:24

As those who belong to God, we too need to rid our 'temple' of any residue from the past, any rubbish that resides in the corners of our thinking, any idolatry that perches in the rafters, before we can possibly hope to restore others. We need to face the challenge of what may need changing within, what may need to be removed, and what curse may be sitting in the darkness that needs reversing and evicting. What have we invited into the house of our life that now needs to be taken out and destroyed? Where has the door been opened to a curse from the enemy through wrong behaviour, fearful thinking, or perhaps through the curse of hereditary iniquities? True worship is restored when there is no competition for space in the room of our hearts and minds. It's time to 'clean the house.'

When I cleaned the 'inner house' of my heart from debris, one of the things I had to remove was the need for the 'approval of man.' I needed to make room instead to seek *God's* approval and His smile upon my life.

 What have you invited into your house that competes with the law of liberty you have in Christ? What rubbish from the past still occupies space in your heart and needs to be thrown out? Today, repent of any unbelief or disobedience, either through your own or your family's actions and receive the cleansing of the blood of Jesus. Clean the house of your heart so worship can be restored — true worship that releases the power of God and the anointing of His Holy Spirit in anticipation of the season to come.

time to connect

Then the runners went throughout all Israel and Judah with the letters from the kings and his leaders, and spoke according to the command of the king: "Children of Israel, return to the Lord God of Abraham, Isaac and Israel; then He will return to the remnant of you who have escaped from the hand of the kings of Assyria."
2 Chronicles 30:6

One of our most powerful needs as humans is to *connect*, firstly with God, and then with others. We are made for connection; to belong, to share, to strengthen and to motivate one another, especially toward the mission of serving Jesus!

Powerful connections flow from our relationship with God. When we personally experience and understand how greatly He loves, values and considers us, every other relationship is enhanced by the flow of God's love in and through our lives. And connection is linked to prosperity! As we do life well *together*, we achieve more! It was written of Hezekiah, one of the kings of Israel, that in all he did, and everything He purposed in God, he prospered! Why? Because he understood the importance of *connection*.

Because Hezekiah had a godly vision, the house of God was reopened, true worship was restored, and the people of Jerusalem and the surrounding nations of Israel were influenced for good. But it didn't end there. *Runners* went out with the good news of the reformation, appealing for God's people to return to Him.

When we make reforms in our lives, our testimony *connects others* to faith and into their own relationship with God. Good news is influential! It spreads and connects!

Connection releases a spirit of celebration. In 2 Chronicles 30:25-27 we read, "The whole assembly of Judah rejoiced . . . there was great joy in Jerusalem, for since the time of Solomon the son of David, king of Israel, there had been *nothing like this* in Jerusalem. Then the priests, the Levites, arose and blessed the people and their voice was heard; and their prayer came up to His holy dwelling place, to heaven." Worship released a celebration, an unprecedented outpouring of joy! When we collectively enter into worship and praise, a supernatural energy in the spirit is released toward the mission of Christ.

Connection releases resources. 2 Chronicles 31:5 says, "As soon as the commandment was circulated, the children of Israel brought in abundance the first fruits of grain and wine, oil and honey, and all of the produce of the field; and they brought in abundantly the tithe of everything." Hezekiah's reforms and his transparent mandate led to a release of resources as the people of God came together to give. You see, resources attach themselves to sincere mission. Godly vision always releases provision!

Connection releases courage and authority. In 2 Chronicles 31:1 we read, "Now when all this was finished, all Israel who were present went out to the cities of Judah and broke the sacred pillars in pieces, cut down the wooden images, and threw down the high places . . . until they had utterly destroyed them all." See how courageous God's people became when they united together around Hezekiah's reforms! The same is true for us. Our obedience to reform what has been damaged, to reinstate truth and engage in authentic worship will release courage when we connect with others.

Today, connect with God and experience the flow of His love and purpose for your life. Take action to reform what God highlights! Then, connect with others to share the good things God has done for you. Connect with the God-given prosperity ordained for you so your reach and influence can be greater. Celebrate in hope because mission has the power to transform communities!

seeing before believing

See, I have set the land before you; go in and possess the
land which the Lord swore to your fathers . . .
to give them and their descendants forever.
Deuteronomy 1:8

The statement, *'seeing before believing,'* may seem at odds with our general call as Christians to believe before we see. Certainly, Hebrews 11:1 tells us that faith is "the substance of things hoped for, the evidence of things *not seen."* Both perspectives exhibit the faith that pleases God; however, in the realm of the Spirit, seeing helps our believing! In scripture, people are encouraged to *see* the victory in their spirit before they experience it. We read in Deuteronomy 1:8, "*See,* I have set the land before you; go in and possess the land which the Lord swore to your fathers . . . to give them and their descendants forever," and in Joshua 6:2, "*See,* I have given Jericho into your hand, its king and the mighty men of valour."

Our mission in life is to take territory for the Kingdom of God, to take back what the enemy has stolen and to take possession of all God has promised. But if we cannot *see it* as a reality in our spirit, we will most likely struggle to possess it. Human nature can be inclined to *diminish the unseen* (Gods' promises) and *magnify the seen* (the issues and obstacles we see before us). Seeing in the spirit is what changes that!

How about today seeing God's promises as bigger than the reality before us? Faith is not a contradiction of reality — faith *acknowledges* reality, but faces it with hope! God is bigger than your financial woes, relational troubles and health struggles. He's bigger than your loneliness, your depression and your self-doubt. God wants you to *see* the victory He has for you, the land of peace, joy and prosperity He gives you to possess.

Seeing in the Spirit is *believing*! So what can you see today? What hope do you hold in your heart? Think of what God has already done! The testimony of God's overcoming power in your life releases courage in your heart to possess your future by faith, causing the enemy to fear and to retreat! Let's build a reputation of being fearsome against our enemies because God is with us—just as Israel did in Joshua 5:1:

> *So it was, when all the kings of the Amorites . . . and all the kings of the Canaanites . . . **heard** that the Lord had dried up the waters of the Jordan from before the children of Israel until we had crossed over, that their hearts melted; and there was no spirit in them any longer because of the children of Israel.*

Perhaps our *seeing and hearing* need challenging? What doubts and fears have become amplified in our ears, and in turn, blurred our vision? Who are we really listening to? Whatever voice we listen to most reflects who really is in charge of our vision. In the Old Testament, Moses *saw* a burning bush—not an unusual sight in the wilderness—only this time it was different. The bush was not being consumed! Moses needed to take *another look* at what was happening!

> *Then Moses said, "I will now turn aside and see this great sight, why the bush does not burn." So when the Lord saw that he turned aside to look, God called to him from the midst of the bush and said, "Moses, Moses!" and he said, "Here I am."*
> *Exodus 3:3-4*

God spoke this very verse into my heart when Bruce and I were planting a church in London. I had initially been viewing this new church as something small—but God wanted me to *look again*, to *see* the supernatural phenomena within the DNA of this fledging church and what it would become because of the power of God's presence resident within. You see, God speaks when we *take another look*, when we pause to enquire. When we choose to *see in the spirit*, we catch a glimpse of what God wants us to possess by faith!

What difficulties are magnified in your sight right now? Which voice has your ear, causing you to doubt and diminish the authority of God in your life? Today, look again, hear God speak, and allow Him to open your eyes to the supernatural power contained in His promises.

and so say all of us

> *Hezekiah became king when he was twenty-five years old*
> *and he reigned twenty-nine years in Jerusalem . . . and he*
> *did what was right in the sight of the Lord, according*
> *to all that his father David had done.*
> 2 Chronicles 29:1-3

A song that was often sung years ago, and is occasionally heard today goes:

> *For he's a jolly good fellow, for he's a jolly good fellow,*
> *for he's a jolly good fellow . . . and* **so say all of us.**

People may complement us on our birthdays or on our achievements while here on earth, but when our lives are over, what are they really going to say about us? That we were pleasant, open-hearted and generous, or that we were grumpy, selfish and mean-spirited? During his reign as king of Israel, King Hezekiah was commended for his leadership. What did Hezekiah do that gave him the recognition and credibility of being a good and godly man? What caused him to receive the *'so say all of us'*? We find the answer in 2 Chronicles 31:21: "In every good work that he began in the service of the house of the Lord, in the law and commandment, to seek his God, he did it with all his heart. So he prospered."

Hezekiah had a *godly focus*. In the very first month of his reign, he *opened the doors* of the house of the Lord and repaired them. He didn't delay, didn't waste time or procrastinate, but began to restore the house of God, knowing the nation's prosperity and posterity was linked with God and His house.

Hezekiah also had a *godly purpose*—to restore true worship in Israel, making God number one priority again. It's the same for us. When we open the door of our heart in worship to God, God opens doors to us. We get to experience God moving powerfully and supernaturally on our behalf! As God's people, we can be good at hearing messages, but how good are we at opening doors to activate them?

Finally, Hezekiah had *godly courage*. He had no problem facing what was 'out of order' or 'out of alignment'—and he started with the dilapidated doors, the entry point to the temple. Sometimes, we don't want to look at what's wrong in our lives and we avert our gaze from our present reality.

But Hezekiah publicly *flung open the doors*. Maybe that invited ridicule from some, but it inspired many! With courage, Hezekiah stated clearly what He wanted to do: "It is *in my heart* to make a covenant with the Lord God of Israel that His fierce wrath may turn away from us" (2 Chronicles 29:10).

Hezekiah wanted to reverse any curse to which Israel had become subject, so the nation could once again experience the favour of God. Hezekiah's desire was to reverse the damage done prior to his reign so that Israel could prosper once again in God's presence. You see, when we open the door to God's vision with courage, we shut the door on the enemy!

What is in our heart? Are we door-openers or door-closers? We can close doors by our doubts and our fears, discouraging others from rising with faith and hope to apprehend their God-given future. Or, we can *open the doors* of conviction, take action, and inspire others to do the same!

Maybe today we are viewing the brokenness or impossibility of a situation rather than seeing the *doors of opportunity* before us! Doors that are opened with faith and obedience release the blessing and prosperity of God. Are there doors in our lives that need to be reopened or restored so that greater faith, richer worship, better marriages, healthier families and better health will result? Let's be door-openers, like Hezekiah!

🍃 *Will you be credited at the end of your life with prosperity of heart, and action—or with poverty of spirit and a lack of action? What will be the 'say so all of us'? What doors have you closed that need to be reopened to see God's favour once again? What vision of restoration is in your heart? What can you state confidently in God? What door could you open today to release worship, restoration and healing?*

how big is your embrace?

So it was, when I heard these words, that I sat down and
wept, and mourned for many days; I was fasting and
praying before the God of heaven.
Nehemiah 1:4

We can have great ideas about outworking mission, but in reality, it is the compassion that flows from the heart that will cause God's mission to succeed. You see, mission needs to be *embraced* not just with the head, but from the heart.

Nehemiah took on the huge task of rebuilding the wall around Jerusalem because his heart broke when he heard the report regarding the state of the city. The wall surrounding Jerusalem was in total disrepair, leaving the people open and exposed to the reproach of the enemy. But Nehemiah didn't just see the task—he felt the desperate need in his heart. Getting down on his knees before God, he arose in power and godly authority to take action. In a record time of fifty-two days, Nehemiah successfully rebuilt the wall. A huge task, which the majority had viewed with despondency, had become a reality under Nehemiah's leadership and guidance.

As we look at our world, we can all see the need and the suffering, and some can envision what needs to be done. But how do we find the capacity to fully embrace the sheer size of the mission? Human effort is necessary to help rebuild that which is broken, but a more powerful combination is *compassion* and *skill* working hand-in-hand. God's grace comes powerfully as we embrace His heart of compassion, enabling us to go well beyond what we would have deemed possible.

Compassion is the catalyst for miracles! We read in the Bible that every time Jesus' heart was moved with compassion, significant miracles resulted. It's the same for us. In mission, we can labour in our own strength to practically fix and meet needs, or we can embrace mission from a heart of compassion that seeks to see God move in the midst. You see, God's grace answers compassionate faith! Compassion for the cause of Christ keeps us persevering beyond simple good intentions, leading us to rely more fully on God's grace to supernaturally and miraculously intervene.

Do our hearts need to grow to embrace God's mission? Most likely! In my younger years my heart was not large enough to embrace the full picture God had for my life; my focus was too much on myself, my inadequacies, and my perceived need for constant personal improvement! As a result, I constantly 'tripped over myself' in my effort to fulfil the mission which God had purposed for me. An important principle I learned through this season was to focus on God's ability rather than on my own; to embrace *His* heart for the need and to call on His Name for the help and anointing required. As I did, my heart began to enlarge beyond my own limitations, enabling me to deeply feel the burden, yet to carry greater expectation and faith to see God heal and restore individuals, communities, churches, cities and nations.

When our hearts fully embrace the mission, God graces us with the skill, the strategy and the endurance to go well beyond what we could have imagined possible. In other words, "If our *heart* can get around it, our *arms* will get around it." God wants to work supernatural feats and spiritual interventions through all of our lives. Let's *embrace* His mission! To 'embrace' means, "to draw near, to feel the heartbeat and sense the need." From a position of closeness, compassion is birthed, strategy is received and divine power is released.

*Today let God and all His fullness embrace **you**! Then, reach out with compassion and **embrace** the need of a community, a city, a nation! Where are the broken walls? Allow your heart to stretch around the mission before you so that God's grace can strengthen you. Feel deeply what moves the heart of God, and know today His empowering presence backing you to achieve supernatural results.*

part three:

healing

a stitch in time

The Spirit of the Lord God is upon Me, because the Lord has anointed Me to preach good tidings to the poor; He has sent Me to heal the brokenhearted, to proclaim liberty to the captives, and the opening of the prison to those who are bound; to proclaim the acceptable year of the Lord, and the day of vengeance of our God.
Isaiah 61:1-3

Have you ever had a garment with a visible loose thread, and in your mind, you purposed to mend it, but because you didn't attend to it, the whole hem eventually unravelled? The old saying, *'A stitch in time saves nine'* is true—not only in terms of broken threads, but in the broken areas of our lives as well. Perhaps we haven't responded to a timely healing touch from Jesus, and now the unaddressed issue has become a gaping, festering wound internally.

A while ago, I fell and broke my arm. I picked myself up and was driven by a friend to a nearby Accident and Emergency Clinic, not requiring any painkillers. But when I was informed that a hospital visit was required to realign the bones in my wrist I didn't feel so brave, even though the procedure was necessary to pull my arm back into its rightful position; otherwise, the future function of my arm would have been severely compromised. I certainly didn't welcome the idea of *extra pain* to address the *existing pain!*

It's the same with the wounds in our spirit. Sometimes, we would rather just put up with low-level pain because we can't face the prospect of our wound being touched. We may consider it easier to ignore the pain under the surface and opt to function as best as we can in our current condition, but if we do, we will never experience the full reality of God's freedom. Jesus' healing touch, when welcomed, will minister to our brokenness, challenge our attitude, expose any bitterness, and yet comfort our deepest pain! Left unattended, however, these wounds have the potential to destroy us *and* to contaminate other areas of our life. Jesus' deepest desire is to realign us with the love of the Father—to *mend and heal* us so we can live free, and fulfil the greater purpose He has for our lives.

Holding onto present pain limits our future. Pain compromises our ability to fully function. Unaddressed, it leaves us vulnerable to 'unravelling' under pressure and reacting wrongly to others (and to situations) from our deepest level of hurt. Could it be that we are holding onto some inner wounds, deceiving ourselves that everything is all right when really it isn't? Could lingering pain be governing our decisions, and limiting our faith and ability to believe for God's best in our lives? It's time to experience healing for every pain, wound or issue that festers beneath the surface! The anointing of the Spirit of God on Jesus is to heal, to mend, to restore and to release us from our pain, sin and iniquities. Let's refuse to put up with low-lying internal pain any longer!

Today let's allow the anointing that is on Jesus to heal our wounds. By putting in a 'stitch in time,' He can pull together and close every wound that leaves us vulnerable and in pain. Acknowledge that God is present today to heal every wound from the past. Today, choose to live healed and free, knowing that we carry the same 'mending' anointing as Jesus to minister healing to those who are hurting in our world.

glance back

*One day I walked by the field of an old lazybones, and then passed the vineyard of a slob; they were overgrown with weeds, thick with thistles, all the fences broken down. I took a long look and pondered what I saw; **the fields preached me a sermon and I listened.***
Proverbs 24:30-32 (MSG)

It is important to assess what we do with our time. It's true that 'time moves on,' but unresolved hurts and open wounds can also cause us to 'stall' in the forward motion of life. When we spend our days reliving events from the past, still feeling the pain of past trauma 'ticking' continuously in the clock of our minds, or allowing bad memories to disturb the settings of our heart, whole years of our lives can go to waste. Even though natural time does not stop, we can go back to former events with the Holy Spirit, activate forgiveness, and receive healing and deliverance through the blood of Jesus and His anointing, positioning us to move forward in a healthy manner!

When we drive our vehicles, we focus mostly on the road ahead and the direction we are going; we cannot afford to be constantly looking in the rear-vision mirror or we run the risk of colliding with another vehicle or running completely off the road! However, *glancing back* is necessary. When we take a quick look in the rear-view mirror, we can not only see the distance we have come, but we can gauge whether anything is approaching from behind—anything that could be gaining ground on us. A *glance back* is always helpful, alerting us to what we are leaving in our wake. When we leave the house, we often *glance back* so we can gauge what we will be returning to. Every area not attended to, will still be there waiting for us on our return—every dirty dish, every unswept floor, every unresolved argument, every bitter word, every unpaid bill. Ideally our homes should be our haven, so it's a good idea to simply ask ourselves what we would prefer to return home to—harmony and peace, or mess and frustration? If time permits, attending to those needs will make our homecoming that much sweeter! Let's not kid ourselves that troubles, unkind words, unkempt mess and unpaid debts will magically disappear while we escape the house momentarily. What has been left unsaid, undone, unfinished and incomplete will confront us on return. *What we don't attend to, will in time demand our attention!*

When we take a look in the rear-vision mirror, we can see who has been left behind, who has fallen over, or who generally just needs help on their journey. Words of encouragement are rightfully directed toward people who succeed and who achieve great things, but have we considered that encouragement is probably more necessary when people are floundering and struggling? I am sure we all have appreciated a word of encouragement, more so when we have done badly or felt condemned. Proverbs 25:11 says, "A word fitly spoken is like apples of gold in settings of silver." Let's not take for granted our blessings, our environment, or the people in our world. Let's *glance back* to see what or who may be missing. Let's not be in such a hurry to possess our future that we overlook the importance of taking others on the journey also. How we leave a situation or person will determine how well we will personally advance.

When God *glanced down* from heaven, He beheld mankind struggling in sin. Rather than leaving us broken and condemned, He sent Jesus, His beloved Son, to earth, to redeem us and create a way forward for us. There has not been, and will never be, any greater demonstration of love than this!

What are you leaving behind in your wake, in your quest to advance? What might you be missing because you are failing to **glance back**? *Is there a 'field' preaching you a sermon? Listen, and see what it is saying! What do you need to attend to today?* **Glance back** *to gather and help others who may have stumbled in their journey. Today, look back with thanksgiving for all Jesus has done for you and worship!*

humpty dumpty

The steps of a good man are ordered by the Lord,
and He delights in his way. Though he fall he shall
not be utterly cast down for the Lord
upholds him with His hand.
Psalm 37:23-24

I am sure we are all familiar with the Nursery Rhyme, 'Humpty Dumpty.'

Humpty Dumpty sat on a wall
Humpty Dumpty had a great fall
All the king's horses and all the king's men
Couldn't put Humpty together again.

Who was Humpty Dumpty? There are many theories about who the character in this children's rhyme written in 1810 could have been. Some suggest Humpty Dumpty may have referred to a king from that time; the most likely theory, however, is that Humpty Dumpty refers to a powerful cannon that was positioned on the roof of 'St Mary's by the Wall' church during the civil war, to protect it from attack. It is recorded that a gunner fired the cannon, causing much damage to the attacking troops, but in turn, the attackers retaliated by firing onto the church roof, bringing both the gun and the gunner down to the ground. As the story goes, the damaged cannon could never be raised again. Hence, the rhyme. Humpty Dumpty, having been toppled from his position, was irreparable, unable to be put together again.

We praise God that He is able to resurrect us and put us together again, even though the enemy may have toppled us at times. But what if Humpty Dumpy was just one big round egg after all?! Then we have a colourful illustration of the mess that results when an egg is dropped. A mess that only God can clean up! And that's what He does.

Psalm 147:5-6 (MSG) puts it like this:

Our Lord is great, with limitless strength;
we'll never comprehend what He knows and does.
God puts the fallen on their feet again.

We commonly use the words, 'the fallen,' to honour those who have given their lives nobly and sacrificially for their king and country, those who sadly never returned home to family and friends, having been killed in the line of duty.

But the word 'fallen' is also used when we foolishly, through error and sin, allow ourselves to be toppled by the enemy, to be broken and taken hostage by hopelessness and condemnation. Adam and Eve fell into sin in the garden of Eden when the serpent toppled their trust in God. "Did God really say?" the enemy suggested subtly, causing them to believe that God was withholding His best from them!

Perhaps we have been toppled in our faith through unfortunate circumstances. Becoming 'fallen in our spirit' deprives us of courage and commitment, and causes us to view everything from the lowest position of hopeless and despair. But God promises to put 'the fallen' on their feet again! He wants to lift us and put us back together. Only God has the power to do this! Let Psalm 20:7-8 be true of you: "Some trust in chariots, and some in horses; but we will remember the name of the Lord our God. They have bowed down and fallen; but we have risen and stand upright."

What is causing you to topple, to sway and be unsteady in your life? Let God lift you up today. Where may you have fallen in faith—or even into sin? Repent, and declare your trust in God. Allow His hand to heal you, mend you and reposition you again on your wall of faith. Today, God reaches out His hand to lovingly restore, strengthen and reinstate. Let's respond to His love. Let's not remain fallen and broken.

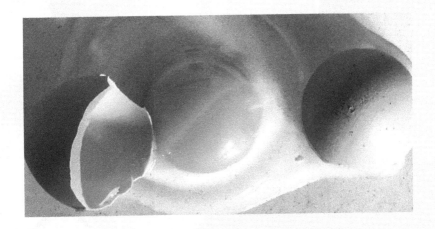

over the fence

> *Thus says the Lord God, "On the day that I cleanse you from all your iniquities, I will also enable you to dwell in the cities, and the ruins shall be rebuilt. The desolate land shall be tilled instead of lying desolate in the sight of all who pass by. So they will say, 'This land that was desolate has become like the garden of Eden, and the wasted, desolate and ruined cities are now fortified and inhabited.'"*
> *Ezekiel 36:33-36*

What is happening here? When did this take place? These are the sort of questions we ask when we witness remarkable changes, either in someone's life or in some location. We just can't help but stop and enquire!

The following passage in the Bible describes people looking *over the fence* in amazement at the transformation they witness! Speaking of the birth of Israel as a nation, God said,

> *No eye pitied you, to do any of these things for you, (cut the naval cord, wash the blood, cleanse with water) to have compassion on you; but you were thrown out into the open field, when you yourself were loathed on the day you were born. And when I passed by you and saw you struggling in your own blood, I said to you in your own blood, "Live!" Yes, I said to you in your blood, "Live!"*
> *Ezekiel 16:5-6 (parentheses mine)*

The compassion of Jesus reaches out to embrace this newly-birthed nation, to *cleanse* her thoroughly from her blood, anoint her with oil, clothe her with embroidered cloth, and bring her into a place of favour and distinction.

> *Your fame went out among the nations because of your beauty, for it was perfect through My splendour which I had bestowed on you.*
> *Ezekiel 16:14*

God's cleansing power enables us to experience life and growth at a whole new level. When God releases the 'immobiliser' imposed over our hearts, such as noxious weeds from the past, confusion, pain or hurt, then we are *enabled* by His grace to transform into His likeness. God's desire for us is to fully experience His freedom, and to dwell, to rebuild, to flourish and prosper!

Do we believe and appreciate that only God can completely fulfil the desire we have to prosper in our lives? We can live in a *desired* place with Jesus or a *despised* place because of negative life experiences. Let's ask ourself the question, "In which place am I living?"

To 'despise' means, "to regard as inferior or worthless; to feel contempt for; to look down on." Are we looking down on ourselves and our situations and therefore failing to see how God has already made amazing provision for us? When Jesus touched and cleansed Israel at her birth, Jerusalem rose in her God-given glory, causing other nations to *look over the fence* and marvel.

Have you ever been to Beverly Hills? It's a lush area where rich and famous people reside. The surrounding districts, however, are barren, dry and unattractive! What makes the difference? It's the belief someone upheld that Hollywood was a great place to live. As a result, people invested into its potential, watering, planting and tending to the land until Hollywood was viewed as a *desirable* place to live. The lesson we learn is that *value and belief change everything!* That's why the love and value God extends toward us makes all the difference.

🍃 *Where are you struggling and need the touch of Jesus? What may you need to look at differently? Today, refuse to despise and loathe your lot! Take another look at what God is offering you and desire His best. Be encouraged that God loves you, believes in you and values you highly. He speaks* **life** *into you so you can flourish and prosper. As you respond to God's investment into your life, people will look* **over the fence** *and marvel at your transformation!*

unclamped

Repent therefore and be converted that your sins may be blotted out, so that times of refreshing may come from the presence of God.
Acts 3:19

What a bother it is when you're ready to go home after some event, only to find your car wheels have been clamped . . . or even worse, your car has been towed away! There goes your transport until you pay the fee for your car to be returned to you. But why was it clamped in the first place? Perhaps we had parked illegally, or breached a time limit?

We can become *clamped* or *immobilised* because we are contravening God's law through sin, violating His word in some manner, or entertaining fear or doubt in the conversation of our mind. The enemy of our soul wants to 'clamp the tyres' of our life in order to keep us from making progress. As a wheel begins to turn, it covers ground—the more revolutions, the more ground! That's why we are thankful for the transport we enjoy these days! Likewise, God has not called us to be stationary or restricted in our expression, but to a faith that is full, alive, mobile and active.

And so, we need to discover the keys that unlock the clamps that threaten to hold us in bondage. One major key is repentance. The Bible tells us that when we take responsibility for our wrongdoing and turn away from sinful actions, doubts or fears, we will experience freedom. In turn, repenting brings about a conversion . . . a refreshing in our soul and an ability to once again move forward. Conversion is about changing from one state to another—from bondage to freedom, from doubt to faith, from sluggishness to possessing energy!

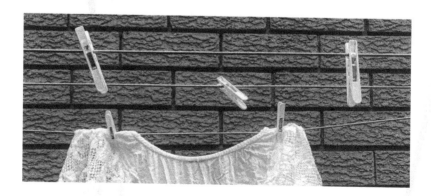

Another major key to living 'unclamped' is to change our conversation and develop a godly ethos. Words have power, and the more we say certain things, the more power they have over our lives. Proverbs 28:21 says, "Death and life are in the power of the tongue, and those who love it will eat its fruit." Sometimes it's our conversation that needs converting! We need to check what is coming out of our mouth, as we will become what we speak.

Many years ago I decided I wouldn't confess tiredness over my life, and as a result I have lived with a fullness of energy generated from my spirit. Of course, we all get physically tired, especially through periods of busyness in life, but there is a big difference between a healthy physical tiredness and a weariness of spirit. People who speak tiredness over their lives, who live in fear of being tired, often end up 'living tired,' with little energy because they have confessed this state of being over their life. Is our negative confession 'clamping' (and therefore limiting) our momentum and expression? If so, it needs converting!

A healthy ethos is also a key to unclamping areas of restriction. Ethos is the characteristic spirit of a culture, era or community, as manifested in its attitudes and aspirations. Ethos is a choice, an atmosphere, a climate, a feeling, a mood! We all have them in our hearts and homes, so let's make sure they are godly and healthy. In one ministry field I was leading, we developed an ethos that remains to this day. Even now, the atmosphere in that area is characterized by a few key statements we introduced, phrases like:

Don't panic—pray! Pray, and God will answer and provide.

Do it calm and colourful! In other words, don't stress—remain calm and creative.

Deep and wide! This reminds us that we will always go wide as a result of going deep.

Are you 'clamped' in your life or feeling 'clamped' in your expression? Find the breach in your thinking or the confession that has clamped you. Today, consider where your conversation and thinking may need converting. Find the keys in repentance, life giving words and godly ethos. Live free!

comfort

*"**Comfort,** yes, **comfort** My people!" says your God. "**Speak comfort** to Jerusalem, and cry out to her that her warfare is ended, that her iniquity is pardoned; for she has received from the Lord's hand double for all her sins."*
Isaiah 40:1-2

In these verses, God was informing Israel that she had served her sentence, that her sin had been pardoned and it was time to move forward in peace, leaving the distress of the past behind. Likewise, we are exhorted to *speak comfort* so that others will know that recovery and hope for the future lies beyond their present suffering and distress.

Everyone suffers at some stage in life, but we have a *Comforter* in the Holy Spirit, one who draws alongside to encourage, assist and hold us through difficult seasons. Then, from the comfort we have experienced, we can embrace others who are hurting. 2 Corinthians 1:3-4 says, "Blessed be the God and Father of our Lord Jesus Christ, the Father of mercies and God of all comfort, who *comforts* us in all our tribulations, that we may be able to *comfort* those who are in any trouble, with the *comfort* with which we ourselves are *comforted* by God."

Let's allow ourselves to be wrapped in the comfort of the Holy Spirit, who empathises with our pain and holds us tight, but gently manoeuvres us to *re-enter the room of life* — only this time, with a greater knowledge of the closeness of His presence. Many people are tempted to stay wrapped in their hurt, refusing to be *comforted*, but this only causes their pain to be prolonged and to become seemingly insurmountable.

David had this very experience when his son Absalom, who was seeking to take David's life, was killed in the battle. David took the blame heavily upon himself and mourned deeply the death of his son, wishing he had died in Absalom's place. But David's prolonged grief had a negative effect on his army; it affected the very men who had fought on his behalf, risking their own lives to save him from certain death. In 2 Samuel 19:2 we read,

So the victory that day was turned into mourning . . . for the people heard it said that day, "The king is grieved for his son."

Instead of being celebrated, David's army felt ashamed! David's grief had blanketed his closest supporters, and scripture tells us the outcome—they stole away ashamed, and fled to their own tents. Thankfully, a man named Joab brought it up with King David. 2 Samuel 19:5-7 (MSG) says,

> But in private Joab rebuked the king: "Now you've done it— knocked the wind out of your loyal servants who have just saved your life, to say nothing of the lives of your sons and daughters, wives and concubines. What is this, loving those who hate you and hating those who love you? Your actions give a clear message: officers and soldiers mean nothing to you! You know that if Absalom were alive right now, we'd all be dead. Would that make you happy? Get hold of yourself; get out there and put some heart into your servants! I swear to God that if you don't go to them, they'll desert; not a soldier will be left by nightfall. And that will be the worst thing that has happened yet."

The message is clear. If we remain wrapped in our grief and *refuse to be comforted*, we stand to lose even more than what we are grieving for. We may also lose the people who have supported us! Although our pain may be genuine, let's not devalue those who stand alongside and fight for our wellbeing. David was exhorted by Joab to speak *comfort* to his servants, or they would be unlikely to remain with him!

🍃 *Do your words bring comfort, helping others arise with hope for the future, or are you stuck in a period of grieving, refusing to be comforted? Have you wrapped yourself in grief, devaluing those who care for you? Today, take heart. Be grateful for the greatest comforter, the Holy Spirit, who is there for you constantly, standing alongside you to help you re-enter the room of life.*

tears into prayers

*Those who sow in **tears** shall reap in joy.*
He who continually goes forth weeping, bearing seed
for sowing, shall doubtless come again with rejoicing.
Psalm 26:5

Sometimes circumstances or people raise their voice against us with intent to hurt and harm. This is painful when we are on the receiving end, but grievous also when we witness someone else receiving this treatment. The fallout affects so many people! In Israel's case, it affected the whole nation. In 2 Samuel 15:23 we read, "And all the country *wept* with a loud voice, and all the people passed over. The king himself also crossed over the Brook Kidron, and all the people crossed over toward the way of the wilderness."

This passage describes the distress of the moment by stating that *"all the country wept."* This was a disturbance of epic proportion, one that rocked the security of the nation. Absalom's treason forced David to leave his place of responsibility and propelled the whole country into a tempestuous time.

Divisive behaviour disturbs everyone. Commonly-held culture, tradition and ethics in Israel were now being threatened by Absalom's treason and anarchy. And it's the same today. Countries around the world are being terrorised and decimated by the selfish and hateful agendas of a few, who through spiteful and revengeful acts, bankrupt, starve and destroy nations.

We too, should *weep* for our nation, crying out to God for healing and a move of His Spirit! 2 Chronicles 7:14 says, "If My people who are called by My name will humble themselves and pray and seek My face and turn from their wicked ways, then I will hear from heaven, and will forgive their sin and heal their land."

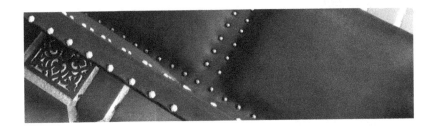

Humility brings healing. Pride breeds division, but humility brings healing. This is why we need to turn our *tears into prayers*! Absalom's attempt to unseat David exposed the whole nation to an ungodly spirit of bitterness and hatred. But we can learn from David's godly responses. In 2 Samuel 15:25, King David said, "Carry the ark of God back into the city. If I find favour in the eyes of the Lord, He will bring me back and show me both it and His dwelling place."

Although David was in pain, his heart was for the welfare of Jerusalem, and he personally chose to trust God for his reinstatement. And so, he chose to send the ark of the covenant and the priests back to the city so they could offer protection and wise counsel in the midst of the chaos. I am sure David would have preferred the ark and the priests to be present with him, but he released them for the sake of the nation, choosing instead to wait patiently in the wilderness, even in his sorrow. Later we read, "So David went up by the ascent of the Mount of Olives and *wept* as he went up . . . and all the people who were with him covered their head and went up *weeping*" (2 Samuel 15:30).

We too may be in pain, offended, hurt, or displaced, but let's choose to make the right response. Are we weeping for ourselves, or for the devastation the enemy brings to a nation through divisive and disruptive tactics? We may be tempted to gather our support systems around us against the offender, *or* we can 'sow in tears,' praying for God to intervene. Let's respond like David, who turned his *tears into prayers*, waiting in that place of dependency on God. David was wronged, but his heart remained right.

Are there any areas of division in your life, any lingering offences? Let's choose to respond today in a godly manner, turning our tears into prayers. Where is our country weeping? Where can we sow in tears for a change of heart and healing for our land? Today, let's be like David, completely dependent on God, not adding to any division but investing in prayer! God wants to heal our land by healing hearts.

part four:

deliverance

no half measures

You crown the year with Your goodness,
and your paths drip with abundance.
Psalm 65:11

God leaves nothing half-finished. In fact, God not only completes what He starts—He crowns it! To 'crown' something is to add the finishing touch, to close off or seal at the highest point. It's a way of adding weight to the existing display of splendour. God wants to *crown our years* with a grand display of His excellence and power! It's like the icing on the cake—the icing just 'tops it off.'

54

But not only does He crown our years—he crowns our lives! The ability to persevere through trials without yielding comes with the promise of receiving the *crown of life*, a recognition for excellence. James 1:12 says, "Blessed is the man who endures temptation, for when he has been approved, he will receive the crown of life which the Lord has promised to those who love Him."

Crowns are also used in coronations, being the recognition of royalty and rule. In Esther 2:17 we read, "The king loved Esther more all the other women, and she obtained grace and favour in his sight more than all the virgins; so he set the *royal crown* upon her and made her queen instead of Vashti." This crown of royal status gave Esther access to certain privileges in the palace, and a special place in the heart of the king.

We too, have been given access into the throne room of God, permission to stand before Him, wearing the royal robes He has appointed us. Let's not waste our access and authority in the Kingdom to rule and reign victoriously with Him!

Even so, those who wear the crown of royalty must guard against living half-heartedly. When Esther first heard about the plight of the Jews and the threat of annihilation, she was distressed, but only made what you could describe as a half-hearted response. Her first attempt to deal with the issue was sadly lacking! She sought to alleviate Mordecai's grievance by offering him clothing to cover the burden he felt for the Jewish people—she came up with a temporary solution, a *half-measure* that could not possibly solve the deeper issue that festered aggressively beneath the surface. Perhaps Esther hoped the clothing would somehow deal with the vulnerability she felt and somehow avert the threat of the enemy?

But Mordecai challenges Esther that a *stronger measure* is needed; she needed to obtain an audience before the king to appeal for the lives of the Jewish people, exposing the enemy's intent. Mordecai reminded her that there was *purpose beyond position, blessing beyond bravery!* In Esther 4:14 we read his words:

> *For if you remain completely silent at this time, relief and*
> *deliverance will arise for the Jew from another place, but you and*
> *your father's house will perish. Yet who knows whether you have*
> *come to the kingdom for such a time as this?*

How often do we offer half measures? Our silence alone is permission for the enemy to rule and destroy lives. A blanket prayer is a half-hearted response that seeks to cover the problem. We need, like Esther to *wear our crown* in the Spirit—a crown of authority, identity, dignity, righteousness, purpose, favour, and power to intervene in the salvation of souls. We must let the cause become greater than any looming threat!

What problem are you simply covering over, hoping it will go away? Where do you need to make a stand, even at your own risk? Don't settle for half measures. Today, know that you are graced with God's authority and have a reception before His throne to take that authority and rule with Him.

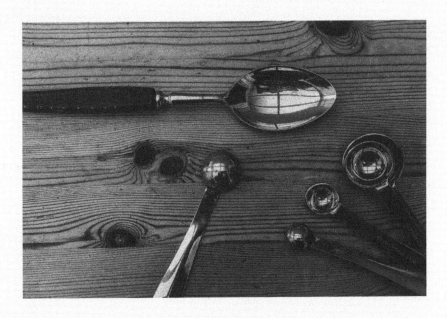

bewitched

*O **foolish** Galatians! Who has **bewitched** you,*
that you should not obey the truth, before whose eyes
Jesus Christ was clearly portrayed among you as crucified?
Galatians 3:1

When Paul accused the Galatians of being foolish, we can be sure he was addressing a fairly serious issue. In the relay race of faith, someone had cut in front of them, pushed them off the track, and knocked the baton out of their hand! In his letter, Paul was addressing the deception they were now entertaining, the mistruth that blinded them from the true message of the gospel. And so, he asks the question, "Who lured them to believe something different from what they had received by faith? Who captured their attention through tempting displays of allure and ease, duping them as with a spell, to gain control over them?" His concern is evident in Galatians 3:3, where he writes, "Are you so foolish? Having begun in the Spirit, are you now being made perfect by the flesh?"

We need to be diligent that no lie or temptation of the enemy cuts in on our path or causes us to deviate from the truth, making us stumble in our resolve to live in the fullness of Christ. Only pure faith in the resurrection of Jesus Christ and the power of the Holy Spirit can help us live triumphantly above our own carnal instincts.

The disciples were filled with the Holy Spirit and ministered in power, but on the journey even they encountered contrary spirits. We read about this in Acts 8:17-21:

> *Then they (the disciples) laid hands on them, and they received the Holy Spirit. And when Simon saw that through the laying on of the apostles' hands the Holy Spirit was given, he offered them money, saying, "Give me this power also . . ." But Peter said to him, "Your money perish with you, because you thought that the gift of God could be purchased with money! You have neither part nor portion in this matter, for your heart is not right in the sight of God. Repent therefore of this, your wickedness, and pray God, if perhaps the thought of your heart may be forgiven you. For I see that you are poisoned by bitterness and bound by iniquity."*

Simon was responding out of his base nature of greed and desire for power. Before his conversion, Simon was a sorcerer, one who was able to command attention from the crowds. Now he was witnessing miracles and signs being done through the apostles and he was anxious to have the same power, even offering money to receive it. Simon wanted to trade on the Holy Spirit to gain further attention and remain 'looking great' in the sight of others. His intention was to use the gifts of the Kingdom for his own selfish purposes. Simon had been converted, believed in Christ and been baptised, but already Satan was cutting in on his life to knock him over, capitalising on the ambition, bitterness and poison within his heart that remained unredeemed.

All sorts of things can cut in on us, seeking to trip us up on our journey of faith and appeal to our base nature as human beings. We need to be aware of where the enemy is trying to 'pull the wool' over our eyes so we cannot see the path ahead clearly. This phrase, *'having the wool pulled over our eyes,'* refers to the woolly wigs wealthy Brits loved to wear in the 17th and 18th centuries. These wigs made them a target for thieves—tugging on the wig, the wool dropped over their eyes, making them easier to rob. In the same way, Satan, who is a thief, tugs at people's minds and hearts in order to obscure their vision and rob them of the ability to discover the truth and power of God that is available to them.

What seeks to cut in on you in your journey of faith? Where is the enemy trying to bewitch you and obscure your vision? Acknowledge any base weakness, that makes you vulnerable to temptation and turn from it today. Let's not be bewitched by the enemy, but be strong and confident in the power of God to help us overcome and run the race appointed for us.

slam the door

In righteousness you shall be established;
You shall be far from oppression, for you shall not fear,
and from terror for it shall not come near you.
Isaiah 54:14

I have never been a 'door-slammer,' but I have heard parents talk about their children slamming doors as a voice of protest against any rule or punishment they consider unfair. In that moment, they are showing their disagreement by a physical response. I am not advocating slamming doors in the natural, but I do suggest that in the spiritual realm, there are times we simply need to *'slam the door'* in the face of the enemy, voicing our non-agreement with his lies and denying him permission to access the rooms of our heart.

When we do not deal with the enemy's lies, they can accelerate until they begin to rule us and dominate our decisions. This was my experience in my earlier years. The enemy's tactic of using fear around expectation and performance would strike my heart—even to the point where I began to 'fear the fear,' which was even worse! The Bible warns us in Job 3:25 that what we fear will come upon us. Clearly, I had opened the door to fear, and the enemy had swept in to dominate that space! And so, I sought God for keys to overcome fear, and strategies to grow strong in my faith and to counteract any faintheartedness. God was gracious—the answers came in many forms to strengthen my resolve and empower my fight of faith.

Answers come to us at times when we least anticipate them, and often through unexpected channels, but we can be confident that if we are asking God the questions, He will always answer.

While watching a movie entitled *Christiana*, a life-changing principle dropped suddenly into my heart. *Christiana* is the sequel to *Pilgrim's Progress*, where Pilgrim's wife, after her husband's departure, makes her own pilgrimage to the Celestial City. On the journey there were many obstacles to overcome; her mercy-heart shrank in fear at the appearance of fortresses and demonic powers. Christiana's first response was to feel powerless and discouraged, fearing she would never complete the journey because of all these setbacks. The children journeying with her, on the other hand, possessed a strong faith. Pushing back every evil manifestation, they called on Braveheart (representing the Holy Spirit), who appeared in a heartbeat to help.

As I watched that movie, God dropped a one-liner into my spirit which caused me to pivot, face the fear, and counteract its presence in my life. He simply said, "Helen, Satan has no power over you—only what you give him." I heard this incredibly clearly, and it became a life-changing statement of faith for me. I had to discern where I was giving the enemy power over me. It was my responsibility to *slam the door* on every lie of the enemy that came knocking on the door of my heart. Isaiah 54:14 tells us that oppression cannot come near us if we first close the door on fear. That verse reinforced my faith. Whenever I was tempted to think fearful thoughts or feel fearful feelings, I consciously, firmly and authoritatively shut the door in the enemy's face, not allowing him entry, knowing that as I did so, no oppression could invade that space and seize territory in my life.

Maybe fear is foreign to you, but are there other lies that oppress you, that weigh you down and worry you? Acts 10:38 tells us that "Jesus went about healing all those that were oppressed by the devil." Let's identify any oppression we are living with, anything that attempts to invade and occupy our emotions or heart, draining us and depleting the full and vital life God has for us. Let's close the door on the enemy of our souls!

🍃 *Are there any areas in your life where you have unconsciously given Satan the right to oppress you? Remember Satan has no power except what you give him through your agreement with fear, doubts and negativity. Today, slam the door on fear, so you will be far from oppression and terror!*

clear the land

*Now Joshua was old, advanced in years. And the Lord said
to him: "You are old, advanced in years, and there remains
very much land yet to be possessed."*
Joshua 13:1

At this point in Joshua's life, he had successfully led the people into the Promised Land and conquered many kings. Now God was speaking to him about the future and the remaining land that needed to be conquered.

However far in our Christian experience we have come, there is still land to take, ground within our own heart, and ground for our families, community and countries. When Joshua was initially commanded to lead the people across the River Jordan, the Lord made the promise that He would,

*". . . without fail drive out from before you the Canaanites
and the Hittites and the Hivites and the Perizzites and the
Girgashites and the Amorites and the Jebusites."*
Joshua 3:10

Sometimes we find enemy forces camping in the land that we are called to occupy, and when we do, we need to clear the land of these squatters! Initially we may need to clear them from the land of our heart, but also from the land God has promised we will inherit. The nations Joshua drove out each represent a specific force we may find resident in our own lives.

The **Canaanites** were merchant people, traffickers and pedlars. In God's economy, money is neither good nor evil, but a commodity for trading. When it takes a grip on the heart, however, it has the power to govern mercilessly. We need to clear our lives of greed and lust for financial gain. The Bible tells us that it is impossible to serve two masters, God and mammon, as we will love one and hate the other (Matthew 6:24). Money makes a good servant but a terrible master!

The **Hittites** were known as timid and fearful people. We need to make sure the emotions of fear and timidity have not pitched their tent on our land, causing us to shrink back from fully serving God. Instead, we need to operate in the opposite spirit of courage and boldness, just like Joshua and Caleb, who brought a good report of Israel's ability to take the land despite the giants.

The **Hivites** were village-dwellers. This can seem positive, but when our ethos includes staying small and obscure and we desire only to make ourselves comfortable, we can become inconsiderate of others and forget God's mission and Kingdom purpose. Then, it needs to be evicted!

The **Perizzites** were people who dwelt in an unwalled city. They were vulnerable to every force that sought to enter because they lived with no boundaries and with independent and unteachable attitudes.

The **Amorites** were prominent folk who spoke against others, but in doing so yoked themselves to their own judgment.

The **Girgashites** were people who turned back from pilgrimage and gave up easily when work and hardship of any kind was involved.

The **Jebusites** were 'down-trodden,' and they trod others down also.

Do you identify with any of these in your life? Remember, the greatest tool of Satan is to undermine and destroy the works of God's creation. So let's take another look at the land of our hearts, the areas of responsibility we have been given, to ascertain whether there are forces illegally squatting on our land. Let's *clear the land* by taking authority in the name of Jesus!

What remaining land needs to be cleared in your life, and in the territory of your responsibility? Are any of the above 'nations' residing on the land allotted to you? Today, identify any struggle or forces you need to resist in Jesus' name. Clear your heart of every imposter so you can fully inherit what rightfully belongs to you!

change of position

*Now He was teaching in one of the synagogues on the Sabbath.
And, behold, there was a woman who had a spirit of infirmity
eighteen years, and was bent over, and could in no wise raise
herself up. But when Jesus saw her, He called her to Him and
said to her, "Woman, you are loosed from your infirmity."
And He laid His hands on her; and immediately
she was made straight, and glorified God.
Luke 13:10-13*

The rulers of the synagogue responded to Jesus with anger, chiding Him for healing on the Sabbath. In response, Jesus challenged them by stating that they would loose their animals on a Sabbath to water them, so why shouldn't a woman who Satan had bound for many years, be loosed on a Sabbath as well?

In the Gospels, we see that Jesus often healed in response to people's faith and confidence in Him as the Son of God. But on this occasion, *Jesus* initiated the deliverance when He saw the woman's inability to raise herself up, discerning the spirit that had bound her for eighteen years. With compassion, Jesus called her to Himself and, taking authority over every demonic power, He released her from every condemnation that had weighed her down.

This woman did not have "an infirmity," but "a *spirit* of infirmity" that manifested symptoms relative to the supposed illness. But Jesus' healing touch brought a change of position for this woman. Her posture changed dramatically and her perspective changed eternally. Her outlook which had been limited, her dignity which had been compromised, and her strength which had been diminished, now yielded to the power of God, enabling her to stand upright and view her future with renewed hope.

Imagine her great joy and gratitude! Jesus brought *'lift into her life'* by releasing her from the load she was incapable of carrying.

Have you ever carried something so heavy that it caused you to buckle over because of the sheer weight of the object? Something that made it difficult for you to stand upright, limiting your view of the direction you were headed? This is the reality for so many people today—people who are walking in hopelessness and bondage, unaware that demonic spirits are weighing them down with heavy burdens of guilt and shame. Sometimes this is through their own wrongdoing; other times it is because of the iniquities of the generations before them. The Bible tells us that the iniquities of the forefathers pass down to the third and fourth generations until they are broken in the authority of the name of Jesus. Without deliverance and Jesus' intervention in our lives, we walk with a 'bend in our spirit,' a disposition of nature that repeats itself generationally in a negative manner. But the good news is Jesus came to change our position! Acts 10:38 tells us,

> *God anointed Jesus Christ of Nazareth with power and*
> *He went about doing good and healing all those*
> *who were oppressed by the devil.*

Jesus can free us from every oppression, every weight and every infirmity! Will we allow Him to *lift* the load from our lives and deliver us from everything we are tied to from the past? This is why Jesus came!

Do you need a change of position and perspective? Are you walking with an unnecessary weight that is bowing you over? Today, Jesus wants to break that oppression and set you free from every condemnation. He sees you and calls you out to deliver you from weights that you were never designed to carry. Walk freely and upright in Jesus today with fresh new perspective and renewed hope for the future!

cold-hearted idols

*The god Bel falls down, god Nebo slumps. The no-god hunks
of wood are loaded on mules and have to be hauled off,
wearing out the poor mules — dead weight, burdens
who can't bear burdens, hauled off to captivity.*
Isaiah 46:1-2 (MSG)

What are we trusting to get us through life? Hopefully as born-again believers, we are putting our trust in Jesus, but sadly in our world today many people still deliberately or inadvertently gaze at *images* and *idols* which are incapable of delivering, saving or securing them.

These man-made gods are weighty and heavy to carry! In comparison, our loving God carries *us* and relieves *us* from loads that are too heavy for us.

He says:

*I've been carrying you on my back from the day you were born, and
I'll keep on carrying you when you're old. I'll be there, bearing you
when you're old and grey! I've done it and will keep on doing it,
carrying you on my back, saving you. So to whom will you compare
me, the incomparable? Can you picture me without reducing me?*
Isaiah 46:3-4 (MSG)

Are we reducing God only to what we can see, hold and handle? To only what our minds can understand? Are we reducing Him or even replacing Him with an idol that has no heart?

Are we comparing the incomparable God to the comparable?

When we do, we discover that:

>**Idols** are heavy to carry; they are a dead-weight because they have no breath in them.
>**God** is strong, committed to carrying us on His back and bearing our load eternally.

>**Idols** are temporal, made by man out of the mind of man.
>**God** always has been! He is eternal, with no beginning nor end.

>**Idols** are motionless. They just sit where placed and never move.
>**God** is continually moving, creating and expressing His glory through mighty deeds.

>**Idols** are mute. If you speak to them, they are never going to speak back.
>**God** is always speaking into our spirit, into atmospheres and into the future.

>**Idols** are powerless. They are incapable of doing anything to help or save mankind.
>**God** is continuously saving and redeeming mankind through His acts of love.

Have you reduced God to a static image in your mind, rendering Him incapable of delivering or saving you? Have you reduced Him to the limitation of your human thinking and reasoning? Have you replaced God with some popular ideal that contains no breath and can't deliver? Today, affirm your trust in a living God who has the power to help and deliver you. Picture Him by magnifying Him for who He is.

a god-storm

But the Lord sent out a great wind on the sea and there was a
mighty tempest on the sea so the ship was about to be broken.
Jonah 1:4

Life is not all continuous blue skies and plain sailing. Sometimes we encounter storms, and the way we respond when storms happen often indicates where our heart is really at. Of course, there are the usual *storms of life* like sickness, workloads, finances and other pressures, and there are *demonic storms* that we need to rise and take authority over. But there are also *God-storms* that He orchestrates to get our attention.

Jonah is an Old Testament example of a man who found himself in such a storm. As a result of deliberately disobeying God and running in the opposite direction, away from the task God had given him, the Lord hurled out a great wind! This was a pretty serious storm which no one could ignore, especially the sailors on the ship. God was seeking to arrest Jonah's attention because he was going the wrong way!

Like Jonah, we too can be going the wrong way in our thinking, our attitude and our behaviour. Often God needs to intervene in such a dramatic way that we notice, respond and turn ourselves around. If we don't respond to the still quiet voice of God's direction, something larger is needed to get our attention. We may be even rebuking the enemy for the storm we find ourselves in, when we need to simply take ownership for any trouble we may have caused. In Jonah's situation, the mariners onboard with Jonah cried out to their god and threw cargo into the sea to lighten the load. But they knew who was responsible. They knew that Jonah was fleeing from the presence of God because he had told them when he stepped onto the boat! In fact, they were aghast that he was sleeping through a storm while they were fighting to save the lives on board.

What a lesson for us! It's time for Christians to awake to the storms around us, and where needed, be accountable. We can choose to ignore the storm or even sleep through it, but unless we take ownership of the chaos we may have caused through our disobedience, lives will be lost and worlds will be thrown into upheaval.

This God-storm located Jonah. It required that he rise and take responsibility; he needed to change direction and follow through on God's mission. Under pressure, Jonah was forced to reveal his identity. Finally, he said to the other men on board, "Pick me up and throw me into the sea; then the sea will become calm for you. For I know that this great tempest is because of me" (Jonah 1:12). And the sailors did just that—following Jonah's instruction, they threw him into the sea, and immediately the waves ceased raging.

You have to come clean if you want to come through! There's no deliverance from a God-storm if we are not truthful and accountable. Life will remain tumultuous, and people (including ourselves) will get hurt if we remain silent. Let's not run from accountability and responsibility before God, but turn afresh to Him with faith and obedience.

Is there any chaos in your life that may be caused through your disobedience to God and His Word? If you are in a storm, discern what type of storm it is and take the appropriate action. Today, repent from any disobedience, any carelessness, if appropriate, and turn to God. He will calm the storm!

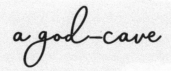

a god-cave

*Now the Lord had prepared a great fish to swallow Jonah. And
Jonah was in the belly of the fish three days and three nights.*
Jonah 1:17

We have all heard the expression *'time out.'* It is a technique that parents use
these days to correct defiant or aggressive behaviour children may have
displayed. This space gives the child time to think about their behaviour,
to calm down and consider what they might do differently in the future.

Caves too, have their place; sometimes they are protective, as in David's
case when he sheltered from the pursuit of King Saul who sought his
life. But the cave that Jonah found himself in, the belly of a whale, was
a cave that represented *'time out,'* a place of discipline, adjustment and
realignment. This was necessary to save Jonah, reset the trajectory of his
life, and preserve the amazing mission God had appointed him to fulfil.

When Jonah took responsibility for the storm that had so violently raised
its head, the mariners at his bidding threw him into the raging sea, which
immediately returned to calm. When we take responsibility for our
actions and repent before God of wrong responses, He graciously brings
adjustment and calm to every disruptive situation. Not only that, God is
able to provide a place to hold us, readjust and commission us once again!

It wasn't a pleasant place to end up in, but God in His grace saved Jonah from drowning, and in His great love gave Jonah a second chance at life by effectively saying, *"Time out, Jonah!"* He gave Jonah time to think about the disturbance his disobedience had caused and how it threatened the safety of those around him, and time to think about the decisions he needed to make for the future.

And Jonah responded. In Jonah 2:1 we read,

> *Then Jonah prayed to the Lord his God from the fish's belly.*
> *And he said, "I cried out to the Lord because of*
> *my affliction and He answered me."*

Jonah cried to God. The inside of a whale's stomach is not that great, and Jonah wanted out! He needed deliverance from his stubborn and judgmental heart, as well as from the physical stomach of the whale-cave. Praise God, this was not the end for Jonah. God spoke to the fish and it vomited Jonah onto dry land.

We may be in a cave, and there is an appropriate time for shelter and reflection. But there is also a time to call on God and come out of that place! If we stay unrepentant and unresponsive in disobedience, we can end up remaining in a vacuum, an airless place where calcification and fossilisation of life and faith will inevitably take place.

The truth is, disobedience is costly. It costs playtime for a child who misbehaves, and it costs freedom for an adult who chooses to stubbornly do their own thing rather than God's. Remember, so many lives are affected when we are deliberately disobedient and hard to motivate.

Are you in a cave, isolated because of your resistance to God's voice? The good news is that it's not too late. Repentance and crying out to God for another chance to fulfil His commands is the response that God is waiting in the wings to hear. He longs to restore you, equip you and send you forth in love and power.

Is God bringing adjustment to your life? Is He asking you to reconsider your responses and direction? Today, respond as quickly as possible so you can resume your best life with Him. Come out of the cave with renewed vision and strength, ready to fulfil His call on your life.

obsessions

And Esau said, "Look I am about to die,
so what is this birthright to me?"
Genesis 25:32

Have you ever mistaken hunger for starvation? Just because we experience a few hunger pangs, it does not mean we are about to wilt and die! But Satan moves in on the hungry, dissatisfied parts of our heart, being the biggest exaggerator of all times. In the book of Genesis, we read about Esau, a man who was, apparently, *starving*.

The truth is, Esau may have been hungry, but he certainly wasn't starving—he lived in a household of plenty! But because of the inner lack of self-control and greed in his life, Esau traded his most important possession, his birthright, for a bowl of lentil stew! How foolish was that? Esau allowed the *starvation* in his spirit to affect his better judgment!

Could the enemy be deceiving us also? We may not be as starving as we suppose; we may just be ready for another meal! Or has our hunger got the better of us and become much more now than the occasional stomach rumble? *Obsessions* in our lives are unhealthy cravings, 'bottomless pits' that have developed because a natural hunger in our earlier years was not met, only now they have become more than just an appetite. They're a fixation!

Like Esau, to comfort our cravings we may look for quick fixes—ways to feel better and achieve fullness—but we often compromise our standards in doing so. The devil is quick to take advantage of any obsession, any persistent, inescapable preoccupation, hooking people into harmful habits, causing them to suffer inner guilt and shame. But the human body and mind was never designed to carry guilt. That's why we need a Saviour who can relieve us of the weight and penalty of sin. Secrets that remain hidden have the power to destroy people and relationships! Obsessions, unmet needs, and outworked fantasy cannot be broken by natural means. They need to be broken through anointed ministry in the Spirit of God, because obsessions touch every part of life, and those who obsess view everything through the starvation they feel in their spirit. Wanting to control their life, they end up getting swallowed by their greed and lust.

In the Bible we read about Korah, a man who began to *obsess* about his position and rank. As a result, he took Moses to task, saying, "You take too much upon yourselves, for all the congregation is holy, every one of them and the Lord is among them. Why then do you exalt yourselves above the assembly of the Lord?" (Numbers 16:3-4a). But then we see Moses' response in Numbers 16:4: "So when Moses heard it, he fell on his face."

Moses responded with an open spirit, stating that if Korah and the discontented people died of natural reasons, it would be evidence that Moses had been doing his own thing, but if God was to take their lives some other way such as the earth opening up, it would be a sign that Korah had rejected the Lord by rejecting His appointment of Moses. Numbers 16:31 says, "Now it came to pass, as he finished speaking all these words, that the ground split apart under them and the earth opened its mouth and swallowed them up, with their households and all the men with Korah, with all their goods."

With *obsessions* comes anxiety, pretence, the fabricating of truth to cover harmful activity, and a bondage to the world of darkness. Obsessions have the power to *swallow us alive* if we don't seek the mercy and help of Jesus.

Is there anything in your life that you are obsessing over? Is there a sense of starvation or lack in your life that demands feeding? Today, acknowledge that Jesus can satisfy your hunger and break any addictive behaviour. He is able to deliver you from unhealthy habits. Ask someone to stand with you as you repent of obsessive thoughts and activity. Be hungry for Jesus and He will satisfy your deepest need!

adjust the levels

People have varied tolerances to different noise levels. Have you ever heard a car coming before you saw it, as the music was thumping through the speakers? Or noticed the disparity between older people and younger people in the same room, where someone will invariably say, "Turn it down!"? There is a need to adjust the noise levels in life, just as we lift or lower the faders on a sound desk to regulate volume. This is something I needed to do in a period of early ministry. Falling prey to a spirit of fear, I needed to adjust the volume on what I was listening to.

We don't always like it when someone lovingly (but maybe bluntly) speaks truth into our life and tells us what we need to hear. We prefer people to think and speak well of us. Viewing myself as a worshipper like Mary, and as someone who loved God and loved reading His word, I was shocked when Bruce spoke forthrightly into my life one day, telling me he was hearing a sound contrary to faith. He challenged my position as a worshipper, as I was often falling subject to fear and timidity. This initially shocked and offended me—after all, his delivery was not exactly soft and gift-wrapped in tissue! However, very quickly I realised that what Bruce had said was true; if I was struggling with a spirit of fear, I was obviously accrediting the enemy with far more power than God. The noise levels in my life were all wrong!

The truth was, I had allowed the volume of the enemy's voice to become louder in my ears than God's encouragement. It was time to adjust the levels and drown out the lies through praise, worship and strong faith. It was time for me to 'shoosh' the enemy altogether, to deny him access to the sound desk of my life.

Occasionally we need a friend who *calls us out*, someone who will interrupt our faulty thinking and challenge our unbelief; someone who is unafraid of the risk of hurting our feelings, whose motivation is purely to see us delivered and set free. Many people choose friends who will only tell them what they want to hear. But in many cases, through their sympathy, this only lowers the sound of truth and leaves the door wide open to the voice of the enemy. The prophet Nathan once came to King David to adjust the wrong sound of entitlement in David's heart and to point out his total blindness to the pain he had caused others. On hearing the sound of God's voice, David responded in deep repentance.

Do be that friend that will sometimes risk offending another, as difficult as it may be, if we can hear a sound that has the potential to lead them astray. We may need to challenge consistent tones of unbelief, fear or criticism, bringing adjustment to the sound levels for the sake and destiny of our friend.

Don't be that friend that blocks their ears from constructive criticism, remaining offended and distant as a result. With every critique that comes our way, we need to inquire of God. Like David, if there is even one percent truth in what someone tells us, let's adjust the sound levels accordingly.

What is blaring in your ears that is not helpful? Where does the level on the sound desk of your life need to be adjusted? Tune out the enemy's voice in your ears by listening to the Holy Spirit and trusted friends. Turn up the sound of praise and worship and release a sound that glorifies Him.

reverse the curse

*"No weapon formed against you shall prosper and every tongue
which rises against you in judgment, you shall condemn.
This is the heritage of the servants of the Lord, and their
righteousness is from Me," says the Lord.*
Isaiah 54:17

Curses spoken in frustration or anger either by ourselves or by others can have a detrimental hold over our minds and the events of our lives. A *curse* is a strong and solemn utterance intended to invoke spiritual powers in order to inflict pain and harm on another person. These *curses* are demonic in nature and are binding until we break them in Jesus' name, exercising authority over their right to influence our life.

Curses directed toward families, individuals or people groups need to be identified so they can be dealt with and rendered powerless to operate. Where previous or current generations have opened their lives to the occult or the demonic realm through cursing, spiritual forces are granted entry and end up governing the lives, not only of the present generation, but of generations to come! We, however, have the authority in Jesus to *reverse any curse* and send it back to where it originally came from.

A vow is often a form of curse, only it is something we speak over *our own* lives—a strong declaration that we will *never* do something in the future, perhaps due to previous failure or disappointment. For instance, a teenager may vow they never want to get married because of the difficulties they witnessed first-hand in their parents' relationship.

But the *vows* we make distance us spiritually from the blessings that God wants us to enjoy, mainly because of the strength of the oath sworn at the time of pain. They give Satan permission to resist us and abort certain blessings in our life. But the good news for all Christians is that by the power of the Holy Spirit we can identify these, repent and reverse them in the name of Jesus. We can change any current climate of cursing to blessing just as Elisha did over bad waters and barren ground.

And Elisha said, "Bring me a new bowl, and put salt in it."
So they brought it to him. Then he went out to the source of the
water, and cast in the salt there, and said, "Thus says the Lord,
'I have healed this water; from it there shall be no more death
or barrenness.'" So the water remains healed to this day,
according to the word of Elisha which he spoke.
2 Kings 2:19-22

Like Elisha, Jesus has spoken words of healing over our lives that we need to claim. We too, can throw the salt of God's word into the source of any bitter waters, reversing every weapon that may have been formed against us.

What weapon has been formed against you that needs reversing? Where do you feel blocked from receiving God's best? What has been vowed by your family or yourself in response to pain? Today, ask the Holy Spirit to reveal the entry point of any vow or curse, and take authority over it in the name of Jesus. Then live free! Speak the Word of God over your life, and experience the fullness of God's blessing!

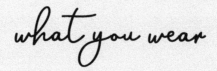

what you wear

I would have lost heart, unless I had believed that I would see the goodness of the Lord in the land of the living.
Psalm 27:13

I love the lyrics of a particular song that describe what a certain person is wearing: a happy and positive demeanour, a harmonious and rhythmical thankfulness, and designer words of life and joy. We all know that life is not always pretty and circumstances harmonious, but regardless of the season, we can choose *what we wear*. The questions we could *all* ask ourselves are, *"Does my clothing reflect the inner belief and state of my heart? Am I wearing hope in this season, or have I succumbed to hopelessness?"* We need to look at what we are wearing. Has a negative feeling become something that now clothes our heart and belies our confession of faith?

The enemy wants to blanket us with despair, depression and discouragement, making us unable to radiate the beauty of Christ who dwells within. The enemy of our soul has a way of riding in on negative events or despair we may be experiencing at any given time. If we allow these negative feelings to linger too long, they can become garments that shroud our hearts yet become visible in our outer responses, our general outlook on life.

During a very short period in our earlier years of ministry, Bruce and I felt discouraged and soon began second-guessing ourselves. As we prayed, God revealed that we had actually become subject to a 'spirit of discouragement' that the enemy was afflicting upon us. His intention was to buffet us, discourage us and dissuade us from our God-given direction. But as we took authority in the name of Jesus, this spirit immediately lifted, and we proceeded confidently on the course and with the 'mantling' Jesus had bestowed upon us. How glad we were for God's revelation and intervention!

Hope and courage worn internally in every season is infectious. It's a powerful motivator! That's why we need to be aware of 'afflicting spirits' on our journey of faith. Is the enemy trying to buffet you, afflict you and cause your struggle to become your everyday apparel? Negative feelings can become what you wear on a consistent basis if unchecked or unresolved. *Feelings of anger* can become a *spirit of anger, feelings of fear* can become a *spirit of fear, depression* can become a *spirit of depression*. But in Jesus we have the authority to break any afflicting spirit that has imposed itself upon us and 'speak it off' our life forever.

Today God may be requiring us to redress, to change our clothes and to put on garments that best represent the hope, love and joy that we have in Him. We have a choice of what we will wear in the next season of our life! How will we dress? Let's choose faith and hope!

Colossians 3:12-13 puts it like this:

> *Therefore, as the elect of God, holy and beloved,*
> ***put on** tender mercies, kindness, humility, meekness,*
> *long-suffering; bearing with one another; and forgiving*
> *one another, if anyone has a complaint against another;*
> *even as Christ forgave you, so you also must do.*

What is clothing your heart and influencing your demeanour right now? What negative thinking and feeling has the enemy moved in on? Today, change your appearance by changing your garments, taking authority over every afflicting spirit. Radiate Jesus today!

start again

Then David and the people who were with him lifted up their voices and wept until they had no more power to weep. And David's two wives, Ahinoam the Jezreelitess, and Abigail, the widow of Nabal the Carmelite, had been taken captive. Now David was great distressed, for the people spoke of stoning him, because the soul of all the people was grieved, every man for his sons and his daughters. But David strengthened himself in the Lord.
1 Samuel 30:4

After David was dismissed from the Philistine army, he returned home to find the city burned with fire, and his wives, sons and daughters taken captive. The loss was overwhelming, and on top of that, the people were threatening him. What was David to do? Well, in spite of the pain, David rose to *start again*. He began where he needed to—inquiring of God what he needed to do next. Immediately, God confirmed that David should pursue the enemy, with the guarantee that they would recover everything that had been taken.

To 'recover' means, "to return to a normal state of health, mind or strength; to find or regain possession of something." It involves bringing that which belongs to someone, back under their rightful covering. When we are under great strain because aspects of our life have faltered or failed, we need to find the strength in God to *start again*, sometimes from the beginning! Like Maria in *The Sound of Music*, we need to *"start at the very beginning—a very good place to start."*

The basic principles in our Christian faith can't be skipped in life's difficulties. We need to go back to the beginning, to the truth of who God is, to enquire from Him, and to receive the wisdom and strength to recover all that has been lost or stolen.

Situations and circumstances can overwhelm us, and too often we may be tempted to stay camped in the overwhelming grief of the moment—or conversely try and handle things in our own strength. Let's not skip the beginning but do what David did instead. In spite of his deep anguish, he looked to the Lord for strength and encouragement. Then he pursued and recovered all, plus some!

Life will knock us down at times but we need to rise to *start again*. Each day is a new day with new strength and mercy! Greet the day with an expectation in God to recover all that we need to live our best life.

Today, do you need to start again by lifting your voice to God and listening for His wisdom for your situation? What do you need to recover? Is it your health? Or your finance? Or something else? Where do you need to start again, to rise afresh with new hope for the day? Praise God today for His help and guidance as you inquire of Him and recover from the enemy all that is rightfully yours!

part five:

healthy soul

love your life

The days of the afflicted are evil, but he who
is of a merry heart has a continual feast.
Proverbs 15:15

There is so much to admire and love in creation and in the creativity of other people! We may admire and fall in love with our spouse, our children, our church and our friends. But do we need to fall in love *with life itself?* Now that may seem like an odd encouragement to some of you, but for others, the reality may be that they don't truly love the life they live. If we don't celebrate the life we get to live, we will lack zeal toward loving God and others. When we live separated from our deepest feelings we run the danger of becoming religious and robotic, tracking in some unappealing rut! Let's determine to enjoy life . . . and if we need to, seek to *'fall in love'* with our life again. What's that going to take? Perhaps we need to ask ourselves some questions.

How good are you at loving yourself? Have you accepted God's design for you and His plan for your life? No person is perfect or has it all together. Everyone has areas of *unlove* toward themselves, but great joy and confidence comes from accepting God's design of us and being truly thankful for who we are! *Inferiority* is simply rejection turned inward, a place where self-hatred and self-loathing exists, occupying our minds and affecting our behaviour. Inferiority is caused by comparing 'unchangeable features.' These days, plastic surgery is available to improve any physical features people may struggle with, but a greater improvement to our beauty shines forth when we accept ourselves inwardly for who we truly are. We are never disqualified from doing life well; rather, we are highly qualified for the full life God has chosen for us. We may just need to come to terms with the areas we cannot change, and work on the areas we can.

Is there *'unlove'* in your heart towards yourself or your circumstances? Then adjust the rhythm of your heartbeat to the heartbeat of Jesus, accepting yourself and every good thing He has spoken over your life. Refuse to waste any more energy worrying about the things you cannot change. In fact, get into party mode and celebrate the *life* you have—and if you still struggle, seek God on how you can change it! Our health depends largely on how we view our life.

How good are we at loving others? Let's love our relationships and look after them! We don't just need 'fair weather' friends; we need friends who we can laugh with, cry with, share with . . . but who will also be honest with us without judgment. The enemy always wants to bring *'unlove'* into relationships. He cunningly uses the smallest tool in his workshop, the wedge to divide and separate people who should be doing life together. That's why many people are doing life alone, and sadly, *'alone'* limits our impact on life. We need to keep our heartbeat in rhythm with the heartbeat of Jesus—a heartbeat of love, acceptance and forgiveness.

We all have the opportunity to be disillusioned in our relationships. Time together allows us to see each other's imperfections! But that shouldn't deflect from our commitment to love as Jesus loved. We need to commit to *loving others*, even if it simply means working on the imperfections we perceive in ourself. Let's not demand one-sided friendships, always withdrawing and never depositing, or be unfaithful with our words, gossiping and relaying information that should remain private. Let's never manipulate others to suit our own agenda or be defensive and quick to take offence. Let's generously *love others* just as Jesus has loved us (John 15:12).

🍃 *Does life to you represent tedious repetition, or joyful expectation? Is there any unlove in your heart toward your life or others? Today, turn from unlovely thoughts and fall in love again with the life you get to live. This is our one chance at life! Let's do it well by loving, forgiving and accepting both ourselves and others.*

isolating insecurity

And Jesus answered and said to her, "Martha, Martha,
you are worried and troubled about many things.
But one thing is needed and Mary has chosen that
good part, which will not be taken away from her."
Luke 10:41-42

When Jesus spoke these words, He was speaking directly to the insecurity in Martha's heart. Little did she know that as she bustled and hassled about the meal she assumed Jesus would have her prepare, her insecurity was all that was on show. The noise in her spirit distracted Martha, preventing her from simply joining Mary in this great opportunity to sit, listen and receive from Jesus. Martha's trouble was that her worth was based in her ability to serve; it was that very insecurity that sabotaged her from receiving what was most important.

Martha needed to grasp the truth internally that she already had a place to stand as a friend and follower of Jesus. Instead, her lack of self-worth drove her to prove her worth by serving. She already had an invitation to sit, but the internal noise in her spirit was louder than the significance of the moment. In Luke 10:40 we read, "Martha was distracted with much serving, and she approached Him and said, 'Lord do you not care that my sister has left me to serve alone? Therefore tell her to help me.'"

Because everything was not going well in the kitchen, she eventually exploded at Mary for not helping her in what she perceived as the most important task of the day. Martha's insecurity was showing!

How easy it is to respond from insecurity, unsure of our place, our 'standing' in any given moment. Insecurity can make us feel unsteady and second-guess our worth, causing us to lean harder on our talents and abilities in an attempt to prove our value. Insecurity has the power to throw us off balance and forfeit the benefits of staying present. It will always raise its voice in some manner and, if not dealt with, insecurity will sabotage environments and prevent growth!

This reminds me of an amusing saying from my teenage years—it was a subtle way to inform someone that their underwear was showing. This saying simply has no relevance today because it is perfectly acceptable (and sometimes even intentional!) to have parts of your underwear visible! But back then we would whisper the phrase, "It's snowing down south" to let someone know that their petticoat was hanging below the hem of their dress, giving the young lady concerned a chance to hitch up the offending item and recover herself from potential embarrassment. Pretty funny as I look back now!

I share that amusing picture because sometimes I think the Holy Spirit may be subtly and lovingly saying the same to us: "Excuse me, your *insecurity* is showing." We may be dressed in the right attire and adopting the right language, but still something contrary may be showing, something that belies our confession of faith. When we are not secure in ourselves and settled in the place God has given us to stand, our insecurity is often visible to others. Insecurity is easy to spot!

So how can we deal with insecurity? Simply hitch up that which is offensive in attitude, thought and deed and bring it to Jesus! We need to do what Martha *failed* to do, and simply take our place at the feet of Jesus, knowing that He welcomes us. Better, more effective service comes from a place of worship. Let's not put our security in our ability to please and perform! Jesus wants us to know that He has already purchased, through His blood, a place for us to stand as His children. We can be fully secure in Him, knowing we are always welcome in His presence.

Where does insecurity show up in your life? What lie or misapprehension is betraying your worth? Today hitch up those offending reactions of insecurity and secure yourself in Jesus!

removing resentment

Now it had happened as they were coming home, when David was
returning from the slaughter of the Philistine, that the women
had come out of all the cities of Israel, singing and dancing, to
meet King Saul, with tambourines, with joy, and with musical
instruments. So the women sang as they danced, and said:
"Saul has slain his thousands, and David his ten thousands."
1 Samuel 18:6-7

King Saul *resented* David when he was applauded for his success in bringing down Goliath, the enemy of Israel. He found this shift of acknowledgment and adoration toward David and away from himself hard to swallow.

Resentment is a powerful emotion that needs to be brought into check before it leads to regrettable attitudes and actions. It surfaces when we feel showed up or challenged by someone else's success. Resentment always feels undervalued and overlooked! That's why resentment looks for vengeance. This was true for King Saul. In 1 Samuel 18:8 we read:

Then Saul was very angry, and the saying displeased him, and he
said, "They have ascribed to David ten thousands and to me they
have ascribed only thousands. Now what more can he have but
the kingdom?" So Saul eyed David from that day forward.

Resentment wants to remove the threat from its presence, and this is exactly what Saul did in demoting David to the rank of captain over a thousand men—all so he wouldn't have to deal with his jealous feelings. In all this

David stayed honourable. The scripture tells us that David behaved wisely in all his ways, and the Lord was with him.

We may be shocked by Saul's response to David, but resentment may be found in seed form in the hearts of many believers when we feel threatened by others. If resentment remains unchecked, it can result in unfavourable reactions and suspicious attitudes towards others.

Resentment causes us to feel angry at circumstances. Resentment wants to *resend* back, things that were initially a blessing. Did you pray for children and feel totally blessed by their arrival, only to resent the time they now demand from you as parents? Or maybe your dream job or mission has now become a burden you resent because you didn't account for the time and effort it would require? As a musician, David was a blessing to Saul when Saul was disturbed by a distressing spirit, but when David rose as a warrior, Saul resented David's success and sought to destroy and eliminate him.

Thankfully, Jonathan had the opposite spirit to his father, Saul. Recognising the anointing on David's life, he bestowed on David the same favour that was on his own life as a king's son, a mighty warrior, a man of faith. Jonathan had no resentment toward David even though he superseded him in rank and file. He simply recognised God's call on David's life, and in 1 Samuel 18:4 we read that his response was to generously bestow on him his own robe, his armour, his word, his bow and his belt!

Let's make sure we don't push away the very blessing God has graciously granted us. Let's not wish away the answers we have prayed for, nor be irritated by the demands God's blessing requires of us. Let's not be threatened by the success of another! God has designed enough space for everyone in His Kingdom.

Is there any resentment in your heart to others or to circumstances? Is there anything you are wishing away that is actually God-sent? Today, remove resentment by showing a generous spirit toward others, recognising God's appointments and celebrating other people's successes.

a way across

For all have sinned and fall short of the glory of God.
Romans 3:23

Have you heard the story of Sir Walter Raleigh, the man who supposedly spread his velvet coat on the ground so that Queen Elizabeth I could walk across a mud puddle without her feet getting wet? Such a gentlemanly gesture, if the account is true!

The Holy Spirit, our eternal companion, is the Gentleman of all time; He helps us across some of the trickier situations in life, keeping us from getting stuck in the mud. We have all fallen short of living righteously before God, and we all need a Saviour! Romans 6:23 tells us, "The wages of sin is death, but the gift of God is eternal life in Christ Jesus." God extended His hand to us in the person of Jesus, who died on the cross for our sins so we could know forgiveness of sin and reconciliation with God Himself. But even after salvation, we continue to need to accept God's hand to help us across some of the more difficult situations in life, across any 'potholes' into which we could potentially fall. That's why God sent us the Holy Spirit as our Helper, the One who would 'lend a hand' when needed.

Others fall short too, and maybe we have suffered as a consequence of their actions! Bitterness has become an underlying disease in our society as unforgiveness, blame and condemnation cause bitter roots to grow in people's hearts. Without God's intervention and Holy Spirit conviction, these roots can spring up and entangle themselves around our hearts, affecting us emotionally, mentally and physically. Unforgiveness in the heart has the power to torment people in their mind, opening the door to physical sickness. This is why Hebrews 12:14-15 tells us:

Pursue peace with all people and holiness, without which no one
*will see the Lord, looking carefully lest anyone **fall short** of the*
grace of God; lest any root of bitterness springing up cause trouble,
and by this many become defiled.

Our heart is a garden, and we need to take care that no bitter thought or emotion is allowed to take root in its soil. Bitterness in our conversations and comments, and condemning statements, need to be weeded out! Will we be tempted toward bitterness? Yes, of course we will! As with every disappointment in life, there is the temptation to dwell on it and find offence.

That's why I love this scripture. It encourages us not to *fall short of the grace of God*! The grace of God through the Holy Spirit has the power to lift us out of our feelings of pain and disappointment in times of testing. Imagine crossing a full river and suddenly finding your life was in danger—you would grasp a hand offering help, wouldn't you?

In my mind's eye, I see the Holy Spirit as a gentleman, offering His hand to me, steadying me through the current, gallantly throwing down a garment of grace so I can walk without soiling my feet or getting stuck in the mud of bitterness. We have a choice in moments of testing—either we let a bitter root find space in our heart or we grasp the offered hand of God's grace which reaches out to assist us over the temptation. Jesus laid down His own life so we could cross from death to life. Now the Holy Spirit offers His hand to help us live a life of health, peace and joy!

*Do you know the power of salvation and what was offered fully to you at the cross of Jesus? Today, walk by **grace** on the provision Jesus made for you on the cross so you can live freely and lightly from a healthy soul! Have you allowed any bitter thought to take root in your heart, defiling you? Are you stuck in the mud of bitterness or regret from the past? Check your conversations and your thoughts for any clues of residual bitterness. Take the hand of the Holy Spirit today, and allow Him to lead you through.*

when the elastic snaps

*And David said in his heart, "Now I shall perish someday by the
hand of Saul. There is nothing better for me than that I should
speedily escape to the land of the Philistines; and Saul will
despair of me, to seek me anymore in any part of Israel.
So I shall escape out of his hand."*
1 Samuel 27:1

The elastic finally snapped. David's resilience and courage eventually succumbed to the relentless pressure of being hunted down by Saul. Even though David's life had just been spared and his enemy had retreated, the forecast of further pursuits brought David's spirit low. He needed a plan.

And so, in desperation, he decided to seek safety among the Philistines. But his plan was an indication of his weariness of spirit, his inability to make wise choices in that moment. David's decisions were in direct reaction to his current plight. As a result, he made an alliance with the Philistines and was given a region called Ziglag as a dwelling place for his household and those of his men.

From there, David planned and undertook raids on the surrounding nations, conquering and depleting those cities of their inhabitants and their livelihood. Something shifted in David's heart and behaviour as a result of his rash decision.

Firstly, he began to *operate in unbelief.* David's faith had just imploded, and in unbelief he resorted to seeking a safe place from Saul's attention in the camp of his enemy! Then, he became *hard of heart.* The once-gentle shepherd become ruthless in battle, not sparing men or women but plundering the livestock and apparel of other nations. And finally, David became *secretive.* He sought to leave no trace of his activities so Saul would not hear of his exploits.

How far David had slipped! How different a man he was from his former days of praising God openly for His help and victory over the enemy! In these raids, God was not glorified; only the enemy got to celebrate David's fall from favour in Israel's eyes. Something had fundamentally changed.

1 Samuel 27:12 says,

> *So Achish believed David, saying, "He has made his people Israel utterly abhor him; therefore he will be my servant forever."*

The anointing for war was still David's life, but as he was positioned wrongly, his efforts now produced different results. David was so 'off side' in this period of his life that his actions belied the call of God on his life!

Sometimes we are at risk of making foolish decisions and projecting negatively into the future when we are in a position of weariness and struggle. Prolonged periods of testing may put pressure on our faith and cause the resilience of our spirit to snap, until, like David, we become vulnerable to poor choices. So stay present in times of testing! Call on God and others for encouragement and strength. Don't allow the enemy to take advantage of your weakness and change the trajectory of your life! David was called to be the king of Israel, and without God's eventual intervention, that call to lead Israel would have been completely sabotaged.

Are you maintaining a resilience and reliance on God to fight on your behalf, or has the elastic snapped, causing you to make unwise decisions in the moment? Where do you need to be self-aware of weariness and vulnerability to the enemy? Are you positioned where God wants you so He gets the glory for the victories in your life? What strategies can you put in place today to prevent the enemy derailing your call in Christ? Today, ensure the elastic doesn't snap, and your faith is not compromised!

clean hands and a pure heart

*Who may ascend into the hill of the Lord? He who has **clean hands** and a **pure heart**; who has not lifted up his soul to an idol . . . He shall receive blessing from the Lord and righteousness from the God of his salvation.*
Psalm 24:3-5

We are all familiar with hand sanitisers today. We use them before treating sick patients, when undertaking common tasks around the home, and often, when we enter or leave public places. Having *clean hands* is a sure way of preventing diseases from spreading from one person to another.

Maintaining a heart that is pure is far more difficult. A heart that is diseased is hard to treat and has a detrimental effect on the overall health of a person. That's why Satan is out to contaminate our hearts! He knows that if an infection lodges in our heart, it has the power to spread to other parts of our body, seriously affecting our wellbeing. Infections to which our hearts can be susceptible are pride, fear, jealousy, condemnation and doubt—just to name a few!

When it comes to our hearts, temptation is not the problem, but yielding to the temptation is. Psalm 24 stresses the need to lift our soul to Jesus and worship Him only. We want the blessings of God and we aspire to ascend into His presence, but the big question is, "What are we really lifting our heart up to?"

1 John 2:15-16 exhorts us with these words:

> *Do not love the world or things in the world. If anyone loves the world, the love of the Father is not in him. For all that is in the world — the lust of the flesh, the lust of the eyes and the pride of life is not of the Father but is of the world.*

There is a tug-of-war for the affections of our heart. What do we love or crave after? The love of the Father? Or the lust of the flesh? The lust of the flesh tugs on our heart and says, *"I want."* The lust of the eyes says, *"I need."* And the pride of life says, *"I know."*

Lust is the focus on self and one's own needs, and is in competition with pure love! Lust seeks to get, whereas love seeks to give. True love, in contrast, comes from *clean hands* and a *pure heart,* and a soul that has not been lifted to an idol.

Are there areas in our lives where we have lifted our soul in futility to an idol or to something in direct contrast to God's pure love and salvation plan for our life? Perhaps there has been a rising of pride stemming from a root of anger, fear or pain, which has subsequently contaminated our actions? The real battle is a battle between *pride* and *grace*. To which will we yield? Pride overrides reason and becomes a slippery slope, while grace upholds us, strengthens our resolve and helps us ascend! Which will you choose?

Today, take the time to gauge where you are at. Do you detect any disease seeking to contaminate your heart? Have you allowed pride and lust in your heart? Today, lift your soul to Jesus and watch Him lift you into places of blessing and righteousness.

keep lifting up

Lift up your heads, O you gates! And be lifted up you everlasting doors! And the King of glory shall come in. Who is the King of glory? The Lord strong and mighty, the Lord mighty in battle. Lift up your heads, O you gates! Lift up, you everlasting doors! And the King of glory shall come in. Who is this King of glory? The Lord of hosts, He is the King of glory.
Psalm 24:7-10

What a beautiful scripture! I am sure we all desire the King of Glory with all His majesty and power to invade our lives, but we have a part to play also, and that is to *lift our soul* to Him. So how strong are we? We all have different capacities in the natural to lift varying weights—some more than others! But as Christians we are called to be strong *in the Spirit*, to be 'weight lifters'—and this is going to take training and practice to develop the spiritual muscle needed. We need to learn how to lift our minds and hearts to the Lord Jesus. Yes, sometimes God moves sovereignly on our behalf, but mostly God wants us to cooperate with Him by responding in faith!

How good are you at responding to His call at the gate of your heart? In biblical days, cities were surrounded by walls for protection, with gates and doors as entrances. It was usual for people or troops approaching the city to cry out to the watchman who sat on the wall, requesting permission to enter. In response, the watchman would enquire who it was that wanted to come in before determining whether entry would be granted or not.

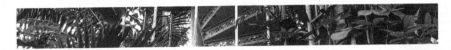

Today, the King of glory approaches our lives, seeking entry. Imagine that! Are the doors and the gates of our heart open for Him to sweep in with all His fullness and all His glory? Or have we 'shut shop' and put a *Closed* sign in the window? Perhaps we are walled in, stuck in a castle of defeat and self-protection because of past invasions from the enemy who brought nothing but hurt and disappointment, and now we have retreated, living instead in anxiety and fear? Perhaps our muscles simply collapsed after too much pressure, and we have given in and pulled up the drawbridge to the castle of our heart?

Psalm 24 exhorts us to *lift up our heads!* The true Answer to our issues is seeking to come in and strengthen us! Let's acknowledge the approach of Jesus, hear His voice, and open the gates for Him to enter. Who is He? He is the King of Glory, the Lord strong and mighty, the Lord mighty in battle, the Lord of Hosts. Let's welcome him in right now!

Where are you at? Enjoying the fullness of Jesus because you have *lifted up the gates* of your heart and welcomed Him in? Or have you battened down the castle of your heart? If we try to protect our hearts in that place of isolation, loneliness and despair, our heart will most likely become hard, brittle and disposed to shattering altogether!

Have you erected walls around your heart through offence and un-forgiveness? Proverbs 18:19 tells us, "A brother offended is harder to win than a strong city, and contentions are like the bars of a castle." Let's stop quarrelling. Let's not remain imprisoned by hurts and offences. Today, Jesus calls for access at the gate of our heart. On entry into our soul, Jesus' presence can love us back to life again, restoring our courage and strength. Let's open the doors and lift up the gates so His love, power and glory can invade our innermost being, strengthening us beyond anything we dreamed possible! Let's keep exercising, stretching and developing muscle so we can carry weight in the Spirit!

What weight or pressure are you buckling under? What hurt or disappointment that has shut you down or caused you to close the door of your heart needs to be exposed again to the love of Jesus? Today, respond to the voice of God and welcome the King of Glory in all His might and power. Find His hand on yours today, strengthening and enabling you to lift every heavy weight with ease.

single focus

*But seek first the kingdom of God and His righteousness
and all these things shall be added to you.*
Matthew 6:33

Every day there are countless messages and signals vying for our attention. Our job is to filter out the ungodly messages, and not respond to those that are simply carnal in nature. God's gospel message is pure: *Jesus came, Jesus died and Jesus rose again* so that we could be reconciled with God, redeemed from our sin, and inherit eternal life.

The gospel of Jesus is a message without adulteration, defilement or corruption. It is a message that speaks straight to our heart about the love of God for mankind. One definition of purity is "to will one thing," to be single-focused in heart and purpose. Jesus talks about this single focus many times in scripture. The necessities of life—as well as the luxuries of life—can occupy so much of our time and attention. In fact, we can get so busy with life that we forget how to really live! But God promises to look after the things we need when we simply focus on Him and seek Him first!

The Bible also speaks about how duplicity can subtly dilute our faith, power and effectiveness. James 1:5-8 says,

> *If any of you lacks wisdom, let him ask of God . . . But let him ask in faith, with **no doubting**, for he who doubts is like a wave of the sea driven and tossed by the wind. For let not that man suppose that he will receive anything from the Lord; he is a **double-minded** man, unstable in all his ways.*

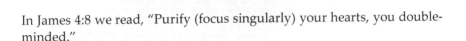

In James 4:8 we read, "Purify (focus singularly) your hearts, you double-minded."

There is a push today for *purity*—environmentally, bodily, and in the foods we consume. It's one reason labels are required to identify ingredients on food containers—so people can make informed choices before buying. We can make so many good choices about healthy living and eating, and yet so many contrasting poor choices in caring for our souls!

When something is pure, it exists in its essential nature—undefiled, unblemished and uncontaminated. When you look at the fruit in a supermarket, you are going to choose an unblemished peach over a bruised one every time, right? Let's choose the same for our lives also. The Bible tells us to "guard our heart" and to keep it pure from manufactured contaminants that seek to destroy. Matthew 5:8 encourages us with the words, "The *pure in heart* shall see God."

Adonijah and Solomon are two sons of David who show us two different motivations and two different agendas. One had a pure heart. The other, not so much. 1 Kings 1:5 tells us that, "Adonijah the son of Haggith exalted himself saying 'I will be King,' and he prepared for himself chariots and horsemen and fifty men to run before him." His heart was set on himself! In contrast, we see the humility and purity in Solomon's heart in 1 Kings 3:7 when he prays, "O Lord my God. You have made Your servant king instead of my father David, but I am a little child; I do not know how to go out or come in."

Adonijah saw position, while Solomon saw people. Solomon's purity of focus caused him to request a wise and understanding heart from God to lead the people effectively. God could respond to the single focus of Solomon's heart, but not to Adonijah's self-promotion. We need to keep the content and the intent of our heart pure! Let's not be double-minded and confused. Whenever we need to discern the quality and authenticity of a message, God says we can ask Him for wisdom and He will give it!

*Are you single-focused, or are you entertaining **duplicity**? Today, take the time to 'read the labels' of the things you are consuming. Are they pure, or impure? Today, choose **purity** of faith and lifestyle so God can back you in all your endeavours.*

part six:

transitions

plant yourself

*Those who are planted in the house of the Lord shall flourish in
the courts of our God. They shall still bear fruit in old age;
They shall be fresh and flourishing!*
Psalm 92:13-14

The key to flourishing and fruitfulness is to be planted in the house of God!
It is not difficult to point out the faults and flaws of the Church, for where
people representing different cross sections of life come together for any
reason, there will always be obvious imperfections. Not one of us has it all
together, but the house of God remains the place He has ordained for us all
to flourish and be fruitful in life together. We need to be connected to God's
house, not just in attendance but by allowing our roots to go deep down.

Bruce and I have always known the strength of this verse being outworked
in our own lives and the blessings associated with being planted in the
house of God. But at times we have needed to *reapply* our commitment—
especially in periods of transition or relocation. In the year 2000, Bruce
and I set off overseas to plant a church in London, one which we saw as
a 'beach head' into Europe. We approached this mission with faith and
expectation, knowing the call and the timing of God was right.

Although I was thoroughly invested into the mission, I realised over time
that I actually needed to plant myself in a whole new way. I certainly wasn't
resistant, but I had viewed the mission as temporary. Subconsciously,
I was awaiting the time when God would whisper in my ear, "mission
accomplished, you can return home now," and as a result, I wasn't as
planted as I could have been. That's when God revealed to me that I was
living with a temporary mindset even while I was fully invested and
desperately keen to see God move and see this church become strong! Is
that even possible? *It is totally possible!* I had to reconcile my commitment
to following the call of God to London with the reality that we might never
return to my home country, New Zealand. For Bruce and I, this wasn't just
about an overseas experience—it was about the call of God on our lives
and our obedience to it. With that in mind, I needed to not just labour in
this 'vineyard' but plant myself fully 'in the soil.'

I love that God speaks in picture form; the image I received was one of
a tumbleweed. If I didn't plant myself internally on a permanent basis, I
would be 'lightweight' like a tumbleweed, with the potential to be easily
blown out to sea. I certainly did not want that to happen!

So many people are 'all at sea' with their emotions, decisions and commitments because they have failed to plant (or replant) themselves in the soil of God's house at certain junctures in life, adopting a temporary mindset because of anticipated changes in jobs or location, and excusing themselves from fully committing and involving themselves in the local church! But suspending commitment in any season of life is unwise, as the enemy's scheme is to uproot us and blow us far away from where the blessing of God is for us. Winds of change come and winds of trouble blow, and if we are not planted deeply in the house of God, we can find ourselves in a place we never thought possible!

"Wherever you are, *be there*," is an expression Bruce and I have always taken seriously. We have chosen to plant ourselves, to let our roots go down deep into the house and the will of God. We want the tree of our life to flourish and produce fruit in every season because of the secure and protected environment we choose to dwell in. God loves His church! And so today's exhortation is to not just attend, but to invest . . . to plant yourself deep so you can experience your best and most fruitful life *now*.

Have you become 'uprooted' and vulnerable to the winds of change? Have you suspended your commitment to His Church because of transitions in your life? Where do you need to recommit and replant yourself? Today, secure yourself, knowing that God honours commitment and devotion to His house.

afraid of the journey

For I the Lord your God, will hold your right hand,
saying to you, "Fear not, I will help you."
Isaiah 41:13

At certain points in life, transitions are needed. To walk on a new path without clear vision is not easy for anyone to negotiate; even the bravest will experience anxiety as they peer into the haze of the unknown. This is especially true when we face unexpected interruptions to normality such as illness, financial collapse or unforeseen disasters. Ageing is another unavoidable transition—a certain amount of trepidation comes with having to let go of familiar routines, certain activities, and maybe a pending relocation from a loved home base. This can be a fearful journey for many as they realise that life as they have known it for many years is now turning a *sharp corner* and heading in a completely different direction.

Life's *sharp corners* demand a change of gear and steadiness of heart to cope with their demand and unpredictability, and knowing when to touch the brakes is important! What *corner* are you negotiating? Perhaps you are staring at a sudden change of circumstances in your life, unable to clearly see what lays ahead. How we approach and anticipate the corner is so important in successfully making it around the other side.

Transitions can place unwanted pressure on us. When the challenge is outside our choice of route or our choice of destination, anxiety may rise, causing us to stall. Whatever you are facing, the Scriptures encourage us that in all our journeying, in all our transitioning, the Lord is with us, holding our hand. He is helping us *negotiate the corners* of life, and He will take us around them and into the new territory victoriously. What a comfort! Just as our parents would take our hands when we were much younger to reassure us of our safety and their presence, so the Lord our God does that for us. He will help us in the place of transition and quieten the accompanying fear!

Perhaps life is on a steady path for you at this time. But could there be people in your life who are negotiating some *tight bends* in their journey right now? Rather than judging their responses, recognise the apprehension that may be present in their hearts and offer your hand to help them. Hold their hand in whatever way is beneficial and imparts courage.

Are there any *sharp corners* ahead of you that need careful prayer and negotiation? We often see signs on our highways warning us of a sudden change of road conditions or potential danger, giving us an opportunity to anticipate the upcoming terrain and make the necessary adjustments. God too, signals any approaching changes to life so that we can seek Him and find what is required to negotiate the challenge before us. If the nation of Israel needed God to hold their hand, so at times will we in the challenges and changes that life may throw our way.

🍃 *Today, thank God that He is your present help in trouble. Put your hand in His today. Remember, He's got you! Ask God for increased skill in negotiating corners that will open into new and greater horizons. Then, look around you and see who needs you to hold their hand and walk with them on their journey. Who in your world is currently fearful of the journey ahead and the challenges represented by life's changes? Reassure them with your presence and prayer today.*

make the frame work

For You formed my inward parts; You covered me in my mother's
womb. I will praise You, for I am fearfully and wonderfully made;
Marvelous are Your works, and that my soul knows very well.
My frame (bones) was not hidden from You, when I was made
in secret, and skillfully wrought in the lowest parts of the earth.
Psalm 139:13-15

Life is constantly on the move. Just as hairstyles have seasons, clothes have eras and methods have expiry dates, time doesn't stop for anyone. There's always a need to update, to stay relevant and relatable to current generations—to change with the season. Seasons come and go throughout our lifetime, and some seasons even reappear but with a new look or feel. Embrace it! New approaches bring fresh appeal and relatability.

Let's not get stuck in a season, growing old on ourselves, drawing the years in on our life and 'freeze framing' ourselves into a moment of time. It's time to come out of the fridge of conservation where we seek to preserve everything that we are familiar with, and instead expose ourselves to the warmth and richness of the current season. It's easy to think this challenge to be relevant applies more to those mature in age, but some young people have old, sedentary mindsets and need revitalising in the spirit of their minds as well! And then there are the older people who have maintained their freshness and vitality throughout life! What category are you in today? Is it time for a revamp of style or a renewal of vision? Wherever you are at, how about today you push the 'refresh button' and view the change God is challenging you with?

Have you ever looked at a painting that was celebrated in its time, maybe of a family member or a meaningful scene that now seems to have lost its appeal? Perhaps the frame that hosted the work of art needs updating to fit the environment. It's beginning to clash with its surroundings! Does that lessen the value of the painting or photograph? *Not at all.* Updating the frame can give the picture more relevancy and appeal. Likewise, we need to be aware of any mismatch between the past and the present.

Let's not confuse changing seasons, however, with changing our identity! There is something permanent God has placed within us that will never change, the very essence and fabric of who we are. But maybe the outer framework has dated and no longer does justice to the magnificence God has placed within each and every one of us. In that case, our frameworks may need updating or repositioning—our placement, or sphere of influence, for example. So let's embrace hope in our heart for an even more fruitful season ahead. God doesn't call us to change just for change's sake, but to experience greater productivity so that others will benefit.

Remember that your value doesn't change, but your style may need to. Check the external framework of your life! What have you frozen into a frame that needs to be revamped? What mindsets are you locked into that may need to be reviewed? Remember that time waits for no one, and you don't want to be left in the wake of yesteryear, bewildered by the changes others are making. Stay relevant, but stay real to who you are!

🍃 *Today, thank God for the person He has created you to be. Think about any changes that need be made in the framework of your life. Transition into the new by thawing any 'freeze framing' around your life and renewing the context. Then thank God for the new and fruitful season ahead. Make the frame work!*

transfer your weight

*It is God who has armed me with strength and makes
my way perfect. He makes my feet like the feet of deer,
and **sets me** on my high places.*
Psalm 18:32-33

No one is exempt from transitions in life. In every stage—moving from school to college, from college to work, from single status to married, from childlessness to parenthood—there is apprehension and excitement for the new season ahead. Some transitions might be relatively easy, while others may take a longer period of adjustment. Transitions can feel like riding a skateboard downhill. When the speed suddenly and unexpectedly increases, we can experience what is known as 'speed wobbles,' a shaking that threatens to throw us off balance onto the sidewalk.

Have you ever felt wobbly? We can feel 'wobbly' wherever there is a change of location, position or even status! I like to view transitions as a time to simply *transfer our weight*. But sometimes we lack the coordination to transition smoothly, incurring a few grazed knees and broken arms along the way, *"ouch"* moments in our journey, when we discover the ground where we previously stood firm is no longer there. That's when we need to transfer our weight into a new season of 'being and functioning.' I believe this is something Bruce and I have done really well through the seasons— releasing our children to marriage, building churches and releasing them to other leaders, and then releasing the leading of a local church to become more apostolic in function.

I gained a great picture of this one day during a tree-top climbing adventure we participated in as a church staff activity. This exercise was conducted approximately five metres above ground level; we were kitted out with a helmet and harness to assist us in crossing from tree top to tree top via the high ropes, and on the odd occasion, across an extensive net. At the beginning of the exercise I felt wobbly, my heart was 'in my mouth' as I climbed to the platform of the first tree which was, horrifyingly, barely large enough for my two feet. What a relief to clip the harness on and know at least I was attached! On the first crossing, a long span between two trees, I found myself lurching back and forth a little uncontrollably. The top and bottom rope were not in sync with one other, and I had to reprimand myself and focus intently on the tree I was heading toward. My apprehension didn't go away completely that day but I improved and I'm pleased to say I completed the course! And, I received a revelation regarding transitions in life.

I pondered the fact that the same harness I had clipped onto the upper rope, become the very means for me to descend from the heights when it converted into a flying fox I could sit on. That's when I had the revelation that if I had put more trust in my carabiner, I would not have put so much pressure on myself to stay on the ropes, trying so hard not to fall! Maybe if I had just tested my carabiner, I would have been much more confident!

The Holy Spirit is our Carabiner in every transition of life. He will uphold us as we learn to walk at new altitudes of faith! I have seen many people flounder at transition points because they mourn too long the passing of a previous season and seem unable to transfer their weight into a new season. As God's children, this shouldn't be so; there may be initial apprehension, but God has made amazing provision for the future which we need to firmly place our feet on. Transitions are all about being able to *transfer our weight* in line with the direction God is leading us into. Let's trust Him to hold us as we transition!

What transition do you face today? Choose to make that transition with faith and expectation in your spirit. Today, trust the Holy Spirit to assist you in your 'wobbly moments' and place you back on the 'high wire of faith' if you fall. Remember, transitioning is not just an age thing—it's a life requirement! Let's transition well so God can be glorified. Stay attached to Jesus, your Carabiner!

recognising seasons

*After these things I looked, and behold, a door standing open
in heaven. And the first voice which I heard was like a trumpet
speaking with me, saying, "Come up here, and I will show you
things which must take place after this."*
Revelation 4:1

God often calls us forth into new seasons that require us to activate greater levels of trust, confidence and reliance on Him, knowing He has the very best in store for our lives. During these times, God invites us into a higher level of understanding and knowledge of Him. In every changing season, we serve a consistent God, a never-changing God who is the *bedrock* of our faith!

Just as leaves changing colour and falling from the trees indicates the approach of autumn, and the budding and blossoming of fruit trees reference the beginning of spring, so in the spiritual God wants us to be able to recognise and anticipate a change of season. He calls us to make preparations. As we approach a new season in the natural, we may stock up on firewood or change our wardrobe to better 'match the conditions.' In the spiritual, we position our hearts for a new season according to the revelation we have received!

For some people a change of season in life makes them feel anxious; others may be daunted by the thought of what lies ahead—especially when a new season is forced upon them through redundancy, death or an illness. We may even describe some seasons as feeling like 'the rug has been pulled out from under our feet.' Perhaps we previously knew where we stood—the rug was familiar, stability was guaranteed, and progress was made while we were positioned there. Have we taken for granted the mat under our feet, that which we have been standing on for some period of time? Have we relied on the 'bounce' of yesterday's revelations to sustain us through new and upcoming seasons? A new and deeper revelation of God will give us the buoyancy we need in the changing season.

During times of change, we also need to *interpret the season*. Transitions can cause issues we had dealt with in a previous season to surface—perhaps an insecurity, causing us to doubt and question ourselves as we recall the loss of stability and victory we may have previously had. We may even question whether we are able to rise to another level of faith, courage and victory. However, these insecurities place us in danger of *misinterpreting the season!*

When I faced this issue some years back, God gave me a way of interpreting the seasons in picture form. I saw that life's challenges are like the alphabet. As a child, we learn to chant the whole alphabet from A to Z. God showed me that just as learning the alphabet allows us to learn to read and write, so the challenges we face in life allow us to mature in our faith. It's a wonderful feeling to have 'learnt the letters' and to move on to greater things! However, it is not so great when a season demands we revisit and relearn some of the elementary letters—letters we felt we had already conquered and were familiar with.

That's why we need to recognise that in every season there is more God wants us to learn when he calls us to revisit a particular 'letter' or challenge. You see, *within truth there is more truth!* Challenges just grant us new opportunities to go deeper in our understanding of age-old truths that have always been! Earlier victories, as amazing as they were at the time, may be insufficient for the season ahead. God has something greater to show us that will sustain us in our future season. Though seasons change, let's choose not to be alarmed, but choose instead to *go higher* in God. We need to receive His invitation to *come and see* what He wants to show us.

Do you know what season you are in? Is a new season pending in your life? Today, refuse to be alarmed by previous challenges. Instead, view them as an opportunity to learn more of God. 'Come higher' with God and receive the interpretation of the seasons of your life!

part seven:

spiritual warfare

it's only dust

*If the household is worthy, let your peace come upon it. But if it
is not worthy, let your peace return to you. And whoever will
not receive you nor hear your words, when you depart from that
house or city, **shake off the dust** from your feet.*
Matthew 10:13-14

'*It's only dust*' is a phrase God whispered in my ear when I was faced with the untimely and disappointing departure from our lives of a friend we had walked together with over many years. These human debacles happen in every aspect of life and are not easy to reconcile at the best of times. They have the potential to knock us off balance, especially when they come at us with speed or from 'left field,' as the saying goes! They leave us reeling, wondering, *what just happened?*

A speck of dust is so tiny but when stirred into a dust storm it has the power to sting our face, eyes, and any other exposed part of our flesh. Such small particles swirling together can have a strong negative impact on us. It was while I was still stunned and knocked back by this event that God whispered, "It's only dust." In other words, *it can sting, but it doesn't have to stick!* You see, while an initial sensation may be painful, it doesn't need to become something you wear permanently. You can shake it off. *It's only dust!*

This is why, when Jesus sent His disciples out to minister, He encouraged them to simply move on and shake the dust off their feet as they went! He knew that not everyone was going to receive the message the disciples were carrying. Not everyone is going to appreciate our best efforts either, even when we have the best intentions at heart. But we don't need to crumble under the sting of rejection or become bogged down by contrary responses. We simply need to move on!

In the natural, dust that has settled on flat surfaces appears harmless enough. It will wait patiently until we get around to dealing with it. But while particles of dust are so infinitesimal, we all know how quickly they can accumulate. Dust sits in our houses relatively harmlessly, but if enough gathers on a filter or in a ventilation system, air flow will be reduced which can result in overheating, equipment malfunction and subsequently, costly repair bills! Dust, along with a little bit of moisture, has the power to corrode, to eat away at surfaces.

Dust can gather also in relationships, settling on hearts and covering surfaces that once were open and transparent. Dust, in the form of unresolved disagreements, disputes and discontent can conceal original commitments and loyalty, forming instead, seeds of betrayal and separation! Perhaps you have experienced layers of dust landing in your heart, weakening your resolve and compromising your commitment? Or maybe you have felt the full-on force of a dust or sand storm blowing up in your face, leaving you stinging and in pain? Sadly, where there is a lack of mature communication, these occurrences can happen. This is a human problem that is all too common; storms stirred by the wind of discontent and selfishness! Let's get better at being 'dust monitors', keeping the surface of our heart clear and clean, free from the corrosive power of dust.

Today, acknowledge any pain you may have collected. Is there an event that has stung you? Exercise forgiveness, shaking off the dust by refusing to allow it to stick to you and corrode your future well-being. Is there an offense that has eaten into your resolves of love and commitment? Shake off the dust of rejection today, and recover your balance and equilibrium. Ask God to help you move forward into your future! Remember, it's only dust!

on team

Then Peter took Him aside, and began to rebuke Him, saying,
"Far be it from You, Lord; this shall not happen to You!"But
He turned and said to Peter, "Get behind Me, Satan,
you are an offence to Me, for you are not mindful
of the things of God, but the things of men."
Matthew 16:22-23

Jesus rebuked Peter! Peter, speaking his concern was totally unaware that his remark to Jesus at that time was like playing 'off-side,' scoring for the opposition! Peter was doing what he so often did—making quick responses to situations, *speaking from his mind and not his spirit*. He didn't realise that if Jesus was to abort His mission, *Team God* would lose against the powers of darkness. That's why Jesus rebuked him so sharply! Peter's mind and heart hadn't fully comprehended the mission Jesus was undertaking or what was involved to win this match against death and hell and to herald in the greatest victory of all time.

There's something powerful about being 'on team,' participating alongside others to see amazing victories against the odds, celebrating the wins *and* standing united together in the tough times. However, with teams—whether a marriage team, sports team, ministry team or work team—boundaries of operation exist so the best can be achieved; there are ethos, ideals and dreams that hold team together! To play outside those parameters is to 'break team,' to damage team morale or team spirit. In fact, to break rank is to hand power to the opposing team!

Not only are God's people a team—we are an army! A well-trained army will stand shoulder to shoulder, march to the same beat, and stay in step with each other, upholding the same belief, hope and confession of faith. Failing to fall into line, support or add weight to the direction and vision of the team is similar to defecting! There can be no loitering in an army, no 'wait and see' or 'playing it safe.' Time matters; there is a mission to accomplish and an enemy to defeat. In God's army, everyone needs to turn up ready and willing, whatever the conditions, to participate and play *on team* in order to win. Together we are stronger! We need to keep turning up!

> *And let us consider one another in order to stir up love and good*
> *works, not forsaking the assembling of ourselves together, as is*
> *the manner of some, but exhorting one another and so much*
> *the more as you see the day approaching.*
> *Hebrews 10:24-25*

When we assemble together on a regular basis, we are 'God's army on parade'; we are making a statement to principalities and powers that God's church is alive and well and on the move, rising up in unity, power and authority over the schemes of the wicked. Let's not operate from a human mindfulness, wanting to stay outside the parameters of God's ordained purpose, and yet still expect to win! Let's check our hearts and minds are not 'off-side,' playing outside God's boundaries for team. God wants you and me *on team*. Let's turn up and add our weight to His cause!

Is there any area where you are refusing to come alongside as part of the team? Today, decide to play 'on team,' to fight 'on team' and subsequently to win 'on team'! Team God always wins!

on god's field

The Lord forbid that I should do this thing to my master,
the Lord's anointed, to stretch out my hand against him,
seeing he is the anointed of the Lord.
1 Samuel 24:6

Wars and disputes, whether between people, communities or nations, have always been prevalent in our world. However they play out, the threats usually sound similar and there is always a great deal of animosity. Hatred is a powerful and destructive force!

The driving motivation of war is simply to take possession of territory from another or to repossess territory that had been taken in the first instance. The Bible describes the warfare we find ourselves in as a spiritual warfare instigated in heavenly places, with spiritual forces seeking to infiltrate, intimidate and dominate. One tactic of the enemy is to take captive people's hearts in the battle so they lose godly conviction and enter the fray of foul play.

David had a very real enemy in Saul, who fought on the field of jealousy, ambition, pride, hatred and self-promotion. Saul viewed David as a threat, and sought to eliminate him. In one particular incident, Saul took three thousand chosen men of Israel with him to search out David, just one man! How incensed Saul must have been?!

Of course, when an opportunity arose to take revenge on Saul, David's men saw it as the perfect chance for David to take advantage of his enemy. But David did not fight on the same field as Saul. Instead of fighting out of revenge, he contended on the field of honour, respect and the fear of the Lord, knowing that wars are not won on the fleshly level but on a godly plane.

In my life I have found the enemy has, at times, sought to hand me challenges, particularly to prove myself worthy or capable when unfairly criticised. At those times, something within me wants to rise up to prove the accusation false and unfounded. God likened this temptation to a 'handle' the enemy was inviting me to take hold of, causing me to enter a playing field I had no business being on. Recognising these carnal challenges early enabled me to make a conscious decision in my spirit to withdraw immediately from any ungodly competition—to just politely decline and retreat, separating myself from any lure or temptation stemming from pride and the desire to prove myself.

David decided the same thing when he said,

> Let the Lord judge between you (Saul) and me, and let the Lord
> avenge me on you. But my hand shall not be against you.
> 1 Samuel 24:12 (parentheses mine)

And to that, Saul replied,

> You're the one in the right, not me . . .
> You've heaped good on me; I've dropped evil on you.
> And now you've done it again—treated me generously.
> 1 Samuel 24:16 (MSG)

David's righteous response stopped Saul in his tracks and caused him to retreat!

What battle or competition have you entered that is not yours to fight? Are you fighting on the field of righteousness and faith or on the field of indignation and pride? Today, invite God to take control of the battle and fight on your behalf. Play on God's field, and you will influence others for what is right!

clap and shout

*Oh, clap your hands, all you peoples! Shout to God with the voice
of triumph! For the Lord Most High is awesome, He is a great
King over all the earth. He will subdue the peoples under us,
and the nations under our feet.*
Psalm 47:1-3

The voice of triumph needs to be heard, to celebrate God and make His victory known! When we attend a sports match and the team we support have a significant win, we don't sit passively, applauding quietly and politely. We *clap* vigorously, making sure others know our team has won! We may even get up on our feet and *shout* for joy, expressing our pride in our team and the players! The win is too good for us to remain quiet!

Could we be too passive when it comes to expressing our praise to God? There are times when we need to get up onto our feet *'clapping and shouting,'* not just for the sake of it, but giving expression to the triumph we have in Jesus! Moments of anointed clapping and shouts of joy in spiritual warfare remind the enemy of his defeat—and God's eternal victory!

A *clap* and a *shout* of faith has the ability to break barriers and limitations. Courage and strength arise in us when we give voice to the victory Jesus has already won and continues to win on our behalf. Like Gideon in Judges chapter 6, we may need to come out of our hiding places of excuses, procrastination and fear into the open spaces to declare how great our God is! There are moments in our life when we just need to *break out*, break the sound barrier and cast off limitations with loud praise and behaviour that is conducive to great victories!

Perhaps we need some 'Gideon-barriers' to be broken over our lives; barriers of self-doubt, smallness in our own sight, intimidation, fear and doubt. Perhaps we need to bring an authoritative *shout* against forces and trials that seek to prevail and weaken us. Concerns for one's safety and fear of danger can keep people blanketed and immobile. Are we buried under the problems of life, living hidden and in disguise instead of on the field of faith, warring in the spirit? We need to declare war on passivity, indifference and intimidation!

> *In the day that I cried out, You answered me,*
> *and made me bold in my soul.*
> Psalm 138:3

Many times, Israel was intimidated by surrounding nations because they did not stand in the victory that already belonged to them. They compromised the inheritance God had promised them through their passivity and fear of opposing forces. Yet the Bible talks about God rising to push back the enemy from Israel, declaring loudly and aggressively, "Enough is enough!" Psalm 78:65 says,

> *Then the Lord awoke as from sleep, like a mighty man who*
> ***shouts*** *because of wine. And He beat back His enemies;*
> *He put them to a perpetual reproach.*

I am so glad that God *shouts* on my behalf and pushes back the opponent of my life, subjecting him to the punishment he deserves! I join my voice with God's in a loud shout of praise, reinforcing the victory in my own life and declaring defeat to the enemy.

🍃 *Where may you be too quiet and passive in your expression? Where may you need to come out of hiding and intimidation to express yourself? Join your voice with God's, to take hold of God's victory for you. Today, lift up your voice and let your praises be heard, releasing faith in your heart and into the environment! Clap and shout loudly!*

back up

And they commanded the people, saying, "When you see the ark
of the covenant of the Lord your God, and the priests, the Levites
bearing it, then you shall set out from your place and go after it."
Joshua 3:3

Finally, the children of Israel were about to cross over into the land
promised to them many years before; a new generation were poised,
ready to possess what their forebears had failed to inherit because of
their disobedient and sinful ways. To cross the river Jordan, which stood
between the people and the land promised them, Israel needed to keep
their eyes firmly on the ark of God's covenant as it went before them.
Joshua 3:11 (MSG) reads, "Look at what's before you: The Chest of the
Covenant. Think of it—the Master of the entire earth is crossing the
Jordan as you watch!"

The ark of the covenant was a symbol of the presence of God. His people
could be confident in their imminent journey through the swollen river
simply because the Lord God Almighty was crossing over before them,
making a safe and sure pathway for the children of Israel. But they had
a part to play also! Joshua said to the people, "Sanctify yourselves, for
tomorrow the Lord will do wonders among you" (Joshua 3:5).

Joshua was instructing the people that they were not to carry any
superfluous weight on their journey to possess the Promised Land.
This was an opportune time for them to unburden themselves of any
condemnation, to rid themselves of any wrong affiliation or allegiances, to
rectify any bad attitude or sinful behaviour that would certainly disqualify
them from experiencing the wonders of God on the journey!

Sanctification is a constant process for us also, as we anticipate new seasons of possession. We get to choose what is not going to be part of our future, which weights we will no longer carry. We get to decide what may accompany us, and what is no longer welcome in our lives.

Jesus too, focused intently on His mission as He approached the cross to gain territory pertaining to our salvation and reconciliation to God. He *set his eyes* on the fulfilment and ultimate triumph of His mission on earth. And we can do the same as we look at His example. In Hebrews 12:1-2 we read, "Let us lay aside every weight, and the sin which so easily ensnares us, and let us run with endurance the race set before us, *looking unto Jesus*." When we do that, we too can take new ground with confidence!

> *When the soles of the feet of the priests carrying the Chest of*
> *God, Master of all the earth, touch the Jordan's water,*
> *the flow of water will be stopped—the water coming*
> *from upstream will pile up in a heap.*
> Joshua 3:11-12 (MSG)

The waters did just that; they *backed up* as the priests' feet touched the water! As we stay focussed on Jesus and the journey He has for us, obstacles will have to *back up*, spiritual forces will have to *back up*, afflictions will have to *back up*! When we keep our eyes on the presence of God and where He is directing us, we can be confident that He will create a safe pathway, even in difficult situations, for us to walk into our destiny. The river Jordan at that time was in flood, bursting its banks, but the waters became subject to God's purpose, piling up in a heap so Israel could cross safely to the other side! What a *wonder* Israel experienced right there! God has so many *wonders* for us to experience too as we watch and follow the presence and promises of God closely.

What weight do you need to refuse to carry any longer? What from your past do you now need to cut from your life? What do you need to see 'back up' by faith—maybe a lie of the enemy, some limitation or oppression you sense, or even a physical restriction? Keep your eyes on God's presence today and simply follow Him! Exercise the authority you have to possess your inheritance in God as you journey forward. Tell the enemy to 'back off' and 'back up' today!

fill the gap

*So I sought for a man among them who would make a wall,
and stand in the gap before Me on behalf of the land,
that I should not destroy it, but I found no one.*
Ezekiel 22:30

When Israel succumbed to the pressures of sin, temptation and lawlessness, God was grieved for the welfare of the nation, and He looked for a man who would 'stand in the gap' on His behalf. God has given born-again believers responsibility to *stand in the gap*, to make a wall through our prayers to protect the land so that God doesn't ultimately have to bring His judgment against it.

Intercession is a powerful weapon against the enemy who subtly aims to steal, kill and destroy. Intercession is not just an office for a certain few but a ministry for every Christian to be actively involved in. We are called to oppose every scheme of the enemy that attempts to rule in God's place!

In the Old Testament we read about Abigail's intervention in the dire situation between her husband Nabal, and David, the next appointed king of Israel. Though there was a pending battle, Abigail didn't remain passive, but involved herself fully to divert the enemy's plans for evil. In 1 Samuel 25:23 we read, "Now when Abigail saw David, she dismounted quickly from the donkey, fell on her face before David, and bowed down to the ground."

She stepped in. Abigail felt the pressure of the need and went to where David was. She *stepped into the fray* by presenting an offering of restitution for her husband's lack of generosity toward David and his men. Abigail intervened by boldly stepping in front of David himself in order to block him from outworking the treacherous plans in his heart and forfeiting the call of God on his life.

When it comes to problems and issues, many people want to step *out* of the way, avoiding any responsibility or discomfort to their own life. Not so with Abigail—nor should it be for us! Far be it from us to moan about issues when we have failed to *step in* to face the challenge in prayer and with authority.

She stepped up. Abigail's deep level of intercession released a strong *prophetic anointing* upon her as she responded with conviction to the need. In turn, she released a powerful prophetic word that caused David to recognise the anointing on her life as from God Himself. She said,

> *". . . a man has risen to pursue you and seek your life, but the life of my lord shall be bound in the bundle of the living with the Lord your God; and the lives of your enemies He shall sling out, as from the pocket of a sling. And it shall come to pass, when the Lord has done for my lord according to all the good that He has spoken concerning you, and has appointed you ruler over Israel, that this will be no grief to you, nor offence of heart to my lord, either that you have shed blood without cause, or that my lord has avenged himself. But when the Lord has dealt well with my lord, then remember your maidservant."*
> *1 Samuel 25:29-31*

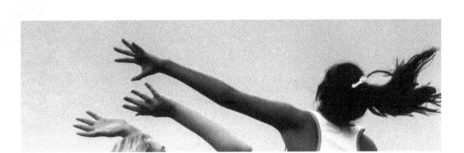

She stepped out. Abigail's focus was on the bigger picture and she didn't mind putting her life on the line! She didn't just stand in the gap—she filled the gap with prophetic ministry, shifting things in the heavens and in David's heart. In 1 Samuel 25:32,33 we read, "Then David said to Abigail, 'Blessed is the Lord God of Israel who sent you this day to meet me. And blessed is your advice and blessed are you, because you have kept me this day from coming to bloodshed and from avenging myself with my own hand.'"

What gap do you need to fill today, not only with prayer but with prophetic ministry? What wall do you need to raise up before God on behalf of others to stem the tide of evil? Prophesy God's word into a situation today. You will see wars won and Satan defeated!

pick a fight — round one

For though we walk in the flesh, we do not war according to the flesh. For the weapons of our warfare are not carnal but mighty in God for pulling down strongholds, casting down arguments and every high thing that exalts itself against the knowledge of God.
2 Corinthians 10:3-5

As God's children, we need to *pick a fight* with the enemy rather than remaining passive while the enemy stirs up chaos and wreaks havoc. We can be far too easily dissuaded, retreating from godly challenges, resulting in isolation and failure rather than aggressively destroying the enemy's right to dominate!

Fights between people normally begin with one person trying to sway the other strongly to their point of view. God, on the other hand, will not participate in any such argument, as He alone possesses the correct viewpoint, based on the unchanging nature of His love and eternal truth. God stands firm! His truth is already clearly stated in His Word, and we need to use it as a weapon to *pick a fight* with every argument that contravenes or contradicts His truth. The Bible calls these arguments *strongholds*, as they become like strong fortresses around us, literally preventing us from stepping forward in faith and victory.

Early in my faith journey, when feeling trapped by my fears, I realised that it was my responsibility to pull these strongholds down by faith, upholding the authority of God's Word against every lie! As I deliberately chose to come into agreement with God's Word, the infrastructure of strongholds around me began to crumble, eliminating the wall to mere rubble around my feet. I was then easily able to step over the rubble into the freedom God had for me.

What arguments are you having with God? Are you trying to sway Him to your point of view, when He already knows best? What intimidating words are causing you to remain hidden and captive behind the walls of fear and self-protection? Words like, "I can't," or "I am not good enough," or "I will never make it." Could it be that the enemy has locked you in behind walls of fear and doubt? The enemy is a relentless, negative, 'nagging' force, and we need to make a decision to stop listening to his lies, and agree instead with what God has said.

Gideon, a young man in the Old Testament, was completely intimidated by Israel's enemy, the Midianites. He would hide on a daily basis in the wine press to prevent the enemy taking away even the little he thought he had! Gideon was living an oppressed life due to the wall of fear around his life. Then, God spoke to Gideon, calling him forth as one who would deliver Israel from the Midianites.

> *Now the Angel of the Lord came and sat under the terebinth tree*
> *. . . and the angel of the Lord appeared to him, and said to him,*
> *"The Lord is with you, you mighty man of valour."*
> *Judges 6:11-12*

Now Gideon had an inner argument going on! He didn't *feel* like a mighty man of valour. He was full of fear and completely walled in by how he saw himself—according to Gideon, his clan was the weakest in Israel and he himself was the weakest member. His argument was, "I can't do this! I'm totally incapable!" Does this sound familiar? If so, we need to *pick a fight*; we need to turn in on these inner arguments by holding the truth of God's word against them and declaring who God says we are!

What fortress have you built around your life that needs to come down? What has God said about you? His words are your weapons! Today, 'pick a fight' with the lies of the enemy, knocking down every wall, every stronghold, and step with freedom into your God-given destiny!

pick a fight — round two

*Fight the good fight of faith, lay hold on eternal life,
to which you were also called and have confessed the good
confession in the presence of many witnesses.*
1 Timothy 6:12

We have a fight on our hands! There are opponents in the ring and we have to knock them out to lay hold of God's best for our life—contestants like fear that seeks to submerge faith, hopelessness that seeks to cloud vision, grief that erodes joy, and despair that overrules our hope. We need to *pick a fight* with these arguments around us that create negative atmospheres and outcomes!

Let's not get so absorbed with our own life that we can't see what is going on around us. Spiritual forces are holding families, communities and nations hostage! Without entering the ring to counteract these forces, we can unwittingly become subject to them ourselves, preventing us from inheriting the fullness of God's blessing and favour toward us. We need to *take a look out the window* of our own life to discern, on a spiritual level, what is really going on around us!

One day in London, I looked out the office window to see a handcuffed youth exiting an armoured vehicle and being escorted by a policeman into the local court room. My heart was really grieved as I witnessed this scene. This young man was somebody's child! Was a parent somewhere weeping for him because of the trouble he was in?

In the surrounding neighbourhood, we recognised a negative spiritual atmosphere, one of resigned hopelessness, an ambition-less mindset, a 'this-is-as-good-as-it-gets' attitude toward life, of being duped by a mist of generational iniquities! The status quo was accepted without ever challenging it. As a result, history continued to repeat itself over and over again, because of a negative pattern of thinking, behaving and believing!

The Psalmist, in contrast, praises God for the choices God has made for him, and recognises the bounty and beauty of God's landscape for his future. In Psalm 16:5-6 we read,

> *O Lord, You are the portion of my inheritance and my cup; You maintain my lot. The lines have fallen to me in pleasant places; Yes, I have a good inheritance.*

We need to *pick a fight* and contend in prayer, shifting these negative spiritual atmospheres so people can see and believe for more of God's best for their lives. One of the responses we made as a church to combat this atmosphere was to organise prayer walks around the estate, taking authority over the spirit of hopelessness and lack of ambition that was holding young people in bondage. Even with technology as advanced and helpful as it may be, many eighteen to twenty-four-year-olds in the United Kingdom admitted to sometimes or often feeling lonely because of it. Negative statistics needed to be changed by breaking demonic holds in the atmosphere.

In the demolition of a large building, a wrecking ball is pounded against a building many times before it falls; so it is in the spirit—we have to fight many rounds to see spiritual atmospheres broken and to lay hold of eternal life in all its fullness, not just for ourselves but for others also. Let's persist in prayer, in authority, in love and action, shifting negative atmospheres and generational lies that hold communities and neighbourhoods in bondage.

🍃 *Today, look out the window and discern any atmosphere that needs to be shifted in your community. Name the prevailing spirit and pick a fight with it, taking authority in the name of Jesus. Persist in prayer until this belief system is broken and faith arises in its place! Today, take hold of your future with hope and joyful praise.*

pick a fight – round three

And Moses said to the people, "Do not be afraid. Stand still and
see the salvation of the Lord, which He will accomplish for you
today. For the Egyptians whom you see today,
you shall see again no more forever."
Exodus 14:13

Pharaoh reneged on his decision to let the children of Israel go so they could serve God in the wilderness, as Moses had requested! Now, Pharaoh's army was pursuing Israel forcefully, striking fear into the heart and minds of the people of God. They had witnessed many amazing miracles in Egypt and in their departure from Egypt, but now they stood in a need of another miracle if they were to survive. The noise of the chariots in pursuit of them were thundering in the background and an impassable sea stood in front of them. What could they do but cry out in fear and defeat?

Instead, Moses exhorted the people to *hold their peace*. He assured them that the Lord would fight for them, and then, in obedience to the Lord's command, he lifted up his rod and stretched out his hand over the sea, dividing it so that Israel could walk through on dry ground. As Moses did so, the Red Sea parted and the children of Israel crossed safely to the other side. Truly a miraculous intervention by the hand of God!

We need to *pick a fight* with the arguments that come against us, the opposition of the enemy that seeks to prevent God's purposes being fulfilled in our lives. The enemy has a plan to pursue us, to knock us out of our God-given position, and to take our God-given authority from us. He seeks to dominate and rule over our lives through intimidation and through striking fear in our hearts!

We need to refute and refuse the sound of the enemy's threat and the noise of his pursuit! We need to stand like Moses did, follow God's direction, and use the authority we have been given to take him down. Isaiah 54:17 gives us this promise:

> "... no weapon formed against you shall prosper and
> every tongue which rises in judgment you shall condemn.
> This is the heritage of the servants of the Lord, and their
> righteousness is from Me," says the Lord.

We have to counteract every attack with our voice, realising the authority and the position we have been given in Christ. It is our right and our responsibility as the children of God to stand up to the enemy!

A weapon formed against me personally was *condemnation*; the noise and rumble of the enemy in the background of my mind sought to distract me, especially as I moved toward the call of God on my life to become an ordained Pastor. As I said yes to the ordination, the noise of the enemy got louder in my ear, reminding me of past feelings of fear and timidity! This scripture, however, enabled me to stay focused, stand my ground, and refute the intimidation of the enemy as I simply 'focused forward' in the direction of God's call on my life and stopped looking behind and listening to the threat of the enemy attempting to chase me down.

As Moses proceeded to lead the children of Israel across the Red Sea, the enemy sought to follow, but Moses, in response to God's command, again lifted up his rod. This time, the sea closed, covering the chariots, the horsemen and the Egyptians, drowning them all in the waters. Israel was delivered! Through this, God showed me that I too was about to step onto miracle land. God was opening a path for me supernaturally, and it was territory that the enemy could not put his feet on! Miracle land does not have the enemy's name on it!

What noise or pursuit of the enemy is thundering in your ears? What weapon is he using to make you crumble in defeat and hopelessness? Today, block your ears to threats and accusations and lift up the rod of your authority so you can walk forward into your destiny. Today, in faith, see the miraculous path God has opened for you to walk on!

disarm the enemy

But David said to Abishai, "Do not destroy him; for who can stretch out his hand against the Lord's anointed and be guiltless?"
1 Samuel 26:9

David, when encouraged on a second occasion to strike Saul and take his life in revenge for the things Saul had made him suffer, refused. David understood headship and wouldn't grieve God by taking things into his own hands. This, however, did not stop him from entering the enemy's territory to disarm him. David boldly entered the enemy's camp and took from Saul the very weapon he planned to kill David with. We read the account of David's words and actions in 1 Samuel 26:10-12:

> *David said furthermore, ". . . The Lord forbid that I should stretch out my hand against the Lord's anointed. But please, take now the spear and the jug of water that are by his head, and let us go." So David took the spear and the jug of water by Saul's head, and they got away; and no man saw or knew it or awoke. For they were all asleep, because a deep sleep from the Lord had fallen on them.*

A warrior's sword was his security in battle, and David humiliated Saul by stealthily removing his spear plus his water jug! But God backed David's bold move with grace, causing a deep sleep to fall on the enemy so the deed could be accomplished.

Likewise, Jesus entered the dominion of Satan by taking the power of sin and death captive on the cross. Colossians 2:15 tells us that, "having *disarmed* principalities and powers, He made a public spectacle of them, triumphing over them in it." Jesus stripped the enemy of every weapon that he would try and use against us. By dying on the cross in our place, He took away Satan's right and power to have any dominion over us!

We too need to face up and enter Satan's domain with the authority we have been given and take from him every weapon he would use against us to defeat us, demoralise us and destroy us.

The Bible talks about words being like swords—and words are what the enemy uses often to intimidate us, belittle us and cut us down from rising up in God. We need to 'walk into the enemy's camp' and refute every lie that Satan is using as a weapon against us, *disarming the enemy* of all power, intimidation and accusation. Satan has always been a liar, and the word of truth is not in his mouth! God will equip us as we boldly take hostage every word of bondage and defeat spoken over our lives, humiliating the enemy in the process by disarming him and giving him nothing to say!

How well do we know God's Word? We need to be ready to counteract every lie of the enemy—every whisper, every suggestion, every insinuation that has previously caused us to recoil from our God-given position. Our offensive weapon is the Word of God!

Have you allowed the enemy to dominate you with innuendos, lies and threats? Are you bold in your spirit to make a stand and disarm the enemy of his deadly weapons? Decide today to walk into enemy territory and take back the authority that is rightfully yours!

hide to be found

You are my hiding place. You shall preserve me from trouble;
You shall surround me with songs of deliverance.
Psalm 32:7

I'm sure we all enjoyed playing games of 'hide and seek' when we were young—taking pleasure in finding a place to tuck ourself away, making it difficult for others to find us! Another favourite pastime for most children was making forts and cubby-houses, places to retreat into for play.

As adults we also need our 'cubby houses,' our hiding place, our safe and quiet haven from the noise of life where we can be found by the One who loves our soul immensely and protects us from danger. When we draw close to God to realign and reposition ourselves, we are engaging in spiritual warfare!

Everyone needs a secret place. Some may refer to that place as a 'garden,' others as a 'retreat,' some a 'war-room,' or simply a place where we can shut the door on the external and internal noise that blares through the surround sound-system of life, a place to find stillness with God to think, speak and be heard, a place to *hide and be found*. That's where we discover refuge, where the refreshing presence of God refuels us to renter the room of life. It's where we *shut the door*—not necessarily a literal door, but the door of everyday hustle that demands our time and attention.

Matthew 6:6 says,

> *But you when you pray, go into your room, and when you have*
> ***shut your door,*** *pray to your Father who is in the secret place;*
> *and your Father who sees in secret will reveal you openly.*

Your *shut door* could be in your car, in your bedroom, in a café—any place where it's just you and God, a place where your life is wrapped in His presence and temporarily hidden from the cares of the world. We *shut the door* so we can connect with Jesus, to create a space where we can hear Him say, "I see you, I hear you, I care for you!"

Some people may find 'aloneness' threatening, and struggle to pull themselves aside, especially if their habit is to seek security in the constant babble of company and conversation. But how about giving away distractions in order to receive supernatural transactions? Hiding in the shelter of God is where burdens are lifted, wisdom is imparted and worship is strengthened. In that place, God finds us ready to listen, to encounter Him and to hear His voice. To neglect the secret place is to neglect the source of our strength.

> *He who dwells in the secret place of the Most High shall abide*
> *under the shadow of the Almighty. I will say of the Lord, "He is*
> *my refuge and my fortress; My God in Him I will trust."*
> *Psalm 91:1*

Let's not wait until we feel beaten up, knocked down or simply battered by life, to seek God out, but instead develop the habit of regularly meeting with Him in the secret place so we can combat every assault and difficulty with faith and freedom. Let's *hide to be found* by our wonderful, loving and powerful God!

Where is your secret place? Where do you meet with God? Do you know how to 'shut the door,' or are you too dependent on the crowd? Make time for Jesus today! He always makes time for you, meeting you with love and strength. Be found by God in that secret place of connection and power. Connect with Jesus and experience His song of love and deliverance over your life.

connect with challenges

A slave girl possessed with a spirit of divination followed him. She cried out saying, "These men are the servants of the Most High God, who proclaim to us the way of salvation." And this she did for many days. But Paul greatly annoyed turned and said to the spirit, "I command you in the name of Jesus Christ to come out of her." And he came out that very hour.
Acts 16:16-17

Sometimes challenges are the last thing we want to connect with; we want to connect with God and with family and friends, but *challenges*? They're the things we would rather ignore, avoid or run from! But resolution and victory can only come when we face our challenges head on.

Paul knew what it was to tackle challenges with the power of Jesus. In this scripture, we read that a girl had been following him around for some days—and although what she said about Jesus' disciples was correct, a spirit was operating in this young lady that was not from God. You see, demons can recognise Jesus, but *we need to recognise demons* when they are in operation! Paul's spirit was disturbed by the presence and interruptions of this girl; he became greatly annoyed. Turning and facing her, he cast the demonic spirit out of her!

Sometimes we put up with disturbances that God wants us to deal with. Instead, we need to get annoyed with them, face the spirit and take authority over it.

Have you ever been followed? If it is not someone we know and trust, it can invoke a certain feeling of dread and foreboding that we may be overcome by force. Satan is threatened when we step out in faith, and will cause certain issues to raise their heads as a deterrent to us presenting a clear message! When we walk with Jesus, however, we can walk with a freedom and confidence in our step, overcoming any opposition before it seeks to overtake or oppress us, but we do need to be observant—to turn and look when we feel uneasy, to be aware of what may be following us uninvited.

What spirit could be following us that we need to deal with? Some folk have noticed financial trouble raising its head unexpectedly as they've reached out in faith; others have experienced sickness, anxiety, fear, fatigue, or other issues that have sought to throw them off balance. We need to be aware of any recurring pattern that regularly disrupts our journey of faith and become annoyed with the spirit involved that seeks to condemn and hinder us. Like Paul, we need to address the disturbing spirit and cast it out in the name of Jesus. And we need to keep the door of invitation to these forces permanently closed!

At the same time, we can be mindful that God's grace pursues us, giving us the ability to discern and deal with any unwanted disturbances spiritually, enabling us to maintain fruitfulness in the mission and direction God has given us.

What deterrent or constant disturbance is annoying you today? What noise is preventing a clear message to be heard from your life? Take action today over any spiritual force that seeks to distract and distress you as you step out in faith. Address this spirit and forbid it from operating and hindering your progress in God. Exercise your God-given authority today, and live in the freedom Jesus has purchased for you!

turn on the light

*We grope for the wall like the blind, and we grope as if
we had no eyes; we stumble at noonday as at twilight.
We are as dead men in desolate places.*
Isaiah 59:10

Have you ever been in a house, shopping mall or even a city, when there
has been an electric power outage, leaving you in complete darkness and
groping to find your way around? For those who are permanently blind
this is the difficult reality they face on a daily basis. As a result, they rely
more heavily on their other senses to get themselves from A to B.

Sometimes life's events cause the 'lights to go out' and the path of our
future to become darkened and difficult to see. Praise God for His
prophetic voice and promises!

Prophetic words spoken under the inspiration of the Holy Spirit are like
the light that shines in a dark place. By illuminating our path, they lead us
to the timely promise spoken by God in times gone by. The light from this
prophetic utterance enables us to put one foot in front of another even in
the more difficult or doubtful times. 2 Peter 1:19 says,

*And so we have the prophetic word confirmed, which you do well
to heed as a light that shines in a dark place, until the day dawns
and the morning star appears in your hearts.*

Sometimes the light just goes out for people in life, making the path ahead difficult to discern. But what causes the light to go out for people on their journey? Sometimes delays in answered prayer, setbacks, disappointment, grief, illness and poverty, can steal faith from hearts. That's why we desperately need to *turn on the light* of prophecy for ourselves and for others so they can find faith and see the path ahead! Spiritual battles are fought with spiritual weapons, and one powerful spiritual weapon God has fortified us with is His prophetic voice speaking into our future!

Prophecy is a source of great strength, defying hopelessness and dejection by injecting faith and courage through the accuracy and sureness of His quickened word. *Prophecy keeps the light on for the next generation, enabling sons and daughters to find their way home!* So 'turn on the light' through prophetic ministry and warfare!

Remember the words of Jeremiah 1:12:

*Then the Lord said to me, "You have seen well, for I am ready to
perform My word."*

God watches over His word to perform it!

Has the light gone out for you? Are you groping in the darkness, unsure what to hold onto? Have you lost vision for the future because you are focussing on present situations? Today, look at the prophetic words spoken by the anointing of God over your life and future. Prophesy the promises of God into others and turn a light on in their heart today!

share and share alike

So David went, he and the six hundred men who were
with him, and came to the brook Besor, where those stayed
who were left behind. But David pursued, he and four
hundred men; for two hundred stayed behind, who were
so weary that they could not cross the brook Besor.
1 Samuel 30:9-10

David was on a mission to recover all that the Amalekites had stolen from him personally, and from the families of Ziglag. God had confirmed the direction to pursue the enemy with a promise that David and his men would recover everything that had been taken, but some of David's men were just too weary to go to battle. And so, David released them to stay behind. Even so, David's mission was successful; he returned having recovered everything and more!

On their return, however, David's men looked at those who had stayed behind with disdain and negativity. They were reluctant to share any of the spoils of war with them. But David had a different spirit. He said,

"... My brethren, you shall not do so with what the Lord has given us,
who has preserved us and delivered into our hand the troop that came
against us ... But as his part is who goes down to the battle, so shall
*his part be who stays by the supplies; they shall **share alike**." So ...*
David made it a statute and an ordinance for Israel to this day.
1 Samuel 30:23-25

David cut across the selfish and self-righteous spirit that prevailed in some of his warriors and set a new standard in Israel that everyone would participate in the spoils, regardless of whether they went to war or stayed home with the supplies.

A powerful spiritual weapon is the ability to *share* what we have plundered with those who were incapable of participating in the battle. David had this quality, not making any distinction between those who went to war and those who genuinely were unable; he shared the spoils with everyone.

Do we make distinctions like David's men, withholding our victories and blessings from those who, in our eyes, lacked courage or fortitude? Aren't we glad Jesus didn't come with a measure of who was 'deserving,' but shared the spoil of His victory on the cross for all of broken and weary mankind! It's so easy in life to give our help only to those we think have earned or deserved it, but how about those who are incapacitated, frightened or just exhausted? *Let's share our spoils!*

Think about it for a moment! The whole purpose of plundering the kingdom of darkness is to take back what the enemy has stolen and to return it into the hands of those who were originally violated—to those who need reviving, sustaining and encouraging. Sharing is not holding onto our successes and keeping the spoils amongst the strong in the camp, but giving to those who struggle, who are too weak to fight, too weary to engage in battle! Our generosity of spirit will encourage them, equip them, and fortify them in their journey of recovery and ongoing personal victories. Who knows whether there may come a time when we are not so strong and need someone to share their spoils of war with us?

A generous spirit warms hearts, people and communities. Deeming someone worthy, irrespective of their participation is the most liberating act of love and kindness we can demonstrate. Sharing blesses everyone, not just some! Why would we want to reserve the blessings just for those who are already strong? *Sharing is a powerful weapon in spiritual warfare!*

What has the enemy taken from you and those around you that needs to be taken back? What have you taken back from the enemy that needs to be shared? Today, ask God for a generous and kind spirit that deems everyone worthy to receive of God's grace.

part eight:

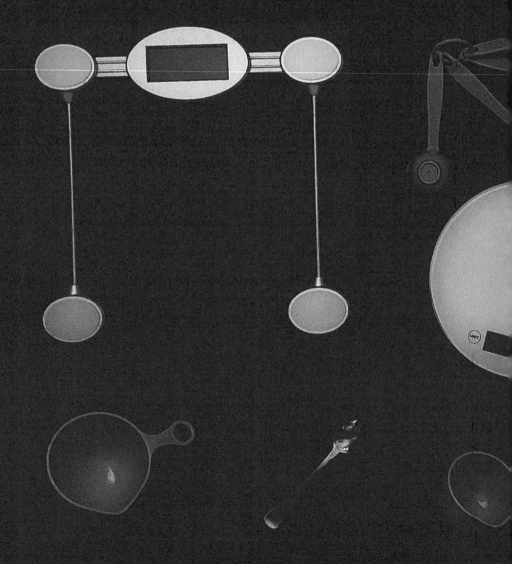

weights & measures

what size?

Judge not, that you be not judged, for with what judgment you judge, you will be judged; and with the measure you use, it will be measured back to you.
Matthew 7:1-2

Metric scales are commonly used for ascertaining weights and measures—to gauge the distance, height, breadth and substance of articles. Other scales are used to judge effectiveness and productivity; these can be so helpful, especially in business, to make necessary judgments about growth and progress.

In life, however, our own preferences and perspectives often become the lens through which we measure and view others. When we project judgment in a critical manner towards people or situations, our negativity restricts our own growth and progress. We need to examine how we think and speak about others. Our words and opinions about what we consider 'faulty' with another, may be binding our own lives!

For a garment to fit the person it is designed for well, measurements need to be taken. What size are they? The quantity of cloth needed for a garment is determined and then cut according to the size of the person. When we look at others, how are we sizing them up?

God has already measured our size! The capacity we each have may be difficult to fully grasp with our finite mind, but God knows the levels and achievements, the impact and influence we are capable of reaching. When we stand in judgment of others, therefore, we seriously impair our future. Matthew 7:1-2 makes it clear that measuring out negative words, thoughts and condemning attitudes toward others will actually determine the size of our own life; our productivity will be reduced to the level we project on others. We, by our judgements, are cutting out a garment for ourselves that will be much smaller than what God had originally designed for us to wear and enjoy!

What sort of judgments are we measuring out? What aspects do we consider 'lacking' in another? What misdemeanours do we see in others that have become a ceiling or limitation in our own life? What we measure out will be what we receive in turn! There is an old saying: "what goes around, comes around." Negativity and judgment have a way of personally repaying the visit—they come knocking on our door!

Perhaps others have judged us wrongly, and this, in turn, has shaped our thoughts, and led us to speak judgments towards others. Romans 12:14 says, "Bless those who persecute you; bless and do not curse." To 'bless' means "to pronounce words in a prayerful way, in order to confer or invoke divine favour upon (or, to ask God to look favourably upon) another." God wants us to make good judgments, to exercise the ability to make considered decisions and come to sensible conclusions. He wants us to be trustworthy and kind in our attitude toward others, even when they seem to be in opposition to ourselves or to God.

When we are tempted to pronounce critical judgment upon another, let's instead turn our words into prayers of blessing! Let's use our words to enhance the wellbeing of another. In so doing, we measure and cut out a far bigger and more beautiful space for ourselves to inhabit!

Today let's consider our words, and the judgments we are making toward life and people? Are our words creative and constructive, or negative and destructive? Choose today to live in a more generous space and enhance your own growth and progress by blessing others.

what shape?

*For I say, through the grace given to me, to everyone who
is among you, not to think of himself more highly that he
ought to think, but to think soberly, as God has dealt
to each one a **measure** of faith.*
Romans 12:3

Have you ever looked at the Christmas presents under the tree and tried
to guess the contents by the shape of the parcel? Maybe you have picked
the present up and given it a good shake, hoping for clues? Even so, it's
difficult to be one hundred percent sure of the nature of a gift until you
remove the wrapping that conceals it.

One of my most enlightening experiences has been discovering the shape
God designed for my life through understanding the 'grace-gifts,' listed
for us in Romans chapter 12:

*Having then gifts differing according to the grace that is given
to us, let us use them: if prophecy let us prophesy in proportion
to our faith; or ministry, let us use it in or ministering; he who
teaches, in teaching; he who exhorts, in exhortation; he who
gives, with liberality; he who leads with diligence; he
who shows mercy with cheerfulness.*
Romans 12:6

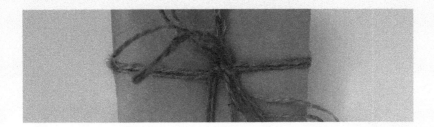

These are base-line graces we can confidently operate from. Bestowed on us, these gifts give language to the motivation of our heart and life. Trying to adapt to the shape and style of an image we hold in our mind—perhaps from a desire to be like someone we hold in high esteem or someone we simply admire—can keep us from discovering the power of the shape and style God has chosen for us.

Don't be a 'shapeless' Christian who continually imitates the flair of another and never comes to the knowledge of their own gift! We are supposed to be different, because of the differing gifts God graces to us. Not one person (apart from Jesus!) has all seven of these motivational gifts. We need each other to make up the full expression of Christ's life, love and ministry. But many gifts lay dormant in Christians' lives as they fail to seek and appreciate the grace gift God has given them. Each of these gifts is powerful—an expression of God's love measured out to us individually. That's why comparing ourselves with one another is unwise; it prevents the individual gift from being unwrapped and powerfully used under God's direction!

As I personally meditated on this passage, I discovered I primarily possessed a gift of *mercy*. That explained the sensitivity of my nature and the natural empathy I have towards those who are hurting. It explains why I have the ability to feel deeply for another, to feel what they are feeling. What I had perceived as a weakness (and, at times, an embarrassing feature of my personality!) was actually a strength and a gift given by God that He wanted me to use for His glory. Being thankful and honouring God for the grace gift bestowed upon me, opened my life more to the power of the Holy Spirit and the operation of the Gifts of the Spirit we read of later on in the book of First Corinthians.

Have you discovered the grace gift upon your life? Give thanks today for the gift God has placed in your life. Do you need to unwrap His gift so you can operate at a new level of power? Today, stop comparing yourself with others, and exercise with joy the gift God has given you!

what height?

As a kid, did you ever wonder how tall you would grow? This preoccupation about height is fairly common today, but it didn't concern me in the slightest growing up, even though I only just exceeded five foot! As the shortest child in my school classes, I always got placed at the very end of the front row for class photos—this was my given position, determined by my height!

God has a different scale to measure height. His assessment is based more on our internal ability to be everything He has called us to be, do all He has called us to do, and rise by faith even in difficult situations. However, when we allow heavy weights to rest on our shoulders, these can restrict us from rising to our *full stature* in God.

The Bible likens these weights that are imposed on us to *yokes*, the equipment placed on bullocks in days gone by to harness them together, enabling them to pull heavier weights because they worked as a team rather than alone. Unbeknown to us, instead of being yoked with God and knowing His supernatural power working in us, we can sometimes be unwittingly harnessed to wrong mindsets, attitudes, reactions and behaviour. Maybe these yokes have been imposed upon us as a result of generational mindsets, but either way we end up carrying heavy burdens that we don't have the strength to bear, causing great strain!

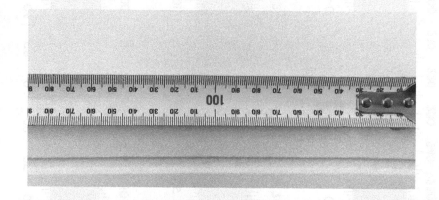

Often we ask God to take these yokes from us when, in certain circumstances, God is asking us to remove them ourselves! He wants us to identify where the strain in our life is, and make the adjustments accordingly.

This scripture encouraged me many years ago to think about what I was harnessed to that might be restricting my ability to rise in God and be all that He had called me to be. As I identified yokes of mistaken beliefs that were in contrast to living a life of faith, I removed the weight of these from my shoulders with God's help and anointing. I also considered what I was speaking out about certain situations in my life!

A common yoke we may be coupled with, and which may be evident through our speech, is *blame*—"the pointing of the finger and speaking wickedness." Maybe we find it easier to excuse our own lack of *spiritual height* by directing blame elsewhere, perhaps pointing our finger toward a lack of opportunity, prevailing negative atmosphere, disadvantaged upbringing or unsupportive people, thinking this will release the weight from our shoulders!

Nothing could be further from the truth. To have the weight removed, we must take the yoke away ourselves and refuse to blame external conditions for our *stunted height* in God. The Scripture declares that if *we* remove the yoke and change our language of blame, our light will dawn in the darkness and nothing will be able to suppress our faith or prevent us rising to new heights of faith and courage. To live in the perpetual daylight of revelation, power and authority in Christ is so appealing!

Reflect on your life and identify any weight that you are carrying today? What yoke of belief or habit are you harnessed to that needs to be removed? What are you blaming for your lack? Ask God to help you remove this weight today so you can grow to full stature in Him.

in deep

*And when the man went out to the east with the line in his hand,
he **measured** one thousand cubits, and he brought me through
the waters; the water came up to my ankles, again he **measured**
one thousand, and brought me through the waters; the water
came up to my knees. Again he **measured**, and it was a river that
I could not cross; for the water was too deep, water in which one
must swim, a river that could not be crossed.*
Ezekiel 47:3-5

For some of us, it may be a frightening experience to be out of our depth in water, unable to put our feet firmly on the bottom of a swimming pool or riverbed, or on the ocean floor. While we may panic a little at first, once we have mastered the skill of swimming, it is not so daunting! Likewise, in our lives as Christians, God has depths for us to launch into in His greater purposes, but first we need to learn how to follow, trust and depend on Him in the adventure of faith.

The book of Ezekiel makes reference to *waters that were flowing from under the threshold of the temple*. These waters could be likened to the worship that flows from the temple of our heart. As each one-thousand cubits was measured, the waters became deeper; a new dependency and greater trust in God was required to stay afloat in the current and direction of the river!

Where are we at with God? Have we learned to let God lead us into deeper experiences and challenges, or are we still hesitating on the edge of faith and trust? We may even be sincere in our desire, wanting to go deeper with God but afraid to step from the shore into the water? Or maybe we have walked into the shallows but are demanding to take our spiritual 'floaty' with us, just in case we drift deeper into waters beyond our control? A spiritual 'floaty' could describe anything that we rely on to keep ourselves safe.

What is God requiring us to let go of? A 'floating device' I had to personally release in order to experience the deeper waters of God, was concern about what others may think of me. Would I, in learning to swim in deeper waters, be considered ridiculous, deemed inadequate, or appear foolish? Was I prepared to look like I was out of my depth, outside the realm of my own natural ability? I had to say goodbye to the floating device of dependency on the approval of others, to fully venture out in faith, adopting a 'never-mind' attitude and a 'focus-forward' mindset so I could move further into the depths of God's flow for my life.

The Bible warns us that, "the fear of man brings a snare, but whoever trusts in the Lord shall be safe" (Proverbs 29:25). We also know that scripture says, "there is no fear in love; but perfect love casts out fear, because fear involves torment. But he who fears is not perfected in love" (1 John 4:18). In God's purposes for our lives, we don't just jump straight into the depths, even if we may prefer to! If we did, we could flounder and be overwhelmed. But entry comes from *measurements*; choosing to go deeper on a daily basis in our faith and worship. A *measuring*, a calculating of our commitment and trust, is required if we are to access and flow in the *immeasurable depths* of God.

> *Along the bank of the river, on this side and that, will grow all kinds of trees, used for food; their leaves will not wither, and their fruit will not fail. They will bear fruit every month, because their water flows from the sanctuary. Their fruit will be for food and their leaves for medicine.*
> *Ezekiel 47:12*

Let's exchange the unhealthy fear of man for the healthy fear of God, which the Bible tells us, is a source of great confidence, enabling us to trust God at a whole new level. God will keep us safe! As we venture into new depths in faith, we will in turn experience more of His supernatural power. There is so much more in God to experience in the flow of His river!

What's your next 'one thousand cubits'? Do you need to measure out another thousand cubits to increase the flow of God's purposes in your life? What spiritual 'floaty' do you need to say goodbye to? Today make some measured decisions to go deeper in God, so that you can experience the immeasurable power of God working in and through your life!

ideals can become idols

And God spoke all these words, saying, 'I am the Lord your God, who brought you out of the land of Egypt, out of the house of bondage. You shall have no other gods before Me.'
Exodus 20:1-3

Sometimes we give too much credence to things that are not deserving! We may not keep graven images in our possession—we know better than that—but we may have tendencies toward idolatry in our heart and mind. What do we elevate above God and His grace in our lives? Ideals, for instance, can be a great source of motivation, but unmonitored or unbalanced, ideals have the potential to become idols that we end up bowing down to!

When ideals become too important, or too heavily consume our thoughts and emotions, they can cease to be measures we simply aspire to, to becoming heavy weights. Should we have ideals then? Certainly! We all need ideals to believe in, to embrace and reach for in order to improve our quality of life and wellbeing. Sometimes, however, instead of ideals being our servant, they move into the position of being a cruel master, merciless and demanding!

Ideals originate from conviction, inspiration and aspiration. Often they are formed in response to a sense of lack, to targets missed in certain areas of our life, causing us to reach out with new ideals to set a new level of achievement! Ideals do matter, but when they matter too much, we should be alarmed. When they become more important than relationships, time keeping, self-care, and responsibility, we may find they have taken hold of us, rather than us holding them!

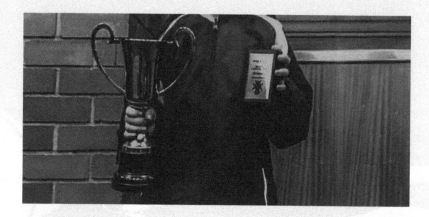

There are many trends in the world that govern the thinking of both young and older people alike, robbing us of our joy in the journey of growing and developing. Some of the more obvious ideals are regarding body image, performance, popularity, friendships and fame. Of course, everyone wants to do well, but our goal as Christians is Jesus; our ideal is to become more like Him!

I experienced a dilemma when I took on board the ideal that I should be able to please people all the time. As a result, I was always attempting to bridge gaps and meet needs. As much as this was a godly and noble ideal, there are some things that only God can achieve in the heart of another. The ideal in my heart was totally unrealistic, a performance that mattered too much!

God will always allow our idols to fail because He wants us to have no other god besides Him. Idols not dealt with will destroy our relationship with God *and* compromise our relationship with others. It's impossible to satisfy a spirit, and an idol will continue to frown on us and be harsh in its appraisal.

I found the ability to overcome this 'performance idol' in my heart by recognising that *God was pleased with my efforts when I sincerely sought to honour Him.* He spoke a comforting phrase into my heart, 'I am happy with the way you do things; *you* are the one that's not!' Knowing that God loved the way I did things, released me from a certain self-condemnation, nervousness and pressure, allowing me to live light and free.

What is your experience of ideals? Have your ideals crossed the line of 'mattering too much'? Today, release yourself from any oppressive thoughts and unattainable goals. Allow the person of Jesus to set your targets and transform you from the inside out!

part nine:

faith

the laugh of faith

A merry heart does good, like medicine,
but a broken spirit dries the bones.
Proverbs 17:22

Life can be serious enough at times without us taking ourselves too seriously and making it even more complicated! God has called us to enjoy the life we have and to be able to *laugh*, even at ourselves, in a good-humoured way!

Growing up, my parents naturally had expectations of us as children. But my father never disciplined us in a stern way—in fact, I cannot remember him ever telling me off! Maybe that was because I was a compliant child, always eager to please! But my father did dish out healthy doses of 'tongue-in-cheek' sarcasm. He was able to make us laugh, and yet gain our attention. "Why don't you lower your voice to a *shriek*?" he would ask, implying the level of our noise was well beyond acceptable or pleasant! Addressing bad manners, he would simply say, "Don't say *what*—say *aye!*" which really meant we should use the word 'pardon' when we wanted someone to repeat themselves. And if we were bothering him, he would say, "Go tell your mother she wants you!"—all dished out with a smile and a *laugh*.

Do you need to lighten your approach, to ease up on your concerns, reserving them for when they are really helpful, like when people are in crisis or in deep need? Faith is the medicine needed for a good life and a positive perspective. Sarah, in the book of Genesis, knew this. She said, "God has brought me laughter, and everyone who hears about this will laugh with me" (Gen 21:6 NIV). And then, in verse 7, she added, "Who would have said to Abraham that Sarah would nurse children? Yet I have borne him a son in his old age."

Sarah invites people to laugh with her; it seems incredulous that Sarah in her old age has given birth to a baby boy! Who would have thought it possible?! How joyous they were! Romans 4:19-20 testifies of Abraham that, ". . . not being weak in faith, he did not consider his own body already dead (since he was about a hundred years old) and the deadness of Sarah's womb. He did not waver at the promise of God through unbelief, but was strengthened in faith, giving glory to God." Faith, in spite of obvious obstacles, strengthened Abraham while he was waiting for the fulfilment of the promise. We have plenty to marvel at when we behold God's works in and through our lives!

> *The stone which the builders rejected has become the chief*
> *cornerstone. This was the Lord's doing and it*
> *is marvellous in our eyes!*
> Psalm 118:22-23

When was the last time you experienced the *laugh of faith* when the odds looked doubtful though the promise proved strong? God has a subtle way of going about things, disproving the odds and coming through triumphant on our behalf. He wants us to laugh in the face of the future, knowing that He can turn the toughest situations around for His glory.

Are you taking yourself and your life too seriously, making it harder than it needs to be? God desires us to smile widely! When was the last time you laughed because of God's goodness showing up in your life? Today, choose to lighten up and enjoy the marvellous things God has already done. Laugh in faith, anticipating the miracles yet to come!

leave the seed

Trust in the Lord and do good; dwell in the land and feed on His faithfulness, delight yourself also in the Lord, and He shall give you the desires of your heart.
Psalm 37:3-4

What an amazing passage! We probably all know, however, that it is one thing to *declare* faith and it's another thing to wait patiently for the answer to come. That's where trust needs to be exercised! Then there are the occasions when God simply answers our longings before we even ask or pray. He listens to our hearts, and delights to surprise us with unanticipated answers.

I remember admiring a handbag in a shop window with a slight sigh one day, knowing at the time we couldn't afford it, only to be surprised when our son came home from Colombia with a gift of the very same leather handbag. God is so amazing! In the words of Isaiah 65:24, "It shall come to pass that before they call, I will answer!"

When answers are seemingly slow in coming, however, we need to make sure our longing for answered prayer doesn't supersede our longing for God. Obsessive longing for results has the power to consume us, overwhelm us, and become an unhealthy pursuit if we don't keep our appetite in check. We need to be hungry *for God* and accept thankfully every provision in the timing He has chosen to release it. If we allow ourselves to become prey to a spirit of starvation, emptied of faith and thanksgiving, we may be tempted to settle for less than God has promised. Depletion blurs people's ability to discern.

Jesus fed His disciples parables so they could understand principles of the Kingdom. In Mark 4:26-29 (MSG), He delivered a parable about trust, saying,

> *". . . God's kingdom is like seed thrown on a field by a man who then goes to bed and forgets about it. The seed sprouts and grows — he has no idea how it happens. The earth does it all without his help; first a green stem of grass, then a bud, then the ripened grain. When the grain is fully formed, he reaps — harvest time!"*

God thinks in *seed* because the seed contains the harvest! We may be praying for the answer to come as a 'fully-grown tree,' but God may answer our prayer with a seed that we need to plant by faith! Then we need to *leave the seed* to do its work. If we become obsessive and anxious about answers to prayer, we may be tempted to interfere by digging up the seed to see if it is growing instead of simply *leaving it in the soil!* Unbelief causes us to rely on self-effort, dissecting, analysing and even adjusting the seed, thereby destroying its full potential. Or perhaps we have dismissed the seed altogether, thinking it may never produce the results we were hoping for?

In the Bible we read of people who yielded to temptation, interfering with the promises God had uttered. Abraham was promised descendants as numerous as the stars in the sky and the sand on the seashore. Impatience in Sarai's heart, however, caused her to take matters into her own hands, compromising the promise, and an heir was produced through her maid Hagar, causing much grief and heartache.

We need to exercise patience, to *leave the seed* in the ground, taking responsibility only for the condition of the soil. To help the seed grow, we need to aerate the soil with thanksgiving, ensure the seed has ample space to grow, water the soil in faith, and keep the soil exposed to the sun! God moves in the unseen (and in the soil of our heart) to bring about His Word. First the blade, then the head, then the full grain!

Today, acknowledge any impatience or unbelief in your heart towards God's promises. Admit where you could be interfering with the purity and power of the seed. Today, choose trust, and leave the seed of God's promise in the soil. Anticipate with patience the reaping, knowing that harvest time is coming!

the fruit of faith

*Now faith is the substance of things hoped for,
the evidence of things not seen.*
Hebrews 11:1

How's our bank account? We may wish it was more 'flush' than perhaps it is! I guess it all depends on how much we have deposited and allowed to accumulate over time, and how much we may have received in dividends from our investment. Faith is a heart attitude and a response of trust toward God that works like a *deposit in the storage unit of our heart*—the more we transact and deposit, the greater the amount our trust and confidence in God grows. First, we exercise small amounts of faith; then, in seeing God answer our requests, we graduate to believe for much larger needs to be met!

Faithfulness is a fruit of the Spirit; as we are reliable, honest and trustworthy in our dealings, both in our work and relationships, it grows as a fruit in our life, stockpiling over the years in the vault of our heart as a result of experiencing God's faithfulness! This speaks to me of having *a reservoir of faith* we can draw from, ensuring we will be faith-full and not faith-lacking when called upon. Are we faith-full in believing, faith-full in praying, and faith-full in our actions? Faith reflects the heart of God and His faithfulness toward us!

Sometimes people get disillusioned in their journey of faith because they may not have experienced or received the answers they were hoping for. But this does not alter God's faithfulness! Sometimes a denial of our request may, in the long-term, benefit us rather than harm us. Maybe God has something better in mind! We don't always grasp the full picture, and a delay may even help us discover treasures we failed to see previously.

Have you experienced disappointment when you have reached out in faith? Could it be that you 'overshot' in your expectation, reaching far beyond your ability to believe? It's difficult to believe for a million dollars if we don't have the faith for ten! We need to implement small steps of faith to begin with and build our capacity to exercise faith for the larger supply. Does this mean God cannot, or will not, do big and amazing things anytime He likes? He can, and He does! But maybe we lack the faith to believe He *will*. Maybe our requests are more like wishful thinking motivated by desperation, a 'stab in the dark' or 'lotto mentality,' hoping God will simply hand us the answer on a plate?

Bruce and I embarked on a faith exercise over the years, believing for financial provision to meet the needs of the vision we carried in our heart. It was so much bigger than what we could humanly produce, so there was a need to first grow faith as a fruit in the belief system of our heart. At the time, believing for one hundred dollars was a stretch in faith for us, but that became easy to believe for once we had seen God honour our faith for a hundred dollars many times over! Over time we grew the capacity within to believe for the 'much more' of God's provision. Now it is not difficult for us to believe for the large amounts needed to fulfil God's vision entrusted to us. In Ephesians 1:18, Paul prayed that the believers would know, "the riches of the glory of His inheritance in the saints, and . . . the exceeding greatness of His power toward us who believe."

We have probably all experienced the *gift of faith,* when we just know, that we know, that we know! In these moments, faith is freely handed to us by God as a gift; we don't even have to stir up our faith to believe, it's just there—a supernatural confidence! But in other areas, we need to *grow faith as a fruit.* So gaze on *God's faithfulness*! He will help us to reflect faith in our journey!

Today, look at your 'faith account.' What has God already done in response to your faith? What may have eroded your faith and confidence? Have you been presumptuous in your belief and missed what God was doing in the moment? Decide today to keep exercising your faith, keep reaching out, keeping being 'faith-full,' growing in your faith and trusting God for 'much, much more'!

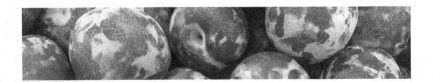

boast in the lord

*For I speak to you Gentiles; inasmuch as I am an apostle to
the Gentiles, I magnify my ministry, if by any means I
may provoke to jealously those who are
my flesh and save some of them.*
Romans 11:13

Have you ever heard someone *boasting,* only to us it sounded like they were bragging about themselves? 'Self-bragging' rarely impresses our listeners or entices them to participate in the conversation! In fact, it can have the opposite effect than perhaps we intended. But on the other hand, we must be careful that we do not shrink back so much that our gifts are not visible and we are not giving any room for God to be glorified through our lives.

The apostle Paul spoke of 'magnifying his ministry.' His goal was not to magnify *himself,* but to *magnify the ministry* God had entrusted to him. Paul was passionate about his God-given responsibility and he wasn't about to shrink back in faith or visibility! In fact, at times he *talked it up* in the hope that the Jews would be stirred by his passion, provoked in a positive way to faith, and restored to their rightful place as God's chosen people!

We all have an area of significant service in God, but if we hide away and remain silent we treat lightly the honour God has bestowed upon us to achieve great things for Him. What is our attitude to serving God? Do we celebrate what we have been given, or do we dismiss it as something insignificant? God gets no glory from our indifference! Paul resolved to take every opportunity to testify of God's goodness. In Acts 26:16-17 he received these words from Jesus Himself:

*I have appeared to you for this purpose,
to make you a minister and a witness . . . I will deliver
you from the Jewish people, as well as from the Gentiles, to
whom I now send you to* **open their eyes***, in order to turn
them from darkness to light, and from the power of Satan to God,
that they may receive forgiveness of sins and an inheritance
among those who are sanctified by faith in Me.*

The Holy Spirit bore witness to Paul's boasts in Jesus as the Saviour of the world, the only One who could save mankind from their sins. You see, God wants us to express *humility* before Him and *confidence* before people!

Are we guilty of judging others, wrongly interpreting another's confidence as pride? Could holding back on our part be even more prideful, as we fear being judged or misunderstood? It's time to stand up in our service for God, to magnify what we have been given so He can be magnified to others. Psalm 34:2-3 says, "My soul shall make its boast in the Lord . . . Oh magnify the Lord with me, and let us exalt His name together!" David was boasting from a position of fullness in his soul, giving testimony to God's grace and goodness, willing others to experience the same level of celebration in their lives. Boasting in God releases power over the struggle, faith for the future, and joy in the present. And, it gives us the ability to overcome every accusation of the enemy! Revelation 12:11 says, "And they overcame him by the blood of the Lamb and by the word of their testimony."

Are you struggling to *boast in God* because you are magnifying other things in your life? What have you 'blown up' in your mind's eye? Is it your fears, your needs, your problems, or the difficulties of life in general? Boast in God and in the manifestation of His liberating power! It's difficult to express worship when the magnifying glass of our heart is focused on earthly worries and human pride. Let's choose today to remember God's goodness and *make our boast in Him*. Let's *talk up* Jesus and every blessing in our life!

*What are you magnifying in your life—God, or your problems? Where are you 'shrinking back,' afraid of being misinterpreted or judged? When was the last time you testified to the goodness of God in your life? Today, break out and **boast in God**—and experience Him bearing witness to your faith!*

winnow to win

You comprehend my path and my lying down
and are acquainted with all my ways.
Psalm 139:3

God understands our thoughts, our processes, our actions and our paths even more than we do. God thoroughly 'gets' us! In the year 2000, God highlighted the word 'comprehend' to me from Psalm 39. To 'comprehend' means "to *winnow*, to sift through to gain clearer understanding." God showed me that He was about to *winnow* my path, and that this was going to involve a relocation from Auckland to London to fulfil God's greater plan for our lives. God allows *winnowing* to create more space in our heart, so things in our life can move to another level.

The word 'winnowing' is generally used in reference to grain; it involves blowing a current of air through the grain in order to remove the lighter particles of dirt and chaff. Sometimes we may need to do some *winnowing* in our pantries by reading expiry dates and throwing out cans or packets of food which have exceeded their 'use-by' date. When an army is recruiting, they will test the candidates to *winnow out* those not fit to be soldiers. Similarly, in talent competitions, judges *winnow* the numbers down to selection of finalists before they choose a winner. We *winnow to win!*

At times in our life, God calls us to winnow our activities to position us for a greater plan ahead. In these situations, some things in our lives need to cease being the main focus because He is calling us to another level of function. Just as in the natural the process of threshing grain eliminates the unnecessary, so it is in the spirit—winnowing streamlines our focus, removing 'lightweight' particles that may restrict our growth.

I remember when we thought it was time for some of our toddlers to be separated from their comfort blankets. We set up a spontaneous game of *"Wouldn't it be fun to throw the blanket in the fire?"* and with great hilarity, the children obliged. Though they may have missed the comfort of their blankets, they never asked for them again!

Could we still be attached to things God has asked us to lay aside even though we have entered a new season in Him that demands a new level of maturity? What thoughts or activities have exceeded their expiry date in our lives? 1 Corinthians 13:11 says, "When I was a child, I spoke as a child,

I understood as a child, I thought as a child; but when I became a man, I put away childish things."

The parts of our life that God *winnows* are not necessarily bad—they could even be good, useful things. But if they are not a good fit for the present or approaching season, we should allow the words of Jeremiah 15:19 to instruct us:

> *If you take away the precious from the vile, you shall be as My mouth! Let them return to you, but you must not return to them.*

There needs to be an extraction from the old, a new way of speaking, a new way of being and believing that adds credibility and authority to our lives. To represent God well, a *winnowing* is required!

What do you need to discard? Is your thinking and activities still relevant to the season you are in? What is God putting His finger on that needs updating and moving up another level? Today, allow God to separate that which is valuable from that which is lightweight and unnecessary, so God can use you at another level. Winnow to win!

deep calls to deep

Deep calls unto deep at the noise of Your waterfalls.
Psalm 42:7

We all desire the deep things of God, but the deep things of God can only call to the deep things within man! God longs for fellowship and communion with us at such a level that He can share prophetic insights and the desires of His heart. Do you wonder why some folk seem to hear God more clearly than others? Perhaps God has designed certain people to be more prophetically inclined—or could it be that some people have simply dug out deeper channels in their heart for the Spirit of God to flow? When we remain in the shallow waters of faith, He is unable to call to the deep things within. His 'deep truths' can get 'beached' in the shallows! That's why we need to develop a *flow of prayer*; we need to increase our depth in the Spirit of God if He is to release prophetic insight and direction in our life.

Have we developed a deep enough channel in prayer? When we are flowing in prayer and godly direction, God is more likely to speak, to add specifics to the current of our life! In the words of Isaiah 30:21, "Your ears shall hear a word behind you saying, 'This is the way, walk in it.'" When I have embarked on faith journeys and been prayerful in the process, I have found that unexpected confirmation, prophecy and provision has come in powerfully behind me.

Do we need to deepen our river of prayer and our devotion to the Word of God? Like workers in a quarry, do we need to loosen and dig out river-rocks that may obstruct the supernatural flow and power of God in our lives? I envision my quiet times in God as not only a time of comfort, communication and revelation, but as an excavation of the river bed of my heart, removing obstacles and creating deeper spaces for the flow of God's anointing.

Proverbs 31:14 (MSG) paints a great picture of the virtuous woman. It says, "She sails away to faraway places and brings back exotic surprises." *Exotic surprises* speak of the deep, yet creative, revelation of God. Some things are found only in the depths of God, and we need to be prepared to sail there in the spirit.

In the Old Testament, Israel called on the prophet Elisha for guidance when they were in trouble. Threatened by the King of Moab and three other heathen kings he had co-opted to fight against them, Israel was understandably concerned. Not only that, they also lacked water for the army and the animals. In response, Elisha (who could clearly hear God speak) delivered this reply:

> *Make this valley full of **ditches** (water canals). For thus says the Lord, "You shall not see wind, nor shall you see rain; yet that valley shall be filled with water, so that you, your cattle and your animals may drink." And this is a simple matter in the sight of the Lord; He will also deliver the Moabites into your hand.*
> *2 Kings 3:15-18*

Elisha heard God speak in the depths of his spirit, instructing the people to dig channels for water to flow, even though there was no rain in sight! With the insight God gave, Moab was defeated! By the power of God, water supernaturally filled those channels, and the threat to God's people was averted!

Do you need to go deeper in prayer and in God's Word? Have you dug deep enough channels in your life for the blessing and prophetic insight of God to flow? Today, know that God wants to fill every channel that you dig by faith, so you can experience the fullness of His supernatural power and supply! Let's go deeper today!

sigh and sign

*Then the Pharisees came out and began to dispute with Him, seeking from Him a sign from heaven, testing Him! But He **sighed** deeply in His spirit and said, "Why does this generation seek a **sign**? Assuredly, I say to you, no sign shall be given to this generation."*
Matthew 12:38

We may be able to communicate well, but because of people's different personalities and interests, we often just don't *get each other*! Even when we give what we consider a reasonably clear, 'why behind the what,' someone may still not seem to get it! Whatever the relationship, this can result in tension or conflict—or even the more mellow response of a simple *sigh*!

When I struggled with improving my technological ability, Bruce would often roll his eyes and *sigh* because it took me so many attempts just to *get it*! Maybe you are teaching someone some new skills and know the feeling? Jesus does. He *sighed* at the lack of willingness the Pharisees displayed to even want to *get it*.

Getting hold of the truth of God launches us into yet another level of understanding and power-filled living. Many people witnessed miracles when Jesus was on earth, but their hearts didn't always grasp the significance of the moment or *who it was* performing them! Even following His amazing demonstration of feeding four thousand people with seven loaves and a few small fish, the Pharisees came to Jesus with questions that were more like challenges! *What didn't they get?!*

The Pharisees were demanding miracles as a prerequisite to believing, yet they already had witnessed so many healings, deliverances and miraculous provisions by the hands of Jesus. Jesus, grieved because of the hardness of their heart, *sighed* in response to their questions; though they had heard His teaching and seen His supernatural power, they remained unconvinced. They just didn't *get it!* Or more accurately, they didn't *want* to get it. Their questions were posed in such a way to trap Jesus; they asked, not because they wanted to learn, but because they wanted to discredit Him.

In reply, Jesus pointed to the people of Nineveh because *they got it!* They were heathens, yet understood the message Jonah brought to them, saw the need for repentance and turned their lives over to God. On the day of Judgment, Jesus said, Nineveh would shame the Pharisees for not repenting, for *not getting it!*

Jesus also pointed to the Queen of Sheba, a ruler who *got it* when she travelled an extensive distance to view Solomon's kingdom. 2 Chronicles 9:3-4 reads, "When the Queen of Sheba had seen the wisdom of Solomon the house that he had built, the food on his table, the seating of his servants, the service of his waiters and their apparel, and his entryway by which he went up to the house of the Lord, there was no more spirit in her." In other words, *she got it!*

How does Jesus perceive us today? Are we *sighing* because we long for more of Him, for greater understanding and for the power to live worthy of Him? Or would He sigh because of our unbelief, longing for us to just *get it*? Acts 5:12 tells us that "through the hands of the apostles, many signs and wonders were done among the people." You see, signs and wonders are granted to those who desire them as *confirmation of their faith*, but denied to those who demand them as a *prerequisite to faith*. Or, in the words of Mark 16:17, "These signs will follow those who believe: In my name they will cast out demons; they will speak with new tongues." Jesus grants us understanding, and *signs* will follow those who believe!

🍃 *What don't you 'get' today? Or are you playing 'hard to get'? Would Jesus sigh over you today because of any unbelief and hardness of heart? Today, let's have a sigh in our spirit to know Jesus more!*

knock, knock

*Behold I stand at the door and **knock**.*
If anyone hears My voice and opens the door,
I will come in to him and dine with him, and he with Me.
Revelation 3:20

"Knock, knock, who's there?" was a game craze several years ago, that sometimes makes a reappearance today; it's a play on words to discover who seeks entrance at the door.

Knock, knock. "Are you there?" we may call out when we stand at someone's front door to ascertain whether they are home. Have you ever stood at someone's door and got the distinct impression that they didn't want you to come in—there was no enthusiastic welcome, no forthcoming smile, leaving you to wonder whether the timing was really inconvenient or perhaps the inside the house was so untidy they didn't want you to see it? We have probably all experienced this at one time or another— knocking on someone's front door to find we haven't been given entry. I wonder if Jesus feels like that when He comes knocking on the door of our heart? *Knock, knock. "Is anyone home?"* Sometimes it is obvious that no one is home, the blinds are down, the door is locked and the occupants are probably away, but we *knock* anyway, just in case!

King David was a God-worshipper and an excellent king, mighty in battle, but David seriously lacked in his role as a father. He was *not home* for his sons when trouble erupted in the family. And though David wept for the loss of life and was genuinely grieved for the wrongdoing of his children, he never went after his son Absalom when, guilty of his brother's murder, he fled to another city. 2 Samuel 14:28 tells us that, "Absalom fled and went to Geshur, and was there three years. And King David longed to go to Absalom, for he had been comforted concerning Amnon because he was dead. After three years, Joab, witnessing David's grief, persuaded the king to grant permission for Absalom to return to Jerusalem." But even then, David did not visit his son. We read in 2 Samuel 14:28, "And Absalom dwelt two full years in Jerusalem, but did not see the king's face." Absalom had requested an audience with his father but none was forthcoming! *Knock, knock. No one was home!*

When a literal door is only partially opened to us, this may be followed by a somewhat superficial conversation on the front doorstep. Jerusalem was like the *front doorstep* for Absalom—he was back in Jerusalem; he was so close, and yet no welcome mat awaited him. There was no open door for him to come back into the family home, nor into the king's presence, until two years later when a particular incident occurred. What was wrong with David?! There is no written account of any communication between David and Absalom and we can only assume, on account of treason rising in Absalom's heart toward his father, that it was seriously lacking! David's lack was Satan's gain. David's inner lack—his inability to communicate, embrace and restore—showed in holding out on his son. In the absence of reconciliation, the door was left open for Satan to move in on the hurts and offences within Absalom's heart, resulting in even more heartbreak for David.

How is our communication? When it comes to our family, workmates, friends and other believers, do we have an *open heart* to welcome them in, or are we just chatting awkwardly on the front doorstep, effectively holding out on them? Have we left people *knocking* because we're *not at home* in ourselves, struggling with discrepancies and unaddressed lack within? *Knock, knock. "Who's there?"* Is it pride, selfishness or inferiority? What is causing us to not answer the door? God is never an absentee Father. His desire is to heal, minister, reconcile and restore us to Himself.

Who have you left knocking at the door of your heart? Today, choose not to be absent but present in all your relationships. Don't settle for doorstep conversations but welcome God and others into your heart.

meet blessing!

The king shall have joy in Your strength, O Lord; and in
Your salvation how greatly shall he rejoice! You have given
him his heart's desire and have not withheld the request of his
*lips. For You **meet** him with the blessings of goodness;*
You set a crown of pure gold upon his head.
Psalm 21:1-3

When people or groups of people struggle to make a decision but are willing to compromise or capitulate on their stance in order to maintain harmony and agreement, they often agree to *meet each other halfway*. The Bible declares that God's ways are perfect and therefore God does not need to compromise or capitulate on any of His decisions. His desire is to *meet* us with the blessings of His goodness, the very best for our lives! We can meet Him anytime—when things are going well, but also when they are not. Are we letting God meet us with His blessings? God wants to answer our prayers and release some of the tensions we are facing in life!

Have you ever looked at a 'Scrabble' board and wondered how you are going to make significant words from all the random letters lying around? When God *meets us*, His desire is to help us, bless us and unscramble any confusion we may have, imparting faith and blessing into our life. God, through the Holy Spirit can make sense of what is unclear to us! He can make visible what is invisible. We just need faith to believe that He wants to meet us and bless our lives. Sometimes the Holy Spirit will exchange and replace unworthy letters and words on the board of our heart and replace them with higher scoring letters, forming winning words that help us conquer in the game of life!

What words are we using about ourselves and our situations? Are they words of faith, worthy words that put us in the right position to overcome and conquer? Are there words we need to exchange, thoughts we need to conform to God's thoughts, concepts we need to unscramble relating to God's blessing? If so, we need to *meet Him*! God will challenge us on any duplicity and impurity of faith that could cause us to struggle and lose in the game of life.

Blessed be the God and Father of our Lord Jesus Christ, who has blessed
us with every spiritual blessing in the heavenly places in Christ.
Ephesians 1:3

God's word in this passage declares that every spiritual blessing is ours! How awesome is that? However, due to our limited concepts, we often mistakenly think that blessings are just what is added to our life—jobs, houses, and similar wants and needs. But blessings are also the things we let go of, the unworthy words and beliefs we exchange in order to pick up the greater, more worthy words that agree with what God has said. Psalm 1:1 says, "Blessed is the man who walks not in the counsel of the ungodly." God's Word *meets us* to ensure that we are perfect candidates for God's blessing whenever we separate from unwise counsel.

Where do you get your counsel or ethos for life from? The psalmist declared that he would "set nothing worthless before his eyes"(Psalm 101:3). Choices keep our faith pure! He also tells us that we are a candidate for ongoing blessing when we seek forgiveness for our wrongdoing, when we are released from our sin.

> *Blessed is he whose transgression is forgiven, whose sin is covered. Blessed is the man to whom the Lord does not impute iniquity and in whose spirit there is no deceit.*
> *Psalm 32:1*

Let's choose blessing in all its entirety, not only for what we gain but also for what we are released from by faith! God will set a crown of pure gold upon our heads when we let God *meet us* with His blessings!

Where could you be demanding God capitulate to your thinking? What words are you choosing that are not compatible with God's blessing on your life? Today, choose to exchange unworthy letters and words! Let God meet you with His blessings today!

listen up!

*Listen, listen to the **wind words**, the Spirit blowing through the churches. I am about to call each conqueror to dinner. I'm spreading a banquet of Tree of Life fruit, a supper plucked from God's orchard.*
Revelation 2:6 (MSG)

We are probably all familiar with *wind instruments*; they have a beguiling sound, traversing effortlessly across a score of music, wooing hearts and enhancing the storyline of the composer. In the same way, the Holy Spirit's breath upon God's Word lifts us to new altitudes of faith, love and power as we recognise God's signature tune of love weaved through the composition. The phrase, *'wind words'* is a metaphor used to depict the words of the Holy Spirit as they blow through the churches. These are the very words that will have the most profound impact on our lives!

Wind words are like a current of air beneath a large bird as it soars at great heights. By simply spreading its wings wide, it allows the rhythm of the current to sweep it effortlessly upwards! The *wind words* of God's Spirit dance and course their way in and through our hearts, gaining an audience and setting new scores of faith, melody and harmony in our heart. We need to *listen up*!

The sound of God's words appeals to our spirit; they surpass the voice of reason that keeps us 'earth bound' and instead open the windows of our heart to unexplored spiritual realities and loftier heights in faith. The sound of God's *wind words* draws us into new dimensions, releasing new songs within our hearts, as the psalmist knew only too well. In Psalm 45:1 he writes, "My heart is overflowing with a good theme. I recite my composition concerning the King; my tongue is the pen of a ready writer." The sons of Korah were bursting forth with emotions of love, being filled and satisfied with the fullness of the flow of God's presence in their life! The same verse in *The Message* goes on to put it like this: "My heart bursts its banks, spilling beauty and goodness. I pour it out in a poem, shaping the river into words."

Do we feel like our hearts are bursting with ready praise? Is a recitation flowing freely from our lips, or have we just settled for the same old score, the same old repetitive recital? In scripture we are exhorted to *sing a new song*, to constantly glorify God afresh and to 'awaken the dawn' of a new day!

Perhaps we need to pull back the curtains on grey days and allow the sunshine of God's words in, 'calling time' on any bland expression of worship and praise! Let's open our ears to the call of God's *wind words* as they weave and wind their way through the storyline of our life, bringing a fuller expression and an ability to *soar higher* in God.

Shakespeare penned the words,

> *"All the world's a stage, and all the men and women*
> *merely players; they have their exits and their entrances,*
> *and one man in his time plays many parts."*
> *('As You Like It', Act II, Scene VII)*

This is our turn to pen the story of our life, to give our own *faith recital* in the play of life! Will our recital be one of complaints, gloom and negativity about all that's wrong with the world, or will it be *a recital to Jesus*, filled with thanksgiving for the beautiful part He plays, not only in composing our life but for His help in the many stages and parts that comprise it? What 'lines' are going to come out of our mouth? Listen up to the *wind words* of the Spirit of God. Attend His banquet! Enjoy His very best as you celebrate the wonderful victories in your life. And then, echo His goodness!

What tune is playing in your heart today? Is it praise—or pessimism? Is the sound of your recital monotonous and lengthy, or is it life-giving? Today, break the banks of conservative worship! Choose to follow God's song sheet, enjoy the colour of His creativity, and then pen your praise to Him!

the line of faith

Faith comes by hearing, and hearing by the Word of God.
Romans 10:10

Faith is a journey—but it is much more than a journey! It's a *lifestyle* we enter when we give our heart to Jesus. This lifestyle begins when we fully accept Jesus' sacrifice on the cross, dealing with the penalty we incurred through our own wrongdoing. We enter this glorious new relationship with our Lord and Saviour, Jesus, through faith, and our faith grows daily through our ever-increasing knowledge of Him—who He is, what He has done, and what He wants to do in the future. Our faith grows in response to His Word as we receive the blessings and provision of God, but also as we let go, giving over what concerns us, and trusting God in prayer for the right outcome.

God revealed to me one day that there was a *line of faith* I needed to adhere to, places in my life where I needed to let go and simply trust Him. He showed me this was *not neglectful, but necessary* –that if I wanted to see God answer my prayers significantly, I needed to grow in faith. This revelation came as a gentle rebuke. God was showing me that at times I was *crossing the line of faith;* I was attempting to do work that rightfully belonged to the Holy Spirit, and wearying myself out in the process. In other words, God was letting me know that I was *trespassing on Holy Spirit territory.*

God reframed my reference of faith, showing me the part I needed to play in terms of 'believing,' and what part belonged to the Holy Spirit. I subsequently adopted a new approach in prayer—I learned to enquire as to where the *line of faith* was in any particular instance, so that once I had fulfilled my responsibility in faith, prayer and action, I could simply let go and leave the matter in the powerful and responsible hands of the Holy Spirit.

In many instances, faith involves holding on tightly; other times, faith involves releasing our grip. Sometimes it even takes a 'forgetting' in the Spirit. Paul wrote of this in Philippians 3:13-14:

> Brethren, I do not count myself to have apprehended; but one thing I do, **forgetting** those things which are behind and reaching forward to those things which are ahead. I press toward the goal for the prize of the upward call of God in Christ Jesus.

Did Paul have a memory problem? Not at all! By faith, he simply chose to *forget* the past—not just the terrible things he had done, but also all the great achievements accredited to him in his lifetime, freeing him to apprehend *by faith* the glorious future and ministry God had planned for him. Paul was pressing on! He needed to adhere to a *line of faith* so that he could live free from condemnation on one hand and pride on the other.

In the natural, lines drawn on the ground often signify starting and finishing points in a race, queue or assembly of people. There are also 'invisible lines' denoting personal space designed to preserve one's expression and dignity. Similarly, in the spiritual realm, the Holy Spirit *draws a line* to protect His territory so He can freely work supernaturally for our good.

Have you crossed the line of faith and taken full responsibility for your life and issues into your own hands? Let's switch off from being overly responsible, and realise the Holy Spirit wants to be commissioned to act on our behalf!

Ask the Holy Spirit to show you where the 'line of faith' is, knowing it sometimes takes more faith to let go and trust than it does to hold on. Let faith work by adhering to the Holy Spirit's prompting today. Let go where you need to! Release the Holy Spirit to do His very best work as you affirm your belief in Him today.

ask big!

Then came the daughters of Zelophehad . . .
and they stood before Moses, before Eleazar the priest,
and before the leaders and all the congregation, by the doorway of
the tabernacle of meeting, saying: "Our father died in the wilderness,
but he was not in the company of those who gathered together against
the Lord, in company with Korah, but he died in his own sin; and
he had no sons. Why should the name of our father be removed from
among his family because he had no son? Give us a possession among
our father's brothers." So Moses brought their case before the Lord.
And the Lord spoke to Moses, saying: "The daughters of Zelophehad
speak what is right; you shall surely give them a possession of
inheritance among their father's brothers, and cause the
inheritance of their father to pass to them."
Numbers 27:1-6

When we find our purpose, we find our *ask*! If our purpose is not very big, nor beyond our own ability, then our *ask* is not likely to be big either. We need to access the favour of God to fulfil His purpose for our life. What are we currently *asking*? Do we desire God's very best for ourselves and others? We need to know what to ask for!

Some women in the Bible knew they needed to *ask big* in order to preserve an inheritance that was rightfully theirs! Although they had no advocate, they boldly stepped forward to manage their own case. Taking a risk, they placed themselves in a vulnerable position before Moses, Eleazar the priest, the leaders and all the congregation. What enabled them to be this bold?

The daughters spoke in honour of their father—who had lived righteously and died from natural causes—requesting that his inheritance be preserved for generations to come! As there were no sons to pass his inheritance onto (as was the usual custom of the day) their father's life's work would potentially be lost. These ladies knew the promises of God; they understood that the tribe of Manasseh was spoken of as God's possession (Psalm 60:7) and that its existence was not supposed to cease at their father's death. They knew there was a line of blessing and inheritance that needed to be claimed!

In the natural, these women were not entitled to their father's inheritance, but God heard their hearts in the matter and granted their request. An age-old law was changed simply because of their *ask*!

What traditions, customs or laws could we change through our *ask*? These women's hearts were pure; they viewed themselves as responsible guardians of the legacy of their father. They were not about to allow his life to have been lived in vain!

Have we allowed things that are rightfully ours to slip out of our hands? Are we stewarding well the line of blessing, both to us and from us? As God's children, we can stand before God for everything that rightfully belongs to us through Jesus' death on the cross. Let's not lose the rightful inheritance that Jesus has gained for us! Hebrews 4:16 exhorts us to "come boldly to the throne of grace that we may obtain mercy and find grace to help in time of need." Let's come on behalf of ourselves, our children, our health, our finances, our purpose. When we come boldly with a pure heart, we find grace and help in our time of need.

How's your ask? Have you allowed what is rightfully yours to slip from your hand? Have you allowed an inheritance that needs to be redeemed, to become obsolete? What is your purpose? Remember, big purpose calls for a big ask! Today, increase your ask, and thank God for the inheritance that is yours!

function

*Then God said, "Let there be light," and there was light. And
God saw the light, that it was good, and God **divided** the light
from the darkness. God called the light 'day,' and the darkness He
called 'night.' So the evening and the morning were the first day.*
Genesis 1:3-5

God has given each of us a *distinctive* so we can function effectively in
the grace He has given us. This will usually take a separation on our
part from the 'norm,' a willingness to operate where God has placed
us and chosen to display His glory. Do we find *separation* difficult? The
word has negative connotations in many contexts, but in God's economy,
separation refers to mindsets, choices and behaviour; a giving away of
the lesser to receive the greater!

We often hear a cry for 'individuality'—along with the need or desire to
be celebrated as such. Yet at the same time, people find it hard to *separate*
themselves from the crowd in order to discover their individuality! Many
people may prefer to follow the 'mass' which in turn may prove to be mindless,
directionless and determined by the minority; whereas God wants us to shine
in our distinctive call and thereby function effectively for the benefit of all!

The first separation we see was implemented in the creation of the world. God separated elements so they could *function effectively* in the purpose He had designed for them. God divided the light from the darkness to make a distinction between day and night.

> Then God said, "Let there be lights in the firmament of the heavens to **divide** the day from the night; and let them be for signs and seasons and for days and for years". . . Then God made two great lights: the greater light to rule the day, and the lesser light to rule the night, He made the stars also.
> Genesis 1:14-18

God set these lights in the heavens, naming them according to their function: the sun to rule the day, and the moon the night. As God's people we want clarification, distinction and individuality, and this often comes as a result of separation. In God's economy, division has a multiplying effect as everyone takes their God-given place and functions effectively. God has a distinct function for each and every one of us, but we have to let Him call it out by name!

We have spaces in our lives we may need to separate from in order to achieve our full potential. Perhaps we need to separate ourselves inwardly from fear of failure, from embarrassment, from sin and condemnation, from unbelief, or from merely wanting to blend in with the crowd rather than standing out for God.

Joseph had to separate himself from any unforgiveness toward his brothers and his false accusers, so that in due time he could be set in a leadership role and lead a nation victoriously through an incredibly difficult period! By separating himself from unforgiveness, Joseph was able to address his brothers with love and wisdom, saying, "But as for you, you meant evil against me; but God meant it for good, in order to bring it about as it is this day, to save many people alive" (Genesis 50:20).

Like Abraham, Moses, Joshua and many of our forebears, let's choose to separate ourselves in order to function and achieve great things for God!

Where might you be hiding in the shadows? What choices do you need to make so that you can operate where God has placed you? Today, let God call you out. He wants to reveal your distinctive and your function. As you separate yourself from fear, take your place confidently, and shine brightly for Jesus today!

cheeky faith

*For You, O Lord, will bless the righteous with **favour**,*
*you will surround him as with a **shield**.*
Psalm 5:12

God has us covered! He has amazing solutions to the issues we face, yet sometimes we act like we are vulnerable and helpless because of our circumstances. We need faith that will be audacious in the face of setbacks and refusals! God causes the scriptures to 'come alive in us' in order to quicken our faith and instil boldness and confidence within.

Psalm 5:12 came into focus in a powerful way for me during a particular season in our church. For five weeks we had to meet in our original venue, which by that time was far too small to house the growing kids' programme! When the Holy Spirit brought this scripture to my attention, it came with a cheeky idea—to approach the manager of a restaurant on the same street, and ask if he would be willing to delay opening his restaurant on Sunday mornings and allow some of the kids to meet there for their programme.

How cheeky was that?! But God had given me a clear picture from Psalm 5 that we were wearing His favour as a shield which would be hard for anyone to resist. That was our confidence! Sure enough, the manager delayed opening the restaurant by an hour every Sunday, allowing us to fill the space with children for those five weeks. And, though I asked for the invoice several time, nothing was forthcoming! I think our presence there invoked God's favour on them too, causing business for them to be better than usual. How fun it was as a team, to don our *favour shield*, knowing that God would push open amazing doors as a result.

In a similar way, during a time when we were praying and interceding for some particular needs, a verse from the book of Esther hit my heart. In it, Esther was seeking a letter from the king revoking the evil decree Haman had instituted regarding killing all the Jews. To her surprise, the king placed confidence in his queen, replying to her in this manner:

> **You yourselves** *write a decree concerning the Jews as you please in the king's name, and seal it with the king's signet ring; for whatever is written in the king's name and sealed with the king's signet ring no one can revoke.*
> *Esther 8:8*

Through that verse, God spoke so clearly into my spirit, *"You write it and I'll stamp it."* God was putting His confidence in Bruce and I to 'decree things' as we sought Him for what was right, good and just in the circumstance! Together we penned three obstacles we wanted to see move, laid hands prayerfully on the piece of paper, and tucked the document away in the office drawer. Within a week, we saw every one of those obstacles move, resulting in breakthrough in the situation!

God is able, and He delights to quicken His Word to us at any particular time, to help us hurdle some of the difficulties that may be before us. We just need to be in prayer and in His Word. When we receive 'rhema' words like these, we will have a confident and somewhat *cheeky faith* that God is about to do something really amazing!

David had faith like that when he took on Goliath, the giant everyone else was afraid of. With great confidence, and knowing the word of faith that was resident in his spirit, David declared that he would take off Goliath's head and feed his flesh to the birds of the air! I believe God smiles when we choose to believe and respond with audacious faith!

Where are you holding back and allowing the enemy to frustrate God's plans? What scriptures have been quickened to you that you need to 'wear as your favour shield'? God smiles on your faith! Realise today, with God on your side, you are irresistible!

god's maths

*Jesus went to the Mount of Olives. Now early in the morning
He came again into the temple, and all the people came to Him,
and He sat down and taught them.*
John 8:1-2

How were your school days? Maths and bookkeeping were some of the subjects I really enjoyed. I found great satisfaction in finding solutions, making sure the numbers added up or balanced correctly. It really just involved being systematic and thorough, and applying the principles behind the theories. God's maths is different to ours—it's sometimes more complicated and puzzling than our learning systems in the natural. But in the greater purposes of God, *God's maths* always adds up to abundant life and provides solutions well beyond what we could have ever figured out!

Because of our limited understanding on one hand, or our overly-structured mindsets on the other, we may struggle at times to grasp the concepts of Jesus' teaching! Will the outcome *equal* the expectation we have calculated in our heart? *Will God's ways really work?* Although this question may be in the forefront of our mind, the *common denominator* we need in the complexities of the calculation, is the simple principle of *trust* in a God, who fully knows what He is doing!

Jesus *taught* at every opportunity, bringing understanding to the hearts and minds of His listeners regarding faith and the principles of His eternal, indestructible Kingdom. John 8:1-2 paints a beautiful picture of Jesus taking the time to sit among the people and to *teach* matters of the Kingdom and principles of life. At other times we read of Him standing up in a boat, a hillside or in the temple to teach. In Luke 4:16 we read, "As His custom was, He went into the synagogue on the Sabbath and stood up to read."

The people in the synagogue that day marvelled at Jesus' teaching. Jesus was anointed by the Spirit of God; the prophetic utterances and scriptures He spoke of *applied* to Him! The power of Jesus' teaching in our lives enlightens our understanding even today, but as in Jesus' day, there are forces that want to deafen our ears and make us resistant to learning God's eternal principles and purposes. In John 8:3-4, we read of Jesus teaching a crowd, and of the Pharisees' attempt to shut Him down by interrupting, seeking to distract His teaching by presenting another issue:

> *Then the scribes and the Pharisees brought to Him a woman caught in adultery. And when they had set her in the midst, they said to him, "Teacher, this woman was caught in adultery, in the very act. Now Moses, in the law, commanded us that such should be stoned. But what do You say?"*

Jesus was not distracted or shut down by this interruption; instead He used this disturbance to take *his teaching* up another level. Bending down, Jesus drew in the sand, making a distinction between law and grace. *Law demands death but grace grants life!*

Jesus invited the Pharisees, if they were without sin themselves, to cast the first stone! We don't know the exact words Jesus wrote in the sand that day, but His words stirred conviction in the heart of the woman's accusers, and they all dispersed and went away. Where they guilty also? We are all guilty and deserving of death, but Jesus in His love and mercy, grants us pardon! A prominent church in Australia expresses it like this: *The Cross = Love*. This doesn't make sense according to human logic, maths or calculation, but the greatest expression of love the world has ever seen *equals* forgiveness and eternal life.

🍃 *Are you bound by law? God wants to show you His grace today. Have you shut down the teaching of Jesus from entering fully into your heart? What side issues or arguments you are lifting up in the face of truth? Today, learn from Jesus. Be taught by Him and watch your life multiply with peace, joy and wellbeing!*

god's map

He left Judea and departed again to Galilee,
but He needed to go through Samaria.
John 4:3,4

God's maths can sometimes be difficult to understand, but so also can be God's map! It may require us at times to walk through unfamiliar land or territory we may prefer to avoid. We need to remember that Jesus willingly walked through hostile territory to make a way for us.

Jesus also went out of His way to meet a Samaritan woman in need, opting to put His life in danger by doing so! Samaria represented a hostile place for Jews, one of opposition, ill feeling, persecution and danger. It doesn't sound like a journey that many Jews wanted to take! Jews usually choose to take the longer route around the edge of Samaria to avoid conflict they may otherwise encounter. But Jesus *needed* to go through Samaria! Why? Because He wanted to connect and bring healing to a woman in need.

Sometimes we are directed through unfamiliar territory because there's a connection to be made, resulting in restoration and healing either for ourselves or others. At times on our journey of faith, God asks us to walk through places we wouldn't select ourselves. We may have a clear destination, but we may not always know the exact paths that will get us there. I have learned through experience that at times God leads us away from what we may consider to be the main track, and ask us to walk on paths that are not only unfamiliar, but also unchartered and potentially hostile! But along that route we will discover God's grace, provision and revelation.

God uses shaky and unfamiliar ground to solidify our conviction, convincing us of *whose ground* we really stand upon and who our true Guide is! Our conviction is shaped more often in the difficult times than in the 'ordinary' routine of everyday life. Negotiating unfamiliar terrain either strengthens our resolve to trust more diligently in God's map, or it can knock us off the correct path because we continue to insist and rely on ourselves to establish right direction.

Planting a church in London was both exciting and challenging as we experienced blessings and growth! In this period of time, as God took me through unsettled terrain and certain contradictions to my expectations, some default settings in my life that I had been unaware of, changed. The

Holy Spirit directed me from serving God *conditionally* to serving Him *unconditionally*, establishing in that territory my *'even if'* surrender and commitment to God! Habakkuk expressed a similar spirit when he wrote, "Though the fig tree may not blossom, nor fruit be on the vine ... yet I will rejoice in the Lord, I will joy in the God of my salvation" (Habakkuk 3:17,18).

During this time, God particularly used the story of Jacob to speak into my heart. When Jacob ran from his brother Esau who he had deceived, Jacob's attitude to God was one of conditional commitment. Jacob declared that if God blessed him, then he would serve God on his return! However, through the landscape of his uncle Laban's cunning nature, God caused Jacob to face up to his own devious nature and to deal with the conditional surrender in his heart. When Jacob returned years later to meet Esau, he was a changed man and, on being confronted with God's presence, he clung desperately to the angel that appeared before him, not wanting to let go or even live without the presence of God!

Queen Esther, when she anticipated going before the king said, "If I perish, I perish" (Esther 4:16). Job too, declared, "Though He slay me; yet will I trust Him" (Job 13:15). Finding themselves in hostile territory, they came to the point of *'even if'* surrender, and committed themselves to following God's map for their lives.

Where is God's map directing you? Are you refusing to go to places that God has ordained for you to walk? What might God want to show you in these new and unfamiliar places? Today, surrender control of the direction of your life and let God bring increase to your life through His direction!

there's more to see 7

Then He came to Bethsaida; and they brought a blind man to
Him, and begged Him to touch him. So He took the blind man by
the hand and led him out of the town. And when He had spit on
his eyes and put His hands on him, He asked if he saw anything.
And he looked up and said, "I see men like trees, walking." Then
He put His hands on his eyes again and made him look up.
And He was restored and saw everyone clearly.
Mark 8:22-25

Sometimes in life, we can get stuck in our thinking and believing. Often, this is related to how we see and perceive things. Perhaps we just need to view our circumstances and our life a little differently, from a new angle or perspective? We need the *touch of Jesus* upon our eyes, revealing to us what we can't see in the natural, allowing His perspective to enlighten our spiritual eyes.

In Mark 8, a blind man was brought to Jesus for healing. Three stages are emphasised in this healing. First, he was blind. Then, he had partial sight; and finally, he received clear vision. Something needed to shift for this man to be able to see clearly. Maybe we too need Jesus to put His hands on our eyes again—to clear the fog, the haze, the uncertainty through which we may be viewing our situation. We need to acknowledge with faith in our spirit that there is *more to see,* that we may not be *seeing it all*.

To receive clear vision however, we need to allow Jesus to lead us. Jesus led the bind man out of town. Why was that? Wasn't Jesus capable of healing anywhere, anytime? Perhaps Jesus wanted to remove this man from the familiar environment, away from the dependencies he had developed to help him cope because he was unable to see. Maybe he had to remove himself from all the voices around him that, with all good intentions, helped to keep him safe.

Today, let's allow Jesus to lead us out of the world we have created for ourselves where everything is accessible, where everything is familiar, where we are able to negotiate our way around even 'with our eyes shut,' as the expression goes—a bit like finding our way to the bathroom in the dark of night! Have we too, developed 'safety nets' around us to secure us, so that we don't need to exercise much faith to survive?

Let's be willing to go where God wants to lead us. He may want to challenge the areas in our life we view as handicaps to our spiritual development—the words, for instance, that we speak over our lives that cripple us, yet have become like security blankets to wrap ourselves in, keeping ourselves covered and excused! It's time to be led 'out of town', into a new zone of vision and direction. It's time to step out of the box of limitations and excuses. Jesus wants us to hear and see something different through the touch of His hand on our spiritual sight. What is your vista like? When it's from a higher perspective, the broader and more glorious it is!

The woman who anointed Jesus with costly oil was criticised sharply by those who were in the room with her. They viewed her actions as wasteful, but Jesus *took a different view*. He saw her actions as honourable, timely, proceeding from a heart of worship and spiritual insight. That's why He responded with the words, "Let her alone. Why do you trouble her? She has done a good work for me" (Mark 14:6). Her 'out of the box' expression of worship, her clear vision of who Jesus was, her prophetic insight of what lay beyond, attracted the attention of Jesus. And, her act of worship, releasing the fragrance of heaven into that room, still attracts people's attention thousands of years later.

Do you need to be 'led out of town' to see more clearly God's perspective? What 'boxed in' vision and excuses need to be broken so you can express yourself more freely? Today, let God lead you, touch your eyes again and extend your vision. There's more to see!

there's more to see 2

*They came to Bethsaida, and some people brought a blind man
and begged Jesus to touch him. He took the blind man by
the hand and led him outside the village.*
Mark 8:22

When a parcel arrives with your name on it, you are entitled to open it. It's yours to have! I love God's postal system—He sends messages straight to the inbox of our heart, deliveries of insight, wisdom and precious promises. Every day, every hour, every second we can hear the computer of our heart beep with a notification, saying, *"You have mail!'"*

The blind man in Mark 8 heard Jesus speak his name *and* he felt Jesus take his hand to move him away from the known, *to a new place* where Jesus could reveal to him what he couldn't previously see. I love this man's response— he willingly allowed Jesus to lead him! Then Jesus opened his eyes!

He was restored and saw everyone clearly.
Mark 8:24

For the blind man to see what he saw, he needed to journey with Jesus *out of town.* My journey 'out of town' was literally to leave New Zealand and go to London to plant a church alongside my husband, Bruce. There were things in this appointed place I would never have been able to see if I had not been willing to go on this journey. I knew I needed God to take my hand and lead me!

We note in the story of the blind man that Jesus checked in with him on his journey about how much he could actually see along the way. For me, the journey 'out of town' began before I physically left New Zealand, as I allowed God to touch my eyes. At the thought of leaving home and family, the blur of tears clouded my vision. I needed to be led by Jesus! For me, alignment was the key. I knew Bruce was seeing something I was yet to see, and when I chose to stand behind him, to remain under his spiritual covering, and to ask God to show me what he was seeing, God spoke immediately into my spirit from Genesis 13. *I had mail!*

And the Lord said to Abram . . . "Lift up your eyes now and look
from the place where you are—northward, southward, eastward
*and westward; **for all the land which you see I give***
***to you and your descendants forever**."*
Genesis 13:14-15

The words that arrived straight into the inbox of my heart were: *"If you can see it, Helen, you can have it!"* This message had my name on it—I had a direct promise from God! Immediately, my vision cleared. As I received the promise of Genesis 13, I ceased "seeing men like trees, walking." I could so clearly *see it!* I knew straight away what to ask! Something I had been believing for over a long time, was about to become a reality. And so it did! Throughout this journey of being led by God, my vision was extended and my faith grew deeper in the knowledge of a God who cared so much about my journey and my ability to see Him at work.

I saw and learned so many things during that period. One of those was that we can never 'out-give' God! As much as we give, God returns, placing even more parcels in the mailbox of our life with our name on them! Isaiah 40:10 says, "Behold the Lord God shall come with a strong hand, and His arm shall rule for Him, behold His reward is with Him and His work before Him." On my journey 'out of town,' I experienced this in great measure!

Is your vision clear, or is it cloudy? Do you need Jesus to touch your eyes so you can receive clarity and courage for the journey? Today, align yourself with the direction God wants to lead you. Check your inbox for mail! God has placed something special and significant there. Discover it today. You have mail!

check-up

The counsel of the Lord stands forever,
the plans of His heart to all generations.
Psalm 33:11

Sometimes we need to pause and *check up* on our spiritual, physical and emotional well-being to see what shape we are in. One summer holiday, this was necessary for me as I was having a continual problem with sinus and an aching back. Why was there tension in my body? Was exercise lacking in my regime? What 'out of shape' habits had I developed? While I was doing well on a spiritual and emotional level, I needed to *shape up* physically and I needed a plan. That's when God strongly convicted me regarding the Sabbath, the importance of resting properly.

In which area of your life do you need to 'level up' into a position of health? Maybe it's your marriage, your finances, your fitness and health, or your relationship with God? In every area we need to *embrace* what we already have to work with, and do our best to ensure we are in peak condition to fulfil God's will for our lives! To do this we need to *embrace the God-shape* He has spoken over our life from before the beginning of time. God *shapes us* individually to fit the area in which He has graced us to function freely and with ease in our call and mission. We need to accept our God-given shape!

From the place of His dwelling He looks on all the inhabitants of
the earth; He fashions their hearts individually;
He considers all their works.
Psalm 33:14-15

Moses' life was shaped by God from the beginning of time as a deliverer of Israel from the hand of the Egyptians. Moses set out with enthusiasm to fulfil this task, and when he observed an Egyptian mistreating an Israelite, he stepped in to intervene—only, he forgot to draw on God's power and operated merely in his own strength. As a result of this failure, and in fear for his own life, Moses fled into the wilderness, disowning the call and the shape God had designed for his life. In a supernatural display of a bush burning yet not being consumed, God called Moses to *pick up the original shape* he had been given. Feeling totally inadequate, Moses objected. That's when God brought Moses' attention to the staff he had in his hand. The staff was a familiar object to Moses, something he used competently on a daily basis, to count sheep, care for sheep and protect sheep!

We can be so familiar with what God has placed in our hand that we take these gifts for granted, perhaps dismissing them altogether. Maybe we are even tempted to seek another 'shaped' ministry or operation than what God has already given and decreed. Each of us need to embrace our *God-given shape*, value it, appreciate it and be thankful of God's choice for us. As with Moses, God wants to show us something amazing!

> *So he cast it on the ground it become a serpent;*
> *and Moses fled from it.*
> *Exodus 4:3*

When Moses let go of the rod in his hand, it took a different shape! Initially, Moses wanted to run from the scene, but God challenged him to take the serpent by the tail, and as Moses grasped it, the serpent became a rod once again! When we want to do great things for God, the gift we release from our hand may change shape as it touches the realm of the spirit— and the demonic! The change of shape doesn't mean the call is wrong. There is simply a need to pick it up with a new godly authority, not out of fleshly strength. God was showing Moses the authority he had placed in his hand to lead the nation of Israel out of bondage through supernatural manifestations. When God spoke into my spirit through this passage He said, "It's how you pick up the call on your life that is important, Helen— don't pick it up with a limp wrist, but with an authoritative grip!"

Do you need to do a 'health check' today? Do you need to embrace your God-given shape more fully? Where have you been afraid, and run from the call on your life? Today, rise and operate in the authority God has placed upon your life! God wants to use what you are already in possession of to defy the enemy and achieve supernatural results!

don't pack too tight!

Do not overwork to be rich;
because of your own understanding, cease!
Proverbs 23:4

It's easy to work *over* an allocated measure, to push past reasonable and sensible limits to achieve a goal, not taking into account when 'enough is enough!' Perhaps we are guilty of trying to pack too much into our life, being overly ambitious, and ending up pushing the limits of our health and wellbeing? We have probably all travelled to other cities or countries and faced the dilemma of choosing what to take with us, only to find we packed way more than was necessary. Then comes the next dilemma— trying to shut the lid on a bulging suitcase by leaning on it or maybe even sitting on it! Climate and proposed activities dictate what we need to pack, but then there's always the temptation to pop the extras in the bag as well, challenging the weight restrictions on our luggage.

My husband, Bruce, has honed packing down to a fine art, being able to travel for three weeks or more with only carry-on luggage that will fit in the overhead locker of an airplane. This is a definite accomplishment, but it's also a high priority for Bruce, as he doesn't want to waste time at airport baggage carousels. The downside, however, is that he needs to be diligent in keeping up with his washing while traveling!

I had been in the habit of overpacking for trips, only to find that many of my clothes never even saw the light of day, and could have easily been left behind. One day in London, while I was still in the mode of cramming clothes into my luggage, I heard the Holy Spirit whisper in my ear, *"Don't pack your suitcase too tight."* I knew what He meant! If I crammed my suitcase too tight, there would be no room for God to slip in any surprises, if He so desired.

This got my attention. I deeply desired all that God had for me, but my habit of 'over-packing' was obviously a hinderance. Sometimes we operate from a premise that we better take all the extras 'just in case!' For some it might be clothing for events, medical supplies to keep in good health, or books for the anticipated free time. For me, it was regarding ministry preparation; God was telling me that I had the potential to 'over-prepare,' and as a result I would miss the spontaneity He may want to download into my spirit at any given time! It was definitely a *faith issue* — I needed to listen for the voice of 'enough,' to check the scales of the Holy Spirit to see if I was in excess!

Many of us don't stop at *enough*, and go over the limit. As our insecurity demands we pack more, our luggage becomes heavier for us to carry—and more difficult to repack at different ports. Maybe we genuinely fear not having enough, so we pack *unnecessary extras* to safeguard ourselves from running short, but in doing so, we run the risk of missing God's best, the God-surprises!

What are your *'just in case'* items or your *'I might just need this'* accessory, which in reality you don't need to pack? Insecurity will cause us to hold onto certain items or attitudes, taking them with us everywhere we go! In so doing, however, we deprive ourselves of the energy and supernatural provision God wants to add to the suitcase of our life. Let's keep room in our lives for His extras, His spontaneous interventions and His revelation!

*Do you **overwork**? Do you push the limits when God says **enough**? What unnecessary weight have you packed into your life that needs to be left behind? What could you **unpack** today to save room for God to slip His provision into your life?*

front foot

Preach the word! Be ready in season and out of season.
2 Timothy 4:2

As children, we knew what it was to anticipate, to have eager expectation for an upcoming event—perhaps a special celebration party, or a special show, or a holiday. As we mature, however, we often lose that sense of excitement for life. Possibly because of the weight of responsibility and chores that now need attention on a daily basis, we fail to 'stand on tiptoe' in expectation for what is ahead!

Faith is an eager anticipation of a hope or desire for what God has already prepared and promised us. It's a feeling of barely being able to wait! We may be adults, but let's not lose that anticipation as God's child! Let's maintain our excitement for the greater things ahead! Let's live on the *front foot* of faith as opposed to the *back foot* of doubt, which has the power to dampen and dull our anticipation for good things. Let's live 'faith-ready,' believing, expecting, and *forward celebrating the victory of a moment yet to come!*

There was a moment in my life when I made a conscious decision to adopt 'front foot' living, as opposed to 'back foot' living! That meant living in a prepared manner, ready to respond and move when called on—as opposed to living unready, unprepared, and slow to respond when the occasion demanded it.

We have all most likely watched sporting events where the competitors are lined up on their blocks, anticipating the starter gun to sound to commence their race. Similarly, in the race of life, we need to live positioned on our blocks of faith so that when we are called on, we are quick off the mark, having a solid base to push from! Victories can be lost in moments of doubt, hesitation, fear, or lack of preparation and training. It is our responsibility to live ready for every good work or great exploit when God sounds the 'starter gun,' and to promptly respond! Maybe we hear the sound, but because our hearts are not poised on the blocks of faith, we miss the moment to run with the baton into the next stage of the relay?

I found that fear and timidity in my life, although negative in some aspects, became a servant to me, a powerful motivator to keep me poised on the *front foot* of faith and expectation! I did not want to be slow in my responses, to be the one who dropped the baton in the relay of faith, or to be the person who let the team of believers down!

My starter block of faith is my testimony, remembering to be thankful for all that God has done for me thus far! The victory of His salvation, His forgiveness of my sins, His overcoming and enabling power in my life, and His willingness to share His revelation with me, all continue to make me live 'ready' and provide the power from which to launch forward!

> *And they overcame him by the blood of the Lamb, and by the word*
> *of their testimony, and they did not love their lives to the death.*
> Revelation 12:11

It is our past (and future!) testimony that keeps us on the *front foot* of faith and expectation, ready to move at God's bidding! In Acts 3, we read the account of Peter and John healing a lame man. Being on the *front foot* of faith as they approached the temple to worship, they recognised that this man was sitting so close to His breakthrough, right at the entrance wall to the temple, yet so far away in faith because of the lameness in his legs. Peter and John were *living ready*. Filled with faith, and with the authority of the name of Jesus, they lifted this man to his feet so he could enter His future healed and whole!

How might you get more faith-ready? Is your faith on the 'back foot,' overrun with worry and daily routine? What testimony or promise are you in possession of, that you can pass on? What promise or dream fills your heart for the future and keeps you on the 'front foot' of faith with excitement? Lay hold of that anticipation today!

god's monitor

"Son of man, I have made you a watchman for the house of Israel;
therefore hear a word from My mouth,
and give them warning from Me."
Ezekiel 3:16

We are familiar with human *monitors*, people who check that systems work and ensure the health and safety of everyone in that sphere! I have observed that when a group of people meet at any time, *monitors* naturally come to the fore—they are concerned that doors are locked, windows are closed and lights are off; they also check people are comfortable, well-fed and well-informed. These people have a natural insight into what needs to be done—it comes from an alarm system within! Others may be appointed responsibilities, and do their very best with the trust that has been placed in them. It's the same in the spirit arena—there are areas where God has given us the responsibility to *monitor* the health and well-being of environments so spiritual growth and progress can take place unhindered!

The Holy Spirit highlighted my personal responsibility as a *monitor* in God's Kingdom through Ezekiel 3:6, defining the call and grace within. This is an internal *monitoring* given by God that I cannot get away from, even if I try! I would love to be more evangelistic, and although I reach out as all Christians are called to do, the results aren't the same as for those people God has graced specifically in this manner. Instead, the scripture in Ezekiel 3 identified the grace I personally possess as an *inner alarm system* that sounds in the place where God wants me to function and serve most effectively—the house of God and God's people! This *monitoring* has come in the form of dreams, impressions, words, prophecies and words of knowledge where I have heard directly from God, His voice sounding in me, alerting me to act, bring healing, ensure harmony, and at times implement teaching, to secure the safety and progress of others.

Years ago, I had a dream regarding a death threat over a young lady who was residing in England. I knew it was a God-dream; the 'Holy Spirit monitor' sounded an alarm in me to pray, which I subsequently did, along with others, exercising authority over any attack against this person's life! Four months later, this young woman was struck with serious meningitis from which recovery was not expected. How amazing that four months earlier God, in His love and mercy, had alerted some women in Auckland, New Zealand, to pray and take authority over this threat to her life! The Holy Spirit is our *monitor,* sounding the alarm in our spirit—in this case, it was to take action in prayer and spiritual warfare.

Today we have elaborate alarm systems for our houses, our cars, even our babies . . . alarms that alert us when there is any potential danger. We also have an inner alarm system activated by the Holy Spirit. Thoughts or insights that come randomly into our hearts and minds, may just be our *inner monitor* telling us to take action in whatever way is required!

The apostle Peter's *monitor* was the discernment of truth—the ability to see in the spirit behind the masks and pretentious facades people projected. In Acts 5:3 the 'Holy Spirit alarm' went off in Peter. In response, he faced off with a couple who were lying to God, saying, "Ananias, why has Satan filled your heart to lie to the Holy Spirit and keep back part of the price of the land for yourself?"

When people are sick, we *monitor* their temperature to gauge the response of their overall physical health; for more serious conditions, scans may be used to isolate and identify the problem. Likewise, let's use our 'spiritual thermometers' to ensure the atmosphere of our lives is conducive to good health and growth!

What area do you have a natural responsibility for? What God-given grace alerts you to what is needed at any time? Are you quick to spot overlooked needs or neglect in any particular situation? Today, thank God for the Holy Spirit's **monitoring** *within, and use it to gauge faith and health for yourself and others.*

good posture

So teach us to number our days,
that we may gain a heart of wisdom.
Psalm 90:12

Have you ever had your posture challenged? *Sit up straight! Stand up straight! Walk tall!* In different settings, we need to adopt different *postures*. Bad posture spoils our ability to move forward with ease into the promises of God, while good posture gives us flexibility and grace to possess all God has for us. The Holy Spirit downloaded the inspiration into my spirit, that in some situations, I am the *leader*, in others I am the *learner*, and in yet other situations I need to be the *listener*. We can assume all three postures at different times if we learn to discern the context.

A leader. We are all leaders, called to bring lift and direction to situations. The first person we lead is ourselves! Can we lead ourselves out of postures of complacency, despondency and complaints when we need to? It's difficult to lead others if we find it hard to motivate ourselves!

Moses was appointed by God to lead more than three million Israelites out of bondage in Egypt, but first he had to lead himself out of a place of fear and defeat by returning to the environment where he had previously failed. This took courage! Moses had become comfortable hiding in the wilderness, away from demands. Now God was restoring Moses to once again lead the children of Israel. What a mission—but what a deliverance through the supernatural power of God as Moses took the lead!

A learner. We are not always the leader in every situation and, in some environments, it is unwise to assume leadership, choosing instead to learn! Some of us may find taking the posture of a learner difficult, maybe due to pride, viewing ourselves as 'independent thinkers' and instinctively resisting being led by others. If that is our *set posture*, we can miss vital instruction and wisdom! Wisdom keeps an open, teachable heart. Pride can blind us; we often don't know what we don't know until we sit with another who knows more than we do!

In 2 Kings 6, Elisha's servant pronounced defeat over his master and the situation they faced because he could not see what Elisha saw. His eyes were only able to see what was physically surrounding them, which was the huge army of Syria! This servant needed to follow Elisha's confident leadership! When he listened to Elisha, his posture changed to one of courage and faith as he saw what his leader saw:

> So he answered, "Do not fear, for those who are with
> us are more than those who are with them." And Elisha
> prayed and said, "Lord I pray, open his eyes that he may see."
> Then the Lord opened the eyes of the young man and he saw.
> And behold the mountains were full of horses and
> chariots of fire all around Elisha.
> 2 Kings 6:16-17

A listener. In some environments, we need to just be quiet and listen—to trust God and maintain a quiet spirit. You don't hear children asking their parents if there is enough petrol in the car before they venture out on a trip; they simply trust it's been taken care of. That's the posture we need before God!

It was prophesied well in advance that David would one day be king over Israel, but there was a period of time when David needed to just sit quietly and play his harp. As he did, he listened and learned the ways of the royal household, which prepared him for his reign ahead. Let's not be all about the telling, but also about the listening!

Is there a leadership position you may you be avoiding? Today, lead yourself first, out of places of procrastination, excuses or fear of failure, so you can lead others effectively! Are there environments where you need to learn from others rather than always assuming the leadership? Today, talk less, and listen from a quiet spirit, preparing yourself for your future!

enter in

*By the rivers of Babylon, there we **sat down**,*
yea we wept when we remembered Zion. We hung our harps
upon the willows in the midst of it. For those who carried us
away captive asked of us a song and those who plundered us
requested mirth saying, "Sing us one of the songs of Zion!"
How shall we sing the Lord's song in a foreign land?
Psalm 137:1-4

Have you ever moved house within the same town or city, only to find yourself, when returning home, driving back to the old address? We need to inform our minds we have a new address and we need to concentrate on the 'whereabouts' of our new location! Perhaps you have never gone onto 'autopilot' like that, but I certainly have, being preoccupied at the time! Sometimes we just need to turn the wheel of the car and steer it in a different direction!

God has so much in store for us! He has relocated us through the blood of our Saviour, Jesus, but at times we can find ourselves returning to old addresses just because it's familiar and it's been our residence in the past. We simply need to remind ourself, *"I don't live there anymore!"*—that we have packed up and shifted camp! At salvation, we were translated from the suburb of Law (sin and death) to the suburb of Grace, (life and peace) by the Spirit of God. Which are you currently living in? We need to consciously direct ourselves and steer the wheel of our heart to our new abode in Christ.

In the Bible, we read of the children of Israel living in the wrong place. They had been taken captive because of their inability to *enter into* the land promised them due to their inability to turn away from old habits and mindsets! The promised land seemed like a distant and hopeless dream in their minds as they lamented their choices in the place of bondage in Babylon.

There was no joy for Israel in dwelling in the wrong place! They were taunted and mocked by the enemy who had taken them captive. Israel had bypassed their God-given destination through their own disobedience and consequently, their song of redemption, deliverance and victory had been lost! They had become captive in a hostile environment.

Israel missed the signs during their exodus from Egypt, and their grumbling had taken them further away from the new location God was directing them toward. This happened because they were *too small* in their own minds, possessing a slave mentality and not fully grasping the enormity of God's love for them as a nation. They failed to *enter in* spiritually and emotionally at their moment of deliverance and relocation, missing the significance of all the miracles and displays of God's supernatural power to free them from the land of the enemy.

They had seen the Red Sea opening before them, giving them a path to walk through great and terrifying waters. They had seen provision in the form of manna falling from the sky. Yet for the children of Israel, there had been a *going but not a growing!* They kept returning to their old address both mentally and spiritually, and missed God's best as a result.

In our journeying with God, we need to access His love and power and fully *enter into* the new land He has purchased for us with His precious blood! Let's reprogram the GPS of our heart if need be, and marvel at the promises and plans of God as we fully *enter into* the new land set before us.

Is there a place you keep returning to? Remind yourself today that you don't live in the old residence of fear, shame and condemnation anymore! What is your new address? Decide today to fully move in, to enter into every blessing and provision God has made for you there! Today, rejoice that God has given you an excellent land to reside in; land that has been designated to you especially! Reset your heart today to 'go and grow' in your new location!

more *than*

The Bible tells us we are not to think of ourselves more highly than we should, but to have sober judgment and appreciate that God has given each of us special graces and anointings! Some areas of our lives are just *'more than'* other areas!

I knew early in life the *'more than'* grace that God had bestowed on me, even before people had prayed or prophesied it over me! I knew my 'flavour,' the anointing on my life. Years ago when I read Psalm 45:7, it confirmed what I already knew in my spirit—that God has anointed me with a *spirit of gladness* that enables me to stay positive even in difficult situations, to possess a buoyancy that keeps me believing. I have been graced with the ability to extract joy out of the mundane and to rejoice over the smallest of blessings! It is an innate choice I possess that enables me to 'bounce back,' sometimes *more than* my companions. This inner grace releases creative strategies for the future and destroys the enemy! Even when I go through challenging times, joy is never that far away! As Psalm 4:7 says,

You have put gladness in my heart, more than in the season
that their grain and wine increased.

Do you know the *'more than'* grace on your life, that special anointing that stands you out above others? Maybe it's your ability to organise *more than* your spouse, friends or flatmates? Maybe it's your generosity in perceiving and meeting needs? We all have an area where God has granted us that extra measure of anointing!

King Ahasuerus recognised that 'X-factor' in Esther when he was in the process of choosing a new queen following the demotion of Queen Vashti. We read in Esther 2:17 that he, "loved Esther *more than* all the other women, and she obtained grace and favour in his sight more than all the virgins; so he set the royal crown upon her head and made her queen instead of Vashti."

In essence, the king recognised and affirmed what Esther already possessed internally, her anointing of God-given grace, something *'more than'* what was in the other young women who had been presented to the king. Before that, even during her time of preparation, Esther's *'more than'* had granted her favour with Hegai, the custodian of the women in the palace.

> *Now the young woman (Esther) pleased him, and* **she obtained**
> **his favour***; so he readily gave beauty preparations to her; besides*
> *her allowance. Then seven choice maidservants were provided*
> *for her from the King's palace, and he moved her and her*
> *maidservant to the best place in the home of the women.*
> Esther 2:9

We have all been given a special anointing, but with God's endowment comes a responsibility to use it for Kingdom purposes. Esther 2:16 tells us that, "Esther obtained favour in the sight of all who saw her!" This is because Esther's anointing wasn't just for herself, but to enable her to appeal for mercy and favour on behalf of the Jews who faced annihilation if no one intervened.

God has placed a *'more than'* anointing in all our lives—an *appeal within us that appeals*, that challenges, asks, rescues, delivers, and brings freedom to situations and people!

🍃 *What is your 'more than'? What 'appeal that appeals' has God placed within you? Identify it and direct it into Kingdom purposes today so God can use you to shift atmospheres and destroy the enemy. Today, thank God for your 'more than' quality, the anointing on your life that stands you out above others!*

no apologies

God designed every one of us exactly as He desired! He had the total
and final say, branding us as His own and gifting us with His grace,
and He remains eternally proud of who we are! God is never going to
apologise for His handiwork in creating each of us to be so unique and
individual. *Let's stop apologising for ourselves!* It is prudent to apologise for
our wrongdoings and our mistakes, but we should never apologise for
who we are! That's an insult to our loving God, our Creator! Satan seeks
to sabotage the fullness of God's likeness within us, tempting us to think
less about ourselves and to compare ourselves unfavourably with others.
But Jesus, as our Redeemer, is able to restore us to God's original design as
we trust Him and His work in our lives! The psalmist encourages us to be
thankful for this, by *saying so.* In Psalm 107:1,2 we read:

When we reiterate God's '*say so,*' we are acknowledging our faith and
agreement with Him. God is good, not only in His works but also in the
plan and design He has for each of us. We need to express our thankfulness
through our '*say so*' and stop apologising for who we are!

Paul totally owned who he was in 1 Corinthians 15:10. So did Peter and
John in Acts 3 as they approached the lame man at the Gate Beautiful.
They were not ashamed to ask the man to *look at them*, to see who they
truly were. They were faith-filled!

In my younger years, there were times I didn't want people to look at me. I
was self-conscious, certain that people would spot all my weaknesses and
flaws! As my faith grew, however, I become confident to say, "Look at me,"
not in a proud way, but *unapologetically grateful* for God's work in my life
that helped me overcome and win in life! I realise now, by faith, that what
people see when they look at me is the grace and power of God within, and

I don't apologise for His grace in my life. With that God-confidence, let me share this excerpt from my journal from many years ago. It is a confession of faith, a way of reinforcing who God made me to be. It is my *'say so'* in Christ:

> *"I am a builder in Christ, creating and forming avenues in the spirit for God to move, connect and empower people. Growth is my DNA—my desire being, 'more love, more power, more of You, Jesus, in my life.' I choose to distinguish myself as a follower of Christ, cutting off all negative thoughts and emotions, being caught up instead in wonder, delight, faith and expectation in my God. My triumph is in God alone that the fragrance from my life speaks about and glorifies Jesus, convincing the most stubborn of hearts. Use my life, God, to appeal to people to be reconciled to Christ! I am not in competition with others. I am a 'stand-alone' masterpiece, equipped for every good work in Christ Jesus. My prayer, taken from Psalm 92, is that I will be 'anointed with fresh oil.' My heart's desire is to triumph through the works of God's hands."*

I share those words as *unapologetic gratitude* for who God has made me to be! My prayer is that you too, will be encouraged to find your *say so* in God regarding His good work in you!

Are you apologising for who you are, and shrinking back as a result? Today, recognise God's 'say so' in the design and plan for your life! How has God presented you to the world? Try writing a statement of faith regarding who you are, and give thanks for His goodness toward you today!

purpose finds you

After these things Jesus showed Himself again to the disciples at the Sea of Tiberias, and in this way He showed Himself . . . when the morning had now come, Jesus stood on the shore; yet the disciples did not know that it was Jesus.
John 21:1,4

God has a purpose for each one of us and *His purpose finds us*! Often, people prefer to determine their own purpose and, in doing so, place a demand on God to release to them all the details first before they 'buy into' His direction for their lives, wanting to base their decision on whether God's purposes will suit them or not.

God has already chosen our purpose, and we need to be careful not to *disconnect* with His carefully-chosen direction! People often say, "I am not sure where I fit," but I have found that it is often *less about fit, and more about flow.* When we flow with vision that already is, we find our fit in the purposes of God. Supernatural convergences happen as we simply follow Jesus!

After Jesus had risen from the dead, He sought out His despondent disciples to restore them once again to His purposes and the greater plan for their lives. The disciples had returned to fishing; it was what they knew, it had been their previous occupation. The scripture tells us, that though they were experienced fisherman, they had fished all night and caught nothing. They were in a place of *disconnect* when Jesus came to meet them! *Purpose* was finding them again! Although they did not recognise His form on the beach, the disciples recognised Jesus' voice as He called to them, enquiring about the catch.

In response to the disciple's reply about the lack of fish they had caught, Jesus said to them, "Cast the net on the right side of the boat and you will find some" (John 21:6a).

Then we read,

> *. . . so they cast, and now they were not able to draw it*
> *in because of the multitude of fish.*
> *John 21:6b*

Jesus was calling the disciples out of despondency and lack into vision. Jesus was revealing Himself to them again! We need to recognise Jesus' voice calling across the waters of our life, summoning us out of the ordinary and into His extraordinary exploits! Peter was no one special—he was just an ordinary fisherman who was about to step into his predetermined purpose and change the course of history!

To Peter and the disciples, God's instruction was simply, "Cast your net on the other side of the boat." These men knew how to fish, and this instruction could have seemed contrary to their natural instincts. The disciples, however, followed this directive from Jesus. The outcome was that they caught more fish than they could ever have expected. There was a *convergence* as the disciples' ordinary equipment connected with the extra-ordinary power of God. That day, *purpose found them,* and their sorrow turned to amazement and worship.

God meets us in the struggle of life to show us how to flow with His purpose. Let's witness God *connecting* the nets of our lives with His supernatural purpose, and marvel at the amazing convergences as we respond. *Find purpose, find flow!*

*Is there an area where you have 'fished all night and caught nothing'? Is there **disconnect** from the purposes of God in your life? Today, **let purpose find you**, as you connect with God. Listen as the voice of God calls you out of the ordinary and positions you for something extraordinary!*

purpose restores you

*There is therefore now no condemnation to those who are in
Christ Jesus, who do not walk according to the flesh,
but according to the Spirit.*
Romans 8:1

Have you ever been on a journey and gone right off track? We have! One year
on a Christmas break in Germany, we took three hours longer than anticipated
to reach our destination because we assumed that we already knew the
way—even though we had landed in a different airport than usual and were
therefore approaching our destination from a totally different direction!

Maybe you have fallen over or tripped up and are now some distance
from God's full purpose for your life? Or perhaps you are only a short
distance away or even right on track! Wherever you are, the good news is
that God is always ready to pick you up and place you back on the path
He has planned for you. *Purpose finds you* right where you are, and *purpose
restores you* to where you should be.

As God-followers, we need to not only recognise God's voice, but also His
heart. Jesus came to the beach where Peter and the disciples were fishing to
restore them! The disciples had lost direction, having been disappointed and
discouraged by His death on the cross. In seeking out Peter in particular,
Jesus' intention was not to mention all he had done wrong nor condemn him
because his courage failed, but to *restore* him and bring him close once again.

Jesus sat on the shore of the Sea of Tiberias. As I sat on that same seashore in 2017, I recognised that in the process of restoring and recommissioning Peter, Jesus needed to lift condemnation and the weight of failure from Peter so he would be able to function freely in the future.

Condemnation is a common spirit that wants to sit on people's emotions and minds, causing them to shrink back. It destroys their purpose and potential. Condemnation causes disconnect on many levels. It is so destructive! It often comes with either a sense of failure or a fear of failure. As such, it has the potential to either keeps us stationary—or traveling around in circles.

Condemnation also produces a spirit of labour, a weariness of heart and spirit. It never produces a catch, no matter how hard one may try! It simply breeds more disappointment, despair and defeat. If we don't remove condemnation, we end up striving in a 'night season,' trying harder, but producing less.

Jesus restored Peter at the Sea of Tiberias—the word, 'Tiberias' meaning "vision"! Condemnation stifles vision, but faith in God's purpose will *restore us*, energise us, and release us into the fullness of His will for our life. We need to see Jesus again in order to see vision!

Maybe today, we need to be released from condemnation, from a spirit of failure that has been sitting heavily on our heart and mind. Let's not allow condemnation to reside in our lives, wearing us down and robbing us of joy and purpose. Let's be fully released by Jesus from any sense of failure, whether it is a faith-fail, parent-fail, relationship-fail or health-fail! Just as Jesus lifted the condemnation from Peter that day, He can do the same for you and me!

Where have you got 'off track' on your journey of faith and godly purpose? Is there any disconnect from God's purpose for your life? Have you allowed failure to bring a condemnation and weariness into your spirit? Today, let God connect you with Himself and with vision. Let Jesus restore you!

speak blessing

Out of the same mouth proceed blessing and cursing.
My brethren, these things ought not to be so.
James 3:10

What are we saying about ourselves? What do we say about the church, about our family, our children, our marriage, our business? What about our health, our circumstances? Maybe unwittingly we are cursing what God has already said He has blessed. God has pronounced us, as His people, *blessed*!

In the book of Numbers, Balaam was called on by the king of Moab to curse Israel because as Israel had increased numerically, he feared their strength! The financial offer to curse Israel appealed to the blemish in his character, the greed in his spirit and the idolatry in his heart. So Balaam prayed 'token' prayers, seeking God's approval to curse the nation, though he already knew what God's answer would be!

God *stood against* Balaam several times on his journey, seeking to get his attention, even using the actions and voice of his donkey to reveal the error of his ways! Eventually Balaam saw what his donkey had seen. In Numbers 22:31 we read, "Then the Lord opened Balaam's eyes, and he saw the angel of the Lord standing in the way with His drawn sword in His hand; and he bowed his head and fell flat on his face."

That's when Balaam recognised that God was *standing against him*, not allowing him to curse His chosen people. Beyond that, God gave Balaam a perspective on how He viewed Israel.

> *Now when Balaam saw that it pleased the Lord to bless Israel,*
> *he did not go as at other times, to seek to use sorcery, but he set*
> *his face toward the wilderness. And Balaam raised his eyes, and*
> *saw Israel encamped according to their tribes; and the Spirit of*
> *God came upon him. Then he took up his oracle and said: "The*
> *utterance of Balaam the son of Beor, the utterance of the man whose*
> *eyes are opened, the utterance of him who hears the words of God,*
> *who sees the vision of the Almighty, who falls down, with eyes*
> *wide open: 'How lovely are your tents, O Jacob! Your dwellings, O*
> *Israel! Like valleys that stretch out, like gardens by the riverside,*
> *like aloes planted by the Lord, like cedars beside the waters.'"*
> Numbers 24:1-5

Balaam's eyes were opened to how God saw Israel. He was overwhelmed with God's perspective and could only say what God said!

We too must be careful to see as God sees and say only what He says! God has already spoken blessings over our lives. He declares, "I have blessed you, I have blessed this child, I have blessed this family, I have blessed this church, I have blessed this nation . . ." Let's not work against what God has declared *blessed*, by uttering careless words that potentially bring our lives and circumstances under a curse!

> *Behold, I have received a command to bless;*
> *He has **blessed it**, and I cannot reverse it.*
> Numbers 23:20

The king of Moab tried over and over again to extract an ill-willed prophecy against Israel but in the end, Balaam could only say what God said. The enemy tempts us to speak destructive, hopeless, negative words over our lives and situations! The Bible instructs us in Proverbs 18:21, "Death and life are in the power of the tongue, and those who love it will eat its fruit." Let's be people who *speak blessing*, speak life, speak God's Word!

*Where may God be standing against you, seeking to get your attention so you will change your words? Have you cursed and limited yourself by saying, "I can't" when God has said that you can do all things through Him who strengthens you? Today, know that God views you with His great love and has pronounced you **blessed!***

suspension

The eternal God is your refuge,
and underneath are the everlasting arms.
Deuteronomy 33:27

If you have ever ridden in a car with bad suspension, you can probably testify to a very uncomfortable ride, when every bump in the road was felt keenly, jarring your body! In a motor vehicle, *suspension* is the system of springs and shock absorbers by which a vehicle is supported on its wheels. Essentially, shock absorbers do two things — they control the movement of springs and suspension, but they also keep your tyres in contact with the ground at all times.

We need to look at the *suspension* of our lives! God is always there to support us, but the enemy wants to give us a rough ride by maligning us, attacking our wellbeing, and tempting us with untruths, causing the shock absorbers of our life to falter and malfunction. I have always envisioned the Holy Spirit, not only as the One who inspires and empowers me, but also as my *'shock absorber'* helping me to negotiate the bumps and unexpected jolts along the road of life.

The word 'suspension' can also refer to a temporary stoppage, one we may have chosen or one that has been chosen for us — a place to pause and observe better ways of responding and thinking!

I love what I call my 'suspended places.' These are often associated with airports and flights where I am 'neither here nor there,' but in-between events, locations and people, and open to observe, see and hear God in a fresh way! For me, it's that place of intrigue between the tension of *doing* and *being*.

God wants to renew the springs of our life, to give us the buoyancy and flexibility we need to live the life He has appointed us to. God certainly doesn't want us to ride heavy in our journey, but to live lightly and freely with the help of the Holy Spirit. He is there to take weight from us, and support us in our endeavours.

In one of my many 'suspended' moments, God spoke so clearly into my heart about the call of God on my life, causing my soul to be at ease. His words to me were:

You *are* a gift! Thus says the Lord, "In an acceptable time I have heard you, and in the day of salvation I have helped you; I will preserve you and give you as a covenant to the people, to restore the earth, to cause them to inherit the desolate heritages" (Isaiah 49:8). You are my covenant, or *gift*, to the city!"

You *have* a gift! You are a watchman with an apostolic and prophetic anointing. But you are not *the gift!* The true gift is the gift of the Holy Spirit, the treasure that dwells within. "But we have this treasure in earthen vessels, that the excellence of the power may be of God and not of us" (2 Corinthians 4:7).

These statements, spoken by the Holy Spirit directly into my spirit, immediately took the pressure from my soul to strive to be someone I wasn't; from trying to satisfy a certain image I imagined was worthy of the call! What a relief to know I could just simply be myself!

In simplicity and sincerity, God simply wants us to know who we are in Him and to release the gift of the Holy Spirit in our lives to accomplish what only He can accomplish! This brought release from any expectation I had placed upon myself, ensuring me an easy ride as I placed full responsibility upon the Holy Spirit to use me as He saw fit.

Where may you be 'riding rough,' feeling every bump, and maybe feeling shocked and jarred? Find your place of 'pause' so God can reveal truth and bring release into your heart and life. God speaks in language you can understand and receive. Today, realise that the Holy Spirit is your 'shock absorber,' the One who can bring ease even into the bumpiest of situations. Find His voice in the midst of the ride today!

take two

So they set the ark of God on a new cart, and brought it out of the
house of Abinadab, which was on the hill, and Uzzah and Ahio,
the sons of Abinadab drove the new cart.
2 Samuel 6:3

Take two! Aren't you glad that God gives us all a second chance, that though we may slip and fall, His weight of encouragement comes behind us to try again? Like a stage performance, or the filming of a movie, *several takes* are often needed before the right results are produced. We can often be discouraged when we fail and could be tempted to just leave the scene. But God is at the stage front, like a director, repeating, *"Lights, Cameras, Action!"* In other words, "Try again! Have another go! Improve your performance!"

This was something King David needed to hear when he was bringing the ark back to Jerusalem. David knew it was time to bring the ark of the covenant back to 'centre stage' in the life and times of Israel. But something was wrong with the scene. Those involved had not read their lines properly nor followed the script correctly; they were 'ad-libbing' as they proceeded, and subsequently they carried the ark in totally the wrong manner! The ark of the covenant was symbolic of God's presence, ordained by God when in their possession to bring blessing to Israel! In their quest to reinstate and transport the ark back to Jerusalem, they simply relegated it to a cart, not giving it the weight of respect the author of the story had designed. This casual, familiar approach cost the 'cast' greatly—when the oxen stumbled, Uzzah put his hand out to steady the ark from falling from the cart, and he died as a result. David was afraid and angry with God for striking Uzzah, and David exited the stage at that point, leaving the ark of the covenant for three months at the house of Obed Edom.

Take two came when David realised that God was fully blessing Obed Edom's house; he reappeared on the scene to collect the ark of the covenant and return it once again to Jerusalem. In this 'take,' David and his men observed the correct method of bearing the ark, lifting it reverently onto their shoulders and sacrificing oxen and fatted sheep as they journeyed.

Then David danced before the Lord with all His might
. . . so David and all Israel brought up the ark of the Lord
with shouting and with the sound of the trumpet.
2 Samuel 6:14-15 (MSG)

There was joy in this 'take' and the Author of the script was greatly honoured as every person followed the story line correctly, resulting in the audience applauding loudly with joy. Such a victory was celebrated that day, as the ark of the covenant took central stage once again in the life and times of Israel.

What takes 'centre stage' of your life? Whose script are you following? There will only be true satisfaction and joyful applause when heaven places its weight behind us, celebrating us as we follow the correct script for our lives. There may be times of stumbling in our Christian walk, times of forgetting our lines and intentionally or unintentionally altering God's storyline for our lives. But God, our Director, wills us to try again, declaring, "Lights, cameras, action!"

Take two, three, four and many more ongoing *takes* have been needed for me to flow and feel at ease in my delegated role in God's plan and purpose. We all have a part to play, and we can be so thankful that God gives us the chance to get up and try again—to repeat, improve, gain confidence and grow so we can take our place! We can do this as we keep Jesus centre stage in our heart; our role is simply to honour Him and carry His presence with dignity so He will be glorified. Our life here and now is a *rehearsal* for the world to come! When the curtain comes down on our lives here on earth, let's be ready to hear the sound of heavenly applause!

Are you following God's script or are you 'ad-libbing', not giving credence to the direction of the one and only Author that matters? Realise today that God wants to give you a second chance. Let God 'call another take'—in your marriage, your interpersonal relationships, your health and in your courage to live fully for Him. Experience the freedom and joy that comes when God's presence is given centre stage in your life.

unveiled

And Jesus cried out with a loud voice and yielded up His spirit.
*Then, behold, the **veil** of the temple was torn in two from top to*
bottom, and the earth quaked, and the rocks were split.
Matthew 27:50-51

There are some things we just can't see unless they are revealed. God reveals to us in the spirit, things we could never see with our natural eyes. When Jesus died on the cross, the veil in the temple was torn in two, creating access into the Holy of Holies, a place previously reserved for the priests but now accessible to every person who expresses their faith and belief in the finished work of Christ on the cross. Every restriction was removed, every obstacle was broken, and blind eyes were opened! Jesus was risen, creating an entrance for all to come into His very presence!

Now even to this day, when Moses is read, a veil lies on their
heart. Nevertheless, when one turns to the Lord, the veil is taken
away. Now the Lord is the Spirit, and where the Spirit of the
Lord is, there is liberty. But we all, with unveiled face, beholding
as in a mirror the glory of the Lord are being transformed into the
same image from glory to glory, just as by the Spirit of the Lord.
2 Corinthians 3:15-16

We need to *behold* Jesus, to stand and stare and absorb His goodness, His grace, and the mercy He has extended to us. Just as a bridegroom may stare at the beauty of His bride at the altar, we too need to stare back at our heavenly bridegroom, Jesus, *beholding Him* who has bestowed His great love and mercy upon us. How good are we at beholding, at allowing our perception to be unveiled so we can step into that privileged place with Jesus?

My mother's name was Dulcie, meaning 'sweet', and so she was! She always had an underlying belief in who Jesus was, but fully committed her life to Him in her mid-seventies while she was staying with us in London. My mother's faith was quiet but resolute, one of strength, knowing the impact and intimacy of the Holy Spirit in her life. As Mum approached her nineties, life got more difficult—her eyesight diminished and her health deteriorated. Then, she had an experience, a moment *beyond the veil* with Jesus. She was 'caught up' in a vision, sitting with Jesus on a grassy hillside, where He sat and talked with her for some hours. It was a glorious experience! When Jesus stood, my mother expressed her desire to go with Him. In response, He reassured her saying, "It's not your time, but I will come back for you; I will touch you on the shoulder and you will come."

As my mother shared this experience, her face lit up with hope and expectation; from that time on, she lived in anticipation of a touch on her shoulder from Jesus! And so it happened early one morning—we believe Jesus simply touched her on the shoulder, and she left to be with Him. That morning there was the most stunning sunrise—the most glorious pink and purple hues painted the sky! It was like heaven was putting on a glorious display to welcome my mother home! Around the same time, one of our daughters-in-law, who was not familiar with Nan's vision had a dream of a much younger Nan running up a soft, grassy hillside with her beautiful red hair flowing, and as she went, she turned her head to look behind, and she smiled!

Jesus wants to meet all of us in a way that is special and meaningful to our life and purpose; He wants to interact with us face to face, just as He did with Moses. We all have that opportunity now, through His sacrifice, to engage with Him and, with *unveiled faces,* receive heavenly revelation of His great love for us.

How long has it been since you accessed the throne of grace and sought His face? Today, choose to behold your Redeemer, your Saviour, Your Lord and King! As you approach Him today gaze at Jesus! He will reveal the secrets of His heart and His amazing love for you!

'bear with'

*And I appeal to you, brethren, **bear with** the word of exhortation*
for I have written to you in a few words.
Hebrews 13:22

We may be familiar with a TV program called *Miranda*. In it, Miranda, the main character, has a friend who has an annoying habit of interspersing her conversation with the phrase, *"bear with,"* suggesting others should wait until she is ready to respond!

In the book of Hebrews, the expression *"bear with"* is used quite differently! It's a positive phrase! The whole epistle was written to exhort the Hebrews not to depart from the living God, but to go on to maturity, and to endure in their faith until the end. The author wrote *"in a few words,"* implying that he could have used many more words to motivate the believers at that time! He was appealing to the Hebrews to be patient with the word of exhortation, to stick with necessary spiritual disciplines and, in good faith, be motivated to move forward into the weightier things of God.

An exhortation can be a challenge to literally move us from one place to another—from one way of thinking to another! Parents exhort us, leaders exhort us, employers exhort us, and the Holy Spirit especially exhorts us with passion to take hold of our God-given future! In Isaiah 60:1 we read, "Arise, shine; for your light has come, and the glory of the Lord is risen upon you!" This exhortation, spoken by Isaiah, was to motivate the people to rise to the glory that had *already risen upon them*; it was a call to faith, action and anointing! Not everyone welcomes exhortation with open arms however, some being apprehensive of the effort that 'rising in faith' may demand. Others may even find exhortation annoying, preferring to 'stay put' while remaining dissatisfied. Paul exhorts the Hebrews to *'bear with'* the word of exhortation; to not be offended by what may seemingly sound like a 'pep talk,' but to fully embrace the encouragement because it would certainly reap rewards in the days to come. Exhortation can also be likened to a 'kick in the pants,' a word to get us moving in the right direction. Between God and Bruce, I have had my fair share of exhortation, pushing me out of my comfort zone and out of any limited thinking that may have restricted me from inheriting God's best.

In Isaiah 49, the exiles complained about the place of their dwelling being too small to accommodate all the children of Israel that were yet to return. The exiles had built far too small a city; the parameters they had made were too restrictive and prohibitive. They needed to be challenged to build a bigger framework in their mind, and on a practical level, to house all that God was wanting to do. In Mark 2, we also read of men who could have been discouraged because the house where Jesus was present was too small and too crowded, preventing them from getting their friend who needed healing to Jesus! But, instead of complaining, these men *exhorted* each other to persevere. They came up with the idea to *'rip the roof off'* in order to gain access, then lowered the crippled man right before Jesus. This certainly gained Jesus' attention, and the rest is history. Motivated by their faith and determination, Jesus healed their friend.

Where may we need to *'rip the roof off'* our too-small lives? To break through limitations and occupy bigger spaces in God? We desire the 'big' of God but we don't always *bear with* the exhortation that goes with the territory of breakthrough! A new level of anointing is going to demand a new level of response and trust. A new level of triumph is going to mean a new level of conflict. Sometimes people just need to be exhorted out of expecting the same results and to defy self-defeating predictions and spiritual opposition by rising up in faith. *What we don't rule, ends up ruling us!*

*Have you succumbed to negative environments and become inactive in faith? What word of exhortation do you need to **bear with**, to embrace, to meditate on, so you can be motivated to greater works in God? What 'roof' do you need to rip off in the name of Jesus? Today receive the exhortation to grow, mature, and experience breakthrough!*

what are you looking at?

My voice You shall hear in the morning O Lord;
*in the morning I will **direct** it to You, and I will look up!*
Psalm 5:3

What a joy it is to experience answered prayer! We need to both pray—and watch for the answer! Could God be answering more prayer than we are aware of? The psalmist not only directed *his prayer* to God at the beginning of the day, but he directed *his gaze* upwards also, continuously looking for the answer. We may be praying diligently, but where are we *directing our gaze?* Do we continue to *look up* after releasing our prayer, or do we shift our gaze to something more temporal to calm us, comfort us and console us while we wait? We need to keep *directing* our thoughts and hearts toward God, reiterating our trust and belief in Him to come through in response to our prayer and petition.

Paul prayed for the Thessalonians to stay in faith and in God's love. In 2 Thessalonians 3:5 he wrote, "Now may the Lord *direct* your hearts into the love of God and into the patience of Christ."

Direction is a strong word. It implies a purposeful course and purposeful decisions. Are we directed toward God, running the course He has set for us, believing to receive our answers to prayer even before they appear? *Faith* and *prayer* talk us into the purposes of God but *unbelief* has the ability to talk us out of them!

In the Bible, one man who strongly directed his gaze toward God was the father whose son demanded his inheritance early, only to waste it all on reckless living! This father would have been praying daily, directing his prayer to God, but also directing his eyes toward the return of this lost son.

And he arose, and came to his father. But when he was still a
great way off, his father saw him and had compassion and
ran and fell on his neck and kissed him.
Luke 15:20

This passage tells that the father's eyes were *directed* toward the son's return and he spotted his boy returning from a long way off. Sometimes our prayers may seem like a long time coming, but we need to keep our sights steadfastly directed into the love of God to restore! We need to stay the course of our prayers, not giving in to second best, or into other options, or even defeat. *Keep looking up!*

We can learn many valuable insights from the father in this story. This father *saw his answer* approaching because he had been watching! Some of our answers may be closer to being fulfilled than we realise. If we have dropped our eyes and are failing to see what God is doing, let's start *directing* our eyes toward the answer!

This father *embraced his answer*. He ran to meet his wayward son and wrapped his arms around him, kissing him! We need to greet our answers! And, the father welcomed and *reinstated his answer*! He didn't dwell on the past, on the wrongdoing or the waste, but offered forgiveness and restored the young man to full sonship.

In the book of Acts, the disciples had been praying for Peter's release from prison, but when their answer came knocking, they were slow to open the door! Acts 12:16 tells us that "they were astonished!" They shouldn't have been surprised—their prayer had been directed toward Peter's release! But they had failed to watch for the answer. Let's direct our gaze towards the answers we are requesting today!

*Is your gaze **directed** toward the answers you are requesting? What course do you need to stay on today? Watch and pray! Today, don't hold your answer at arm's length, but embrace it; give it place and purpose in your life today!*

boss it like bruce

*Having then gifts differing according to the grace that is given to us, let us use them . . . (let) he who **leads** (do so) with diligence.*
Romans 12:6,8 (parentheses mine)

Have you ever wondered why some people are just bossier than others? Did they become bossy through practice, or were they just born that way?! God has given some people the *grace gift* of leadership—and for those people, the latter is true! Because they feel like the boss, they act like the boss, particularly if no one else is leading or taking charge; they just step in to fill the gap! This grace is evident even in a very young child who is able, with ease, to take control of a whole room of people and organise everyone accordingly.

"You *bossed* it" is an expression we use when someone has done a great job, overcome an obstacle, or succeeded in some significant challenge. It's an affirmation that the person has totally owned the challenge and successfully risen to the occasion.

My husband, Bruce, has such a gift! He has 'bossed' the call of God in his life, planting churches and raising significant leaders around the world. He has owned his responsibility fully by maintaining a willing and yielded spirit. The strength of his gift, as I have observed it 'up close and personal,' is a *fearless focus*, an inner resolve that doesn't yield to pressure, and a possession of personal confidence—something I aspire to emulate! Bruce's 'take charge' attitude has brought security and ease to my life! I am totally grateful for his consistent encouragement and support, his championing of me to be all that God has called me to be, and for the many practical areas in our life and marriage that he just naturally assumes are his responsibility, things he 'bosses' on an everyday level! That's *boss* leadership right there!

When this gift and call of leadership is fully surrendered to the Lordship of Jesus, it enables the person in possession of it to direct the crowd, discern atmospheres, gauge efficiency, and confront issues where needed with no fear for their own personal safety and wellbeing! They prefer it mostly plain and simple; in other words, clear and uncluttered, with no frills! Their strong conviction enables them to suffer rebuffs, criticism and persecution for the cause of Christ and the advancement of the Gospel. Bruce's grace-gift operates at a premium in the Kingdom of God as he maintains a soft heart towards God and a thick skin toward unfair criticism. He is totally *bossing* it!

We are all differently graced in our expression of life and ministry, and all our gifts at times need to be tempered for the sake of relationships and effectiveness within the body, or in a family context. At times, the strength of our gift can be 'too much' for the particular setting we are in. For those graced in leadership, discernment is needed to know when to defer and allow another grace gift to come forward—to understand which occasions don't require them to take charge!

"Many roads lead to Rome" is an expression that we are familiar with, indicating there are several ways to get to the same destination, although they may involve different time frames and take different routes. The leadership gift 'shines' in intuitively knowing the best and the fastest route to a destination, or the best and most effective method for a result, but there are occasions where slowing down to incorporate and encourage others along the way is necessary.

I have learned so much from observing Bruce '*bossing it*'. His life and faith, and his devotion and obedience to the call of God, has rubbed off on me, helping me become more confident, decisive and resilient in my life and leadership. Let's honour the leaders in our lives, give them room to operate, and thank God for those who lead and direct us into all God intended for us!

Today, take the time to observe a 'boss'. What can you glean from them? Is there an aspect of personal confidence and security you desire in your own life? As you witness their leadership, take the opportunity to learn how to be more efficient and decisive in your own life. Do you have the grace-gift to lead? If so, keep 'bossing it' today!

heart it like helen

*Having then gifts differing according to the
grace that is given to us, let us use them . . .
(let) he who shows **mercy** (do so) with cheerfulness.
Romans 12:6,8 (parentheses mine).*

So much wisdom, joy and strength come to our lives when we understand the way we are wired. God has purposefully graced our lives with a gift, an *anointed flow* that adds value and creates pathways for ourselves and others to experience more fully the freedom of God's work and purpose for our lives. When we appreciate and use this 'grace gift' with faith under the direction of God, it produces supernatural manifestations of the Holy Spirit!

Understanding the strength of the mercy-gift God has graced my life with, helped me make sense of the way I thought and felt. Someone with the 'mercy gift' has a natural empathy for others; they feel deeply, and sense when others are hurting or genuinely struggling with life. They carry a tenderness of heart, but along with this, a vulnerability, as they are able to pick up the full range of emotions present in any environment at any one time, whether they want to or not! This exposure to 'atmosphere' can make us susceptible to fear and anxiety because of the felt responsibility to respond to a need while not always having the maturity or skill to handle it. When feeling under pressure emotionally, the person with the mercy-gift may compare themselves with their strong leadership-gifted friends and question themselves. *What is wrong with me? They look so strong and I feel so weak!* But the exhortation to the mercy-gifted person is to use their gift with cheerfulness, not shouldering the responsibility of healing for another as a heavy weight nor viewing it as an inescapable obligation, but as insight to pray, intercede and release an atmosphere of faith and healing. When we recognise the inherent nature of the grace within, we can operate in the gift of mercy to unlock people and environments! Learning to appreciate my 'grace-gift' has allowed it to shine as I have brought it in submission to the Lordship of Jesus and found freedom to express the desires of my heart through finding my *flow* in loving . . .

Loving peace. When tempted to feel anxious about responsibility, I speak this simple phrase to my soul: *"Just flow from your heart!"* My heart is my asset! Bringing 'heart' to situations can shift atmospheres and release the power of God! My constant desire is to walk in peace and then bring God's peace, harmony and reconciliation into the different environments I occupy!

Loving sincerity. Possessing a genuine, sincere love for God and others, in turn creates a safe place for others to confide and divest themselves of secret struggles without fear of rejection or ridicule. My desire is to have a *'crystal clear heart,'* a heart that is transparent, approachable, inclusive, welcoming and willing to help. I love that the mercy-gift within, has the grace and power to gather and multiply!

Loving faith. A deep love and dependency on the Word of God searches out revelation to counteract any fear or insecurity! This has given me a strong confidence in the answers contained in the Word of God and in the prophetic revelation of the Holy Spirit to break yokes and open environments to God's love. My desire is to 'unlock hearts,' to release healing, and witness transformation. This gift within comes with the grace of creativity to enhance environments and release the energy and the passion of the Holy Spirit.

Loving warfare. A desire to defend territory! Possessiveness is both a strength and a weakness of the 'mercy heart,' but when operating in the right spirit and context, it has the authority to watch, to discern and shift negative and spiritual forces that seek to invade; possessing the ability to forecast a 'move of God.' My personal desire is to labour in the spirit, in prayer and in intercession, believing for amazing victories and significant breakthroughs!

If you have a mercy gift, realise that you are not weak; you are strong in God and His might! Lift off any heavy weight of expectation today, and carry your gift with cheerfulness and faith. Release the creativity of the gift through expressing your desire for God's Kingdom to come into our earthly existence today!

untangled

*Every valley shall be exalted and every mountain and hill
brought low; the crooked places shall be made straight
and the rough places shall be made straight.*
Isaiah 40:4

Have you ever experienced the problem of your hair getting tangled, making it hard to comb, brush or even manage? I can't say this has ever been my experience, as I have fine, straight hair! However, we've all probably had a 'bad hair day,' or woken up with 'bed hair' first thing in the morning. Fortunately for us, hair products are readily available to condition curls and scrunch them beautifully, to spike our hair, or to achieve a silky, smooth look when applied.

Likewise, our thinking and emotions can get all 'knotted up' and complicated. That's when our thoughts need to be *untangled* or *unravelled* through the wise counsel of God, so that wise actions can follow. I am so thankful we can call on God to help us 'iron out' issues, and that the Holy Spirit is available to bring clarity and understanding into the most trying of situations.

God used a man called Daniel to bring clarity to king Nebuchadnezzar after he had a dream he struggled to understand. Because Daniel was able to interpret the dream by the power of the Spirit of God, his reputation of untangling issues echoed throughout the palace! When the next king, Belshazzar, had a similarly strange experience (he saw a finger writing on the wall!), his advisors said,

> "... there is a man in your kingdom in whom is the Spirit of the
> Holy God. And in the days of your father, light and understanding
> and wisdom; like the wisdom of the gods were found in him; and
> King Nebuchadnezzar your father — your father the king — made
> him chief of the magicians, astrologers, Chaldeans and soothsayers.
> Inasmuch as an excellent spirit, knowledge, understanding,
> interpreting dreams, solving riddles, and explaining enigmas were
> found in this Daniel, whom the king named Belteshazzar, now let
> Daniel be called and he will give the interpretation."
> Daniel 5:11-12

Daniel had *distinguished* himself beforehand, his reputation had gone ahead of him, and now Daniel was being called upon once again. The king summoned Daniel, addressing him in the following manner:

I have heard of you, that the Spirit of God is in you,
and that light and understanding and excellent wisdom
are found in you . . . and I have heard of you, that you can
give interpretations and explain enigmas!
Daniel 5:14-16

An interpretation is the ability to bring God's mind to difficult situations, making sense of the moment, season and pressing need, unpacking wisdom and revealing the way forward. This is how we *distinguish* ourselves as God's children. Like Daniel, we have an excellent spirit and an ability to bring God's revelation and understanding into situations to help those who have become entangled in the issues of life.

An enigma is a person or thing that is mysterious or difficult to understand. Daniel was known as one that had the ability to explain enigmas. He had the ability to 'untie knots', untangle complexities, and give an explanation regarding their existence. Daniel could do this because the Spirit of God and revelation was in him.

Life can present 'knotty' problems, but gnarled and twisted perspectives can be solved and smoothed by the counsel of God who has given us access to His wisdom! Let's bring those issues to God today, seeking Him for the wisdom to explain them, untie them, or resolve them!

What problems need to be smoothed out in your life? What has become tangled and complex? Do you have an **excellent spirit** *that can bring interpretation and the explaining of enigmas to other people? Seek God for His wisdom today! Then release insight and understanding into the 'knotty' areas of life!*

unwrap the gift

But we have this treasure in earthen vessels, that the excellence of the power may be of God and not of us.
2 Corinthians 4:7

Some people are just so talented when it comes to gift wrapping! When the wrapping around a gift looks spectacular, it immediately raises our expectation for what the parcel may contain. For some people, the effort that goes into the wrapping is almost as important as the content of the gift! They wrap it with so much love, thought and effort that it creates delight and expectation for the receiver even before they open it. This is the same as God—He wraps us in His love, His creativity and His promises, inviting us to go deeper and discover the true gift of His power and presence within!

Despite any perceived lack of external lustre, we are the package God has chosen to carry His glory! We contain the gift of His power within, a gift that needs to be released supernaturally into situations! When receiving a gift, we may linger initially at the impressive external appearance of the parcel, but we need to delve deeper to discover the real gift within. Likewise, God desires that we individually discover the fullness of the powerful treasure He has placed within every one of our lives.

Perhaps the gift God has placed inside you has remained hidden because you got too *wrapped up* in the 'trimmings' of life, leaving the true gift covered and suppressed? Or perhaps you are *'wrapped in concern'* rather than *'covered with thankfulness'* to God for His blessings and the gift of His peace within!

What are you wrapped in? We live in a world with many pressing issues, but when external worries overwhelm us, they hinder the brilliance of the gift within us from being activated. When we allow ourselves to become overly consumed with concerns for family, relationships, finances, careers, or even our appearance, the gift of faith and God's power within can lay unnoticed and untouched. One definition of concern is *'to be about.'* What are we 'about' in our thinking, acting and believing? Are we, in our own strength, carrying concerns that have the power to disturb, unsettle or distress us, and possibly cause physical problems in our bodies?

When Jesus went missing as a child, he responded to His parents by saying, "Why did you seek Me? Did you not know that I must *be about* my Father's business?" (Luke 2:49). In essence, Jesus was saying that He shouldn't really have been that hard to find, because He was wrapped up with passion for His Father's house! His concern was to be *about* His Father's business. We, like Jesus, need to be wrapped in a godly concern that will cause us to draw deeply by faith and release the supernatural gift of God within to function!

How do you know what a person is about? By what is wrapped around their heart, what shows in their conversation, attitudes and action! Are they wrapped in faith, or in fear? Job was a man whose concern was wrapped in fear for his children. This was an open invitation to the enemy to touch him in the area he most feared! In Job 3:25 he admits, "The thing I greatly feared has come upon me, and what I dreaded has happened to me." Job had to tear the wrapping of fear from around his heart, the concern that had blinded him. To release the deep grace of God within through faith, Job needed to repent! In Job 42:5-6, we read his words:

> *I have heard of You by the hearing of the ear, but now my eye sees*
> *You. Therefore I abhor myself and repent in dust and ashes.*

As Job's story attests, when we rid ourselves of the wrapping of fear, the potential for greater glory is released in our lives!

What concerns have you wrapped yourself in, preventing the power of God from working in and through you? What are you 'about'? What consumes you—the power of God, or the worries of the world? Today, tear off the layers of carnal concern and discover the powerful treasure of God's power within to meet every need!

don't push the plate away

Oh, taste and see that the Lord is good;
Blessed is the man who trusts in Him!
Psalm 34:8

When we were children, I'm sure we were all made to eat something we didn't like. In their younger years, our children used to gag whenever they were served cauliflower! We can set up a resistance in our mind to a food due to our childhood experience only to discover, as we mature in age, that we actually like that food after all. This was my experience with custard, which I had an aversion to as a child because I didn't like milk, only to find as an adult that I actually love custard!

God often serves us dishes that we don't like. Because of past experiences, we can be guilty at times of *pushing the plate away* because it's not our favourite food, or because it's not on our menu! God knows that if we partake of what He is setting before us, there are nutrients and strength within that meal that will sustain us, and that by consuming it we will discover and develop new taste buds! Some adults still refuse to eat fruit and vegetables, yet wonder why they may be struggling with their health! Likewise, we may refuse to partake of God's choice of what is presented on our plate, fearing the discomfort and the energy it will entail! Have you ever heard people say, "I have too much on my plate"? This may be a fair and true statement, and in wisdom they may need to eliminate the glut, the excess from their lives—but when it's God who is dishing up the food, we can be sure it will lead to prosperity and growth.

It is true, however, that some of God's food may, at first, not look that tasty or easy to digest!

How about this verse?

> . . . *whoever compels you to go one mile, go with him two.*
> *Give to him who asks you, and from him who wants to*
> *borrow from you do not turn away.*
> *Matthew 5:41*

Or this one?

> *But I say to you, love your enemies, bless those who curse you,*
> *do good to those who hate you, and pray for those who*
> *spitefully use you and persecute you.*
> *Matthew 5:44*

At one time I heard God speak this phrase into my spirit, *"Don't push the plate away."* This was in relationship to an area of ministry where God wanted me to extend myself further. As I looked at the opportunities and challenges presented before me, there was something in me that just wanted to slide the plate away and say, "I'm not having that." We have all seen children refuse to eat, even when they are being encouraged to *just give it a try*! God was asking me to pick up my knife and fork and receive what He had dished up for my life in public ministry. God believed I would like it, that this menu would suit me, and sure enough, as I received it with thanks, I discovered a depth in God, *an explosion of flavour* in my mouth, a receptivity to the greater purpose of God that I would never have experienced if I had pushed the plate away.

We may be familiar with a prayer of *grace,* often said around a table before a meal is consumed: *"For what I am about to receive, may the Lord make me truly thankful."* Let's not bluff, but apply this prayer to God's command and direction in our lives! Being thankful for what God dishes up is key to our growth and development. As His child, He sets before us only what will boost our health and wellbeing!

Has God placed before you something you are 'refusing to eat'? Are you telling God you don't like it, that it doesn't suit you, that it's not one of your favourite dishes? Today, 'pull the plate toward you,' pick up your knife and fork and begin to eat the food God has set before you! It will do you good! Thank God that He is dishing up only His best for your life! Make some discoveries! Today, let your taste buds explode as you partake of the good things of God. Choose God's menu and don't push the plate away!

buy in

She considers a field and buys it.
From her profits she plants a vineyard.
Proverbs 31:16

The book of Proverbs contains many inspiring passages about investments! In this verse, a woman considers a field and she *buys it*! She has done her homework thoroughly, checking on the potential of the property. When she is satisfied, she buys in! God has set so many good investments before us that we need to *buy into*—marriage, family, friendship, church, business and mission. All demand our best commitment to see the best of returns!

We may initially take hold of projects with a great sense of responsibility and enthusiasm, only to let our commitment wane over time, rendering the project less effective and less productive. It's going to take *buy in* if we are to reap a full harvest from our investment! A good attitude to adopt regarding our responsibilities is, "If we are in, we are fully in"—not just part of us, as the 'Hokey Tokey' dance suggests, but *our whole self!*

Are we *all in* in our marriage, *all in* with our children, *all in* with our work commitments? Or are we half-hearted and slack in some areas? It's easy for people to have the attitude of 'this will do; this is good enough,' especially when their gifts and opportunities are taken for granted. In all our responsibilities we need to be personally invested, not from a distance or from afar! Our field is our mission, our assignment, so let's take another look at how we are operating. Are we *buying in* fully from the heart, realising that how we personally invest matters if we are to produce the right kind of results?

We need the same approach to our mission or the 'field', the special task and responsibility God has called us to fulfil. For example, writing this devotional book, was a field I needed to *buy into* heart and soul; affirming this was a God-idea which I considered carefully in prayer before beginning! It has taken a big *buy in* for me to write and finish this project. Did I wane in the process? Absolutely! There were times I doubted myself and could easily have given the project away. But knowing this was my 'God-field,' even if it was just a memoir of God-experiences for myself, I needed to keep putting my *whole self* in!

In this scripture we can see this woman's investment paid off. From her *profit*, she planted a vineyard. From her full *buy in*, she made the land work. She was not depleted from her purchase; she retained enough energy and resources to plant it. That is so much like life! As we invest wholeheartedly into plans and projects, *and work them*, our good plans have a way of returning us profit. God's ways are *even more* like this. He lends His supernatural power to our diligent and faithful efforts in obedience to His bidding.

We need to identify the field before us, not only in terms of the natural responsibilities that require our full investment, but also the field beyond us . . . in mission. When there is a cost involved, or the going gets hard, we still need to choose to fully buy into the field.

> *She girds herself with strength and strengthens her arms.*
> Proverbs 31:17

When we diligently *work our fields*, there will be a yield that pushes beyond the natural into the sphere of the supernatural! When attitude meets opportunity, harvest results! And with that, comes thankfulness, joy, and celebration!

*What field have you considered that has your name on it? Are you 'buying into' life and mission wholeheartedly? Where do you need to push through with diligence in order to see a full return for your **buy in**? Give yourself thoroughly to the task before you today, knowing you will reap in time to come.*

keepsakes

*For this reason I also suffer these things; nevertheless I am not ashamed, for I know whom I have believed and am persuaded that He is **able to keep** what I have committed to Him until that day.*
2 Timothy 1:12

In life, there are things we want to have close by and not lose hold of— items we *keep in our possession*. Maybe we have photos of times we have enjoyed, souvenirs from a wonderful holiday overseas, letters from a loved one, or maybe trinkets of a departed one that bring back memories or hold special meaning for us.

I have several crystal serving bowls and platters that belonged to my mother who passed away a few years ago. When I use them, I am reminded of her 'vital' days, how she loved to serve her family and friends, putting her time and best effort into every meal we shared. I also have her recipe books written in her beautiful handwriting. These bring such precious memories of a sweet-spirited lady who loved to serve and minister to the needs of others. We also have my parents' grandfather clock in our lounge, a reminder of days gone by. I love to hear it chime, even through the night if I am awake!

Although I live fully in the present, these keepsakes remind me of another era. Different items have different meanings to different people, but we call them *keepsakes* because they help keep the person who gave it or originally owned it in our memory. I have also many keepsakes in my spiritual journal, a record of specific truths God lovingly imparted from His Word into my life that held me strong in testing times. These scriptures *prompt memories* of the strength, hope and joy they brought in that moment. They are precious *keepsakes* of truth that I will treasure and use for a lifetime.

Blessed be the God and Father of our Lord Jesus Christ, who according to His abundant mercy has begotten us again to a living hope, through the resurrection of Jesus Christ from the dead, to an inheritance incorruptible and undefiled and that does not fade away, reserved in heaven for you, who are **kept by the power of God** *through faith for salvation ready to be revealed in the last time.*
1 Peter 1:3-5

In this scripture, Paul expresses his utmost confidence in God, even in a time of imprisonment. These verses came alive to me at a time when the environment seemed unsure and unsteady. Though it was a time of testing, I literally knew I was being *kept* by the power of God in the face of uncertainty; I was surrounded and held by His power! It was a tangible feeling from a very present, powerful God.

God can hold you also, as you keep and treasure His promises in your heart, knowing He is a *promise keeper!* That's why Paul wrote,

I . . . am persuaded that He is able to keep what I have committed to Him.
2 Timothy 1:12

Paul was persuaded. He was sure of his ground! God *keeps* His promises and regards faithfully the commitments we have made to Him. He *safe-keeps* them for a time yet to be revealed. Let's rejoice in the knowledge that God takes seriously every commitment we have made to Him, and that we can trust Him to act on them at the appropriate time!

What keepsakes do you have in your possession that remind you of former good times or people you loved? What keepsakes of scripture and encounters with God have you tucked away in your heart to remind you how good God is, and to reassure you of His continual keeping power? Today, seek a fresh encounter with God, and receive some new keepsakes from His Word!

235

legacy

A good man leaves an inheritance to his children's children.
Proverbs 13:22

In *The Message*, this verse reads, "A good life gets passed onto the grandchildren." We all need to ask what will follow after us. Do we want ourselves to be reproduced in another generation? I have often used the phrase, "If I wasn't me, would I be happy to follow me?" On some counts I can confidently say "yes," but in other areas I acknowledge the need for improvement, so I focus on building strength into these spaces.

A *legacy* is the story of someone's life, the things they did, the places they went, the goals they accomplished. It is the stories we leave behind that we will be remembered by! Sadly, some legacies read only of the failures and associated disappointments of a life lived foolishly. With this in mind, we should be more determined to pass on a good and godly legacy to our children and grandchildren, who in turn will build on these foundations.

We also need to look back and recognise the legacy we have been blessed with from generations before. I am thankful to stand on a foundation of positiveness, adventure, strong determination, and an ethos of hard work! *Legacy gives me a place to walk!* Good legacy is like solid ground beneath us—it has the power to sustain us and lift us to greater levels. Legacy that is negative, on the other hand, can be challenged, healed and changed in the next generation!

Are you embracing the good legacy that has been passed down through the generations, or are you despising it? We read in Luke 15 about a young man who had an excellent legacy, a great foundation on which to build his life, but instead of valuing it, he despised it, discounted it and disowned it, wanting instead to make his own way in life. This young man left his place of security and blessing, thinking he knew better and freeing himself from his supposed restraints—only to find that the ground underneath him gave way and the storyline of his life became one of desperation, deep need and poverty. This young man was financially, emotionally and physically bankrupt! Thankfully, he came to his senses and returned to his father.

> *I will arise and go to my father, and will say to him, "Father, I have sinned against heaven and before you, and I am no longer worthy to be called your son. Make me one of your hired servants."*
> *Luke 15:18-19*

This young man realised that his blessing lay in His father's house, upon secure, established foundations! On his return, he was lovingly embraced and restored into sonship. Our blessing and advancement lies in the house of Father God and the legacy He has chosen to pass down to us through the sacrifice of His Son, Jesus, who redeems us from every failure and mistake! *God grants us a new beginning!* Let's not despise this legacy, or elevate our own thinking above our heavenly Father by doing our own thing. God's *legacy* for our lives is solid ground, a foundation of faith we can stand firmly on today!

Today, think about the legacy passed down from your hereditary line. Is there u need to change the storyline in your generation? Recognise the good legacy passed down. As you stand firmly upon that secure foundation, reach up to your own unique destiny! As you recognise any resistance or despising within, repent and return today! Embrace your legacy of good and godly examples, but more importantly, embrace the rich and full legacy passed down by your heavenly Father and thank Him for it today.

lift to fit

*For this very reason, giving all diligence, **add to** your faith virtue, to virtue knowledge, to knowledge self-control, to self-control perseverance, to perseverance godliness, to godliness brotherly kindness, and to brotherly kindness love. For if these things are yours and abound, you will be neither barren nor unfruitful in the knowledge of our Lord Jesus Christ.*
2 Peter 1:5-8

Have you ever felt you weren't big enough to fit the challenge that God (or life!) presented to you? Sometimes, there is a genuine need for us to *lift to fit* that which God has spoken over our lives, and all that it requires!

Many years ago, we were amused by my father who, unable to fit his new motorhome into his existing garage, came up with a solution which probably not many of us would have entertained. Determined to house this motorhome for the periods of time when my mother and he were not traveling the country, he simply decided that he would *add height* to the existing garage—not a simple task at all! A crane was required to access the property then uplift and suspend the whole garage in the air while my father built a whole new framework at the base below, onto which the existing garage was then lowered. Now the garage had the necessary height to store the vehicle! This was a huge effort, but the will and the focus were certainly there!

At times, God calls us to *lift in order to fit* the call of God on our lives—to stretch upwards and add strength to the base of our life and beliefs, so that we can house all that God has proposed for us. In 1994, I was given a word through a significant prophetic ministry that God was calling me to carry the *"mantle of a General"* and to function in that authority to strengthen the women of this nation! At that time, I certainly didn't feel at all like a General; I didn't consider myself big enough to fit this word! That prophecy was well beyond where I stood and how I felt at the time! However, God is faithful, and as we fix our eyes on Him, He lifts us on a daily basis, willing us to grow in faith, to believe bigger, to increase capacity, to act more courageously, and to pray more consistently with the authority we have been given! It dawned on me one day some years later, that I was *standing in that prophecy!* For well over a ten-year period, I had, from a heart's desire, initiated and established women's leadership summits throughout New Zealand, imparting strength and championing women! Who knew that this desire had been there all along?! Jesus did! He spoke into it years beforehand, and while I had focussed simply on growing in Jesus, the fulfilment of the prophetic word had come about as a result of me strengthening my base and *lifting to fit* on a daily basis!

Has God spoken words over your life about an area where you may need to *lift to fit*? Is an 'addition' or an 'extension' needed to house and fulfil the call He has given you? Sometimes we just need to *lift to fit*!

Let's add to our faith the virtues that Peter described in 2 Peter 1:5-8. Let's consistently *lift to fit* in accordance with God's directives! The great apostle Paul wrote:

> *I am the least (worthy) of the apostles, and not **fit** to be*
> *called an apostle, because I (at one time) fiercely oppressed*
> *and violently persecuted the church of God.*
> *1 Corinthians 15:9 (AMP)*

Although he didn't feel fit or worthy, Paul chose to *lift to fit* the call of God on his life and left an amazing legacy that we all can access today! He chose to *lift his game*—and as we do the same, we too will fulfil all God's good plans for our lives!

What needs strengthening in your life to fit the call God has placed on your life? What do you need to add to your faith to build capacity within? Where do you need to lift your faith and obedience in response to God's directives? Today, choose to focus on Jesus, grow in Him and you will see His words over you come to pass!

wake up!

Awake, my glory! Awake, lute and harp! I will awaken the dawn.
Psalm 57:8

When I accepted the role of leading the kids' ministry in our church, I heard God plainly whisper into my spirit during a regular Sunday evening service that He wanted me to *wake up* the children's spirits! The children were well awake in the natural, but there was an extra dimension in the spirit that God desired to awaken them to. Consequently, the first curriculum series I wrote for kids' ministry, was called the *'wake up'* series!

We too may be awake in the natural as we go about our everyday activities, but we may well be asleep or slumbering in our spirit, oblivious to the energy, strength and revelation available through the Holy Spirit. God wants us to *wake up* our spirit so we can access all His benefits!

Praise awakens our spirit. We choose to put on the garment of praise as we enter His courts! Our flesh may not feel like praising, our bodies may protest giving expression to praise, but *praise is the key* that unlocks our heart and our understanding to the fullness of God's grace and mercy. A thankful heart is a full heart!

The Psalmist knew that our souls need to be *awakened* to God's glory already present in our life through praise! As our soul awakens, we in turn, are able to 'awaken the dawn,' to wake up our environments, our emotions, our hopes and our attitude to a new day and new possibilities in Jesus. Let's be door-openers to the presence of God through our praise!

When I was a young mother with four children, the eldest being six and the youngest two, I discovered the power of praise in my home as I chose to sing my way through the busyness and sometimes hectic moments of life. I would sing the same song over and over again until faith was *awakened* in my soul through praise! The song I sang regularly at one particular time was:

He's setting me free, this Holy Ghost power
He's setting me free this very hour
He's flooding my soul, He's making me whole
He's setting me free, free, free, this Holy Ghost power!

The more I sang this song, the more the Holy Spirit flooded my soul, the closer I felt to God, and the more freedom I experienced as truth entered my heart, releasing an abundance of strength and joy to handle endless chores and demands! An exchange took place as a result of faith being 'quickened' through the awakening of praise! *Praise opens the door to the very presence of God!*

Throughout the Bible, we witness praise opening doors—and opening the heavens! In Acts 16, the doors of the prison flew open in response to Paul and Silas's praise. In Matthew 21, the multitude gained revelation of who Jesus really was, as they welcomed Him into Jerusalem shouting, "*Hosanna!*" The heavens opened at the sound of their praise!

When we *wake up* to the power of praise, we introduce the presence of God, not just to our own lives but to the lives of others. What do you wake up to in the morning? Birds outside the window and the smell of coffee, or an annoyingly loud alarm clock? Let's not wait for something major like a disaster or a significant loss in life to awaken us spiritually, but choose to *stay awake* to the powerful presence of God's Holy Spirit within us, equipping us, strengthening us, empowering us, teaching us, guiding us, comforting us and leading us day by day!

Does your spirit need to awaken to God's best for your life? Are you sleeping your life away, not experiencing God's liberating power? Today, put on the garment of praise, sing your song, and watch God lift the platform of your hopes and dreams. Wake up to the Spirit of God within who can empower you as you choose to praise Him today!

search for the hero

Then the Lord turned to him and said,
"Go in this might of yours, and you shall save Israel from
the hand of the Midianites. Have I not sent you?"
Judges 6:14

'*Search for the hero inside yourself*' was a popular song several years ago, suggesting that within us, there is a powerful person that can rise to overcome in all situations. In the Old Testament, God spoke a similar thing over Gideon, but Gideon's challenge was not only to unlock his own potential but to defeat the Midianites, a fearsome nation who had oppressed Israel for seven years!

Gideon certainly didn't feel strong enough for the task—all he could see was what and where he was lacking. He was seriously afraid! But God's words intimated that Gideon already had the might within to step out in faith and take on this challenge. As far as God was concerned, all Gideon really needed to know was that God was with him, that God believed in him, and that he *already possessed* all he would need for the battle ahead.

Have you ever watched sheepdog trials? Sheepdogs are judged on their performance as they muster sheep in the direction of a pen. Usually there is at least one sheep who 'balks' and darts off in a different direction from the main group! This is similar to our thoughts when under pressure—they dart off in many directions and become difficult to muster into the same space, difficult to unify in the face of the challenge before us! When our minds are tempted to run 'here, there and everywhere,' we can remain confident because we have a *hero* who lives within, a person we can call on who is able to unite our thoughts and emotions! This is the Holy Spirit, who Jesus sent to abide in us as our Teacher, Friend, Comforter, Guide and Helper. *The Holy Spirit will add His supernatural strength to our might* when we step out in faith and obedience to God's command. Are we drawing on the Holy Spirit as much as we could be?

Don't be distracted looking for the hero outside yourself, looking in many different directions, but instead, look within. The Holy Spirit within you longs to manifest God's glory through you. Knowing this gives us the courage to go where God sends us and do what He instructs us. Have you noticed that God makes no small plans, but always promises big?!

> And the Lord said to him, "Surely I will be with you,
> and you shall defeat the Midianites as one man."
> Judges 6:16

The chorus of the 'Hero Inside' song says, "Search for the secrets you hide, and you will find the key to your life." Inside us all are hidden great God-secrets that the Holy Spirit will make known as we search Him out. Like Gideon, we will discover that they are much bigger than we could have ever anticipated!

Who would have known that within Bruce and I there would so many churches in many countries, as we began to take small faith steps in the might God had given us? Who knew that God would supernaturally release burdens for nations into our hearts and open the doors for us to travel to them? As we search the Holy Spirit out, He releases *keys* to our life, unlocking His deep passion and purpose within. Just like Gideon, *God chooses to live His big life through you and me!*

How well acquainted are you with the Holy Spirit? Are you searching out the Holy Spirit to find the keys to your life? Do you know that the Holy Spirit can muster your thoughts together and impart courage? Today, affirm your faith in God's Holy Spirit—your Hero who backs you with His supernatural power!

footprints in the sand

But as for me and my house, we will serve the Lord.
Joshua 24:15

Footprints make an impression on surfaces, particularly on soft surfaces like sand. As people walk the beach, they will often attempt to place their feet into the indentation of another's footprint, endeavouring to follow the track they have marked out.

Joshua sought to make an imprint on his household by the choice he made for his whole household to walk and live a life of dedication, of service to God. As parents, kids' leaders, pastors and Christians, we make a choice for our households to bring up those in our care in the ways of God.

> *Train up a child in the way he should go,*
> *and when he is old, he will not depart from it.*
> *Proverbs 22:6*

As a couple, Bruce and I desire our lives to be godly examples to our children and grandchildren through our choice to be God-seekers, God-followers, Church-lovers, and ones that seek to fulfil the mission God has entrusted us with. Have we done this perfectly? Not at all. But I fully believe, through our dedication to God, we have left footprints in the sand for others to follow.

God also has made footprints in the sand of life for us to follow!

Ephesians 2:10 says, "For we are His workmanship, created in Christ Jesus for works, which God prepared beforehand that we should walk in them." Are we placing our feet in His footsteps, into those good works that He has prepared for us to walk in? Are we walking where He walked, in love and compassion, and in relationship with God the Father? Are we, like Jesus, walking in the power and anointing of the Holy Spirit?

Several years ago, Bruce received a prophecy relating to his already-existing ministry in Europe. The word given was, "that he would walk with big feet through Europe, shaking existing traditions that in turn would cause religious demons to scream; that in that place, Bruce would leave a footprint, an impression, an imprint in which others would establish and build churches."

I smiled at this prophetic word, knowing how Bruce walks with heavy footsteps at home, shaking the whole house! What a good and descriptive analogy this prophetic word was in relation to his ministry and effectiveness in Europe! Have you noticed how God always talks prophetically in a language we relate to? This word is truly coming to pass as Bruce continues to be obedient to *go* and *walk* where God has already walked before him. None of us are able to fulfil God's call, unless we go where He has walked before us!

What imprint are we leaving for others to follow? What footprints are we leaving in the heart of another because of our choices? Today, identify the footprint God has left for you to step into. Match your foot to His indentation, follow the direction He has already walked in, and watch God increase your sphere!

nevertheless

*And the king and his men went to Jerusalem against the
Jebusites, the inhabitants of the land, who spoke to David, saying,
"You shall not come in here; but the blind and the lame will repel
you," thinking "David cannot come in here."* **Nevertheless,**
David took the stronghold of Zion (that is, the City of David).
2 Samuel 5: 6-8

I love the expression *'nevertheless'* in the Bible. It means despite what has been said or referred to, we need to reach forth to possess our God-given inheritance! It denotes an attitude of courage, tenacity and boldness! God has placed before us all that is necessary to prosper in life, work and relationships, and we simply need to reach out and take hold of every provision He has made.

Growing up, you may have been taught a family practice of waiting for others—particularly visitors—to be served before you took any food for yourself; firstly, to ensure that the visitors had enough, and secondly, so that, hopefully, good manners would be instilled in you! Maybe there were daily rations on food in your household, ensuring the provision would stretch over the week or for the allotted period of time? Maybe there were restrictions on certain items, the reason being that if one family member took more than their share, others would miss out? We were the family (particularly when the kids were teenagers) that ate all the bananas on the same day they were bought! How about your family?!

In the Kingdom of God, the *opposite* principle applies; the more we *take*, the more there is for everyone else. When we avail ourselves of God's bountiful provision of faith, strength, financial provision, joy and peace, there is simply *much more* to go around! People benefit from our faith, our consumption and receptivity toward the blessings and favour of God on our life. God is never going to 'run out' of what we need! So come on, just take what is already yours!

King David understood this in relationship to his reign over Israel. He needed to *take every advantage* available to him to rule well so Israel as a nation under his leadership would prosper. David couldn't lead well from a compromised position but needed to take an elevated position, a vantage point for over-seeing the nation. To do this, David firstly needed to dispossess the inhabitants residing there, those whom the tribe of Benjamin had previously failed to drive out.

That's when we read this word, *'nevertheless'*! In spite of the words spoken and the discouragement shown toward David, he *still took the stronghold!* By positioning himself for the sake of Israel and taking the stronghold, David brought increased blessing to the nation and attracted favour from those around—even the king of Tyre, who gifted David resources to build his house. 2 Samuel 5:9-10 (MSG) tells us:

247

> *David made the fortress city his home and named it*
> *"City of David." He developed the city from the outside*
> *terraces inward. David proceeded with* **a longer stride, a larger**
> **embrace** *since the God-of-the-Angel-Armies was with him.*

We need to know that God is with us, and we need to *take back* the provision that God has made for us, all that the enemy may have seized, refuting every word of arrogance and opposition. Let's proceed today with a longer stride and a larger embrace!

🍃 *What words spoken over you have caused you to shrink back from taking your inheritance? Where do you need to exercise your 'nevertheless' today—choosing to proceed in spite of what has been said of you? Today, seize your appointed position in God so you can rule and reign with godly oversight and authority. Take your portion in God today knowing there is more for you to share with others. God never runs out of provision!*

learning to lean

*When Jesus saw His ministry drawing huge crowds, He climbed
a hillside. Those who were apprenticed to Him, the committed,
climbed with Him. Arriving at a quiet place, He sat down
and taught His climbing companions.*
Matthew 5:1-2 (MSG)

Jesus needed to breathe, to distance Himself from the crowd for a time so
He could relax and bring His disciples 'up to speed' for the journey ahead
by teaching them the principles of living responsibly and sincerely before
God and toward others. These teachings, which would hold the disciples
steady in their journey, are commonly referred to as the Beatitudes. For
the carnal minded, these teachings are difficult to grasp; they are in
sharp contrast to human nature. But if we want to live *blessed,* these clear
principles of the Kingdom are instructions we can depend on!

Have you ever walked up a steep mountain or hill? Perhaps you felt
yourself breathing more heavily than normal, and your muscles began to
ache, but did you persevere, putting one foot in front of another as you set
your sights on the summit? Maybe as you travelled upwards, you stopped
to rest and catch your breath, or leaned against a tree or a rock for a while
to relieve some weight and pressure from your weary body.

In our journey of faith, there are times where an *uphill climb* is necessary
to overcome unbelief or random fears, to gain new perspectives of faith,
or to change behaviours! The new height requires extra energy and
determination to push through barriers to reach the top. As we ascend a
mountain in the natural, we experience the air becoming thinner, affecting
our breathing. Panic may set in, which may result in us abandoning the
goal of reaching the top and heading back down the mountain! The better
option, when the going gets tough, is to pause, allow our breathing to
adjust to the higher altitude, and then to continue 'ascending.'

The Beatitudes are a call for us to live at a higher level of godly attitude and
behaviour. As we strive and persevere to outwork these godly responses
in our lives, we find ourselves living more freely at a higher altitude of
faith and wellbeing. The Bible described this state as 'blessed.'

As I sought to surmount fear and carnal responses in my life, the journey
often felt like an uphill trudge, but the words of this song encouraged me

and reminded me that the strength I needed for the journey, was found by simply leaning more on Jesus:

Learning to lean, learning to lean,
I'm learning to lean on Jesus.
Finding more power than I ever dreamed,
I'm learning to lean on Jesus.

Many people view 'leaning' as weak, opting to find the strength in themselves to rise to new levels, but as a result, they find themselves struggling or failing in the process. *Leaning* is a faith response to Jesus' invitation to trust Him; it involves simply letting go, and in that place of trust, finding His power to sustain our weight, release the pressure, regulate our breathing, strengthen our resolve, and ease our aches and pains! This is not weakness, this is *faith*! As I learned to lean more on Jesus in my journey, I truly did find more power than I ever dreamed.

Is the 'going' getting tough for you? Are you struggling with carnal responses and the weight of unbelief? Does the challenge of change appear too steep an incline? We can conquer any uphill challenge as we let go self-effort and simply *lean on Jesus* and witness Him lifting us to new heights!

Is there an area where God is challenging you to rise to new heights? Are you a committed 'climbing companion' of Jesus? Have you learned to lean on Him? Jesus can take your weight—He's got you! Allow Him to add His breath to your spiritual lungs so you can enjoy living at a higher altitude of faith and wellbeing today. Choose to live blessed!

open your eyes

Oh, how great is Your goodness, which You have laid up for those who fear You, which You have prepared for those who trust in You in the presence of the sons of men!
Psalm 31:19

Have you ever been disappointed when you have given someone a gift and the receiver didn't appear to appreciate it? Perhaps they didn't take time to look at it properly, or dismissed it fairly quickly. I wonder if God feels like that when we take for granted the blessings He has *already* bestowed on us—and those He has stored up for the future?

God's cupboard is full of great blessings that He has prepared for all His children; there is more than enough for our entire lifetime. Imagine that! Why are we so slow to access His storeroom by faith to find what we need? Not only does He have what we need *now*, but He has anticipated and ensured there is a ready abundance for all we will ever need. And if we don't need anything, God's goodness is *still* there! It's available *just because!* Just because He loves us. When we look into the face or heart of God, we see *His storehouse of love,* the goodness He stored up for us for a lifetime even before the beginning of time. That's who He is—a good, good Father. Today, open the door to His storeroom and receive all He has for you with gratitude and thankfulness.

Sometimes we go through life with our eyes shut! Have you ever been somewhere only to hear later that friends spotted you from a distance, but you didn't spot them amongst the crowd? You didn't hear them calling your name, so you missed the opportunity to connect as you would have liked to? Perhaps you were so intently focused on all the activity or where you were going in that particular moment, that you failed to lift your head, and moved on before they could engage with you? Or maybe you made plans to connect with friends, but the details were so vague that you failed to arrive in the same place at the same time?

God's goodness waves at us! Jesus highlights His blessings and favour to us so we can't miss them! Why we don't always spot them? Maybe because, with our heads down, locked deeply into our own thoughts, we fail to look up and spot His blessings! How much easier life would be if we looked up and availed ourselves of all that He, in His favour, has prepared for us. Sometimes we need to ask ourselves, "What was I thinking? What took so much of my attention at that time?"

On one occasion I had to seriously ask myself that question after attempting to fill an already-filled petrol tank. *"Where was my brain?! How did I view the gauge as empty instead of viewing it as is really was? What was wrong with my vision?"* Sometimes we view ourselves and our situations as lacking, casting our eyes downward instead of realising there is already a fullness to access. I am sure the same question was in God's mind when he asked Adam and Eve, "Where are you?" God knew where they were, but He wondered if *they* really knew where they were! What were they thinking?! They had just forfeited complete freedom and abundant favour, in their selfish appetite to fill their stomachs! Adam and Eve's unbelief in God's goodness and bounty had caused them to look beyond God's best.

It's time to look up and recognise God's goodness. He's been so good in the past, and He will continue to be good in the future. We are never too old or too mature to open God's cupboard, peer in with faith and expectation, and find the good things He has in His heart to bless us, encourage us, strengthen us, and equip us to live our best life.

Do you have your head down, and as a result are missing out on God's best? Are you operating on empty instead of being filled with God's goodness and grace? Today, open the doors to God's heart by faith. See the provision of His goodness within, already with your name on it, and be thankful!

Desire

Have you ever wanted something? It is fairly easy to see things we would like, such as food, clothes, cars and houses, and label these as our desires. But *desire* is another level altogether from just *wanting!* Desire is an aspiration that lives deep within that we may be totally unaware of at first. It is a deep longing that needs to be awakened in us by the Holy Spirit—it requires uncovering. Have you discovered desires that you didn't even know were in your heart?

Desire is a conception of God's desire in our hearts that He wants to outwork through our lives, knowing that we will be delighted by the outcome! Firstly, we need to delight ourselves in the Lord for who He is, so that, in response, He can bring to life our deep, latent, heart-desires. Imagine reaching heaven without ever seeing those aspirations met or accomplished!

The Holy Spirit is the Revealer of desires! In the Gospels we read about God's desires being awakened in the heart of a young woman, Mary. This was perplexing for Joseph, her husband to be! In Matthew 1:20-23 we read:

> *But while he thought about these things, behold an angel of the*
> *Lord appeared to him in a dream, saying, "Joseph, son of David,*
> *do not be afraid to take to you Mary your wife, for that which is*
> *conceived in her is of the Holy Spirit. And she will bring forth a Son*
> *and you shall call His name Jesus, for He will save His people from*
> *their sins." So all this was done that it might be fulfilled which was*
> *spoken by the Lord through the prophet, saying, "Behold the virgin*
> *shall be with child, and bear a Son, and they shall call His name*
> *Immanuel, which is translated, 'God with us.'"*

God revealed His deep desire to send His Son to redeem mankind back to Himself. Because Mary's desire was for God, God knew He could commit His plan safely to Mary, to carry His desire to fulfilment! He found a worthy vessel in Mary.

What starts with a seed of desire can grow and flourish! Sometimes we are unaware of our God-desires until they start growing and moving within. Sometimes desire can be born out of adversity, when a lack experienced or a misdemeanour exposed, highlights a serious need for God's intervention. Through this passage in scripture, the Holy Spirit revealed to me that I was the blockage to some family members coming to salvation because in my mind I couldn't really believe this would ever happen—I was governed only by their external response!

Mary conceived Jesus by *the Holy Spirit overshadowing her!* I needed to conceive a miracle in my heart, a reliance on God to do what only He supernaturally could do. That day, I opened my heart and conceived a miracle for the salvation of my family. A miracle is *a miracle*—it is beyond our natural ability to perform. Our job is simply to believe for God's supernatural intervention in the matter. Over the years, the miracle in my family appeared a long way off, but because I had conceived it, I held that miracle close within my heart and was thankful to God that in time He was going to perform it. And so He did—nearly fifteen years later!

Are you confusing 'want' and 'desire'? Desire is much deeper, and needs the Holy Spirit to uncover it. What have you conceived in your heart, maybe even through adversity, that you know will be birthed in God? What miracle do you need to hold onto, and trust God to fulfil? Ask the Holy Spirit to awaken **desire** *in your heart to conceive and believe for supernatural miracles today!*

send trouble packing

*For this cause everyone who is godly shall pray to You
in a time when You may be found; Surely in a flood of
great waters they shall not come near him. You are my
hiding place; You shall preserve me from trouble;
You shall surround me with songs of deliverance.*
Psalm 32:6-7

We live in a stressful world, with time pressures, work pressures, and unrealistic expectations troubling hearts and taking a toll on people's health and wellbeing. Trouble may be taking centre stage in your thoughts and emotions, while God, who promises to be your help in trouble, is being pushed into the background.

"Time is of the essence" is a saying that indicates something needs to be done as soon as possible—like an ambulance speeding to get to the scene of an accident in order to save someone's life! Potential delays and obstructions need to be eliminated to ensure a safe and speedy passage to the destination where help can be accessed. A siren is often activated to clear the road and help with this process. At critical times like these, speed is a priority, but when we extend this principle too wide in our everyday lives and rushing becomes a normal response, life can become increasingly harried and regimented as a result.

Has time become a competitor in your life? Are you struggling with unrealistic time frames and deadlines that cause you to stress and worry? A moment in God receiving His wisdom can help you prioritise, eliminate stress and solve the issue! You just need to slow down! Personally, I had to decide to *'make friends with time'* instead of viewing time as my competitor—one that constantly sought to rob me! I have learned that as I trust in God, time is on my side!

In Psalm 32, David calls on God in his time of need—he was desperate for release from the pressures that were draining his life of vitality and strength. David's sin weighed heavily upon His heart and replayed over and over in his mind. David knew God could be found, that God had time for him, and God would prioritise His healing and release!

The questions we need to ask ourselves are: *"What is featuring too large on the main screen of my mind? What movie is playing repetitively before my eyes, what constant worry or bother, what stress? What has shifted from being just a small trailer on the sideline to now being the main feature in my mind's eye?"* Identify the demand that is making you anxious or causing you to feel pressurised—that which causes internal angst and has the potential to spill frustration over onto others. Has that stress moved from the periphery and become the main feature, crowding your vision and depleting your energy? It's time to *send trouble packing!*

The scripture says,

> *Pour out all your worries and stress upon Him and leave them there, for He always tenderly cares for you.*
> 1 Peter 5:5 (TPT)

Jesus has time for us, and we *will* find our answers in Him. It's time to tell trouble to *pack its bag* and leave; that it's not welcome to stay any longer!

What is constantly troubling and worrying you that you need to send packing? What scenes are playing on the main screen of your life? What time pressures and unrealistic expectations are robbing you of energy and vision? Make time your friend! Today, pour out your worries on Jesus, unburden yourself of sin and trouble, and find His strength and help in your time of need!

stop squirming

The Lord has appeared of old to me saying,
"Yes I have loved you with an everlasting love;
therefore with loving kindness I have drawn you."
Jeremiah 31:3

There are many things we will miss in life if we adopt a rushed, 'busy, busy' attitude to our days! If we don't slow down, we will soon be asking questions like: *"When did our kids grow up? When did I get these wrinkles? When did that view become so breath-taking?"*

Activity is great, but constant busyness dulls our eyes and mutes our hearing, until we don't notice what is happening around us and therefore miss vital connections and cues. Life is about activity, but it's also about breathing and observing. There is so much to be learned, felt and enjoyed by observation!

The question is, "Are we *still* enough to take in our surroundings, to enjoy the people in our lives and the beauty of nature that God has created for us to enjoy?" I remember a line of a song that spoke to me when in my twenties: *"I need to be still and let God love me."* In the rush and bustle of life we sometimes fail to pause, to simply breathe so we can fully inhale the love of God. So often, we don't let God love us! God is not a quick fix, a dispensable source of strength that we call on in haste when needed, but a living, loving God who is ever present and longs to embrace us.

Have you tried to hug a child while they are playing? It is virtually impossible as they are fixed on their game and absorbed in the moment. But there will come a time, maybe later in the day, when they will want to be held and reassured by a parent's love and embrace. We need to do the same thing. God's love cannot reach our heart the same if we continue to squirm, hassling about our schedule and refusing to pull aside from activity, people and pleasure.

Does that mean that sometimes God can't reach us? It totally does! We miss moments of closeness when we embrace a stance that says, "I'm too busy to stop. My work and play are more important." Without love coming *to* us, love certainly can't flow *through* us, and this defeats our purpose of impacting others with the love of Christ. We are in danger of becoming wooden and mechanical, deluding ourselves that we are really achieving what God wants. We need to be still and let God love us!

Maybe we struggle because of internal doubt, wondering whether God really does truly love us? If we don't be still, we will never know! I heard a testimony once of an ex-hippy who, although he had been radically saved and had surrendered his life to Christ, continued to struggle with the concept of God's love for him personally. In his own words, he "constantly hassled God to prove it" by some external evidence; until one day he had a revelation that he needed to settle this issue by *faith*! If God's Word said that God loved him, then he would make a choice to believe it! It took a decision of faith on his part to believe. The day he settled this issue by faith—declaring what Scripture says, that God *loved him*—was the very day, he said, that God's love came to him. God just loves us—there is nothing we can do to make Him love us more, and there's nothing we can do to make Him love us less! God *is* love!

Let's not push away from God's love because of our doubts or the demands of life. God loves us with an everlasting love! What a great source of joy and confidence it brings to our hearts as we allow God to come close.

What issues do you need to settle by faith, so God's love can come to you? Where do you need to stop squirming and seek closeness with God? Today, determine to be still and let God love you!

maturity

For though by this time you ought to be teachers, you need someone to teach you again the first principle of the oracles of God; and you have come to need milk and not solid food. For everyone who partakes only of milk is unskilled in the word of righteousness for he is a babe. But solid food belongs to those who are of full age, that is, those who by reason of use, have their senses exercised to discern both good and evil.
Hebrews 5:12-14

Paul could discern where the Corinthians were at spiritually. They hadn't progressed at all and needed to be taught again the basics of the Christian faith. They were still immature in their responses, with an inability to digest the fuller revelation of God.

We all come to a stage in our lives where we learn to feed ourselves, first as a toddler, then as a child, and eventually as an adult who needs to resource our own food. In the natural, you never see a grown person still being bottle-fed milk by their parents! But this is the image Paul paints regarding the immaturity present in the Corinthians. He is urging them to grow and mature!

Sometimes we need to be *'called into maturity'* just as Paul exhorted these believers. Life itself demands us to mature, to take our place as responsible adults in the world; likewise, spiritual leaders may call us to maturity, providing us with spiritual food so we can grow strong in our Christian faith and belief. Sometimes it is our spouse who is willing us to grow, to make more mature decisions and display less selfish responses in the relationship. Responsibilities also appeal to us to grow, whether as a parent, an employer or employee, or as a leader of any sort. Maturity means to be fully developed, responsible, skilled and able to lead with the wisdom of God and the ability to make wise choices.

Some children experience *'growing pains'* particularly in their legs as their body stretches extensively over a short length of time. Have you ever seen a child grow so fast that every time you saw them, you were amazed? Fast growth spurts, such as these, obviously put pressure on their young bodies.

Sometimes we liken the pressure of physical growth to the *call to mature* as God's children; it requires us to *stretch beyond our current status, behaviour and belief* into the more mature level God desires us to operate in. Maturity accepts God's healthy diet without complaint or protest. It doesn't demand an easier option to swallow! God's Word contains sustenance, variety and texture, and we need to know how to chew it thoroughly and digest it slowly to gain the best nutrients and benefits from it!

Maturity is not dependent on age. Some kids display an incredible maturity at a young age—they know how to hear God's voice for themselves, and consequently stand out as young leaders who possess strong, internal discernment. Come on, people! It's time to *embrace the stretch* and heed God's call for us all to *mature!* Today, let's praise God that He wants to feed us with the best, to establish us as the healthy and mature Christians He has called us to be. Let's welcome His call to mature in Him today!

How's your spiritual digestive system? Could you be choking on something God wants you to digest simply because you refuse to embrace a change of diet? What may you be 'spitting out' that God wants you to chew on? Is God speaking to you, calling you into maturity through situations or other people? Thank Him today for the stretch of faith! Embrace the growing pains and take your place with wisdom and maturity.

not now

*A little later John's followers approached, asking, "Why is it that
we and the Pharisees rigorously discipline body and spirit by
fasting, but your followers don't?" Jesus told them, "When you're
celebrating a wedding, you don't skimp on the cake and wine. You
feast. Later you may need to pull in your belt, but **not now**. No one
throws cold water on a friendly bonfire. This is Kingdom come!"
Matthew 9:14-15 (MSG)*

In Ecclesiastes 3:4 we read that there is "a time for every purpose under
heaven, a time to weep, and a time to laugh, a time to mourn, and a time to
dance." We need to discern the '*Kingdom-come*' moments—the times when
heaven invades earth. Jesus's presence on earth was a '*Kingdom-come*'
moment not to be missed but to be fully appreciated and celebrated! Jesus
likened it to a wedding in the natural, where the bridegroom is present.
This was not the time to be secluded and locked into normal routines. As
good and necessary as they may be at other times, they were '*not for now*'!

I once heard the saying, *"Don't let a good thing hide a sinful thing."* In this
case, an outward show of religiosity and duty could be used to hide a

serious lack of generosity and gladness toward God's goodness and favour toward another, a spirit that is too rigid and unable to yield to the spontaneous nature of the Spirit of God. This spirit not only says "not now" to celebrating the presence of Jesus, but has the potential of becoming a "not now, not ever" attitude that lacks the capacity to express joy.

How good are we at spotting moments when the Kingdom of God invades our present and God's glory is on display for us all to enjoy? Can we rejoice with those that rejoice? Can we share in the celebration of 'Kingdom-come' moments?

Have you ever been to an occasion where the quantity of food has been sorely underestimated for the size of the crowd? Maybe it left you wondering how everyone was going to enjoy even a little piece of the celebration cake?! When it comes to our bridegroom, Jesus, parties and celebrations are to be extravagant. Don't skimp on the cake! Don't cut your life too small, or bring a stingy attitude to fun and spontaneity. Make it bigger than is needed so everyone can enjoy plenty. This is a true party!

In Matthew 9:14-15, Jesus encourages us to turn God-moments into feasts and celebrations. Don't be a party-pooper! Don't be like the Pharisees who couldn't see the significance of the occasion or understand the cause for the celebration. They lacked the party in their heart! Where Jesus is, there is liberty; that alone is reason for a party! God's continual presence fills us with great joy within.

> *All the days of the afflicted are evil,*
> *but he who is of a merry heart has a continual feast.*
> *Proverbs 15:15*

Routines are necessary to thrive, but as good as they are, they can be paused for a moment to celebrate! Recognise when it is time to simply say "not now" to routines and duty, and "yes" to celebration and thanksgiving! Let's not throw cold water on a friendly bonfire! Let's keep it burning with praise and celebration. More can be achieved through pausing and worshipping with the presence of God in our midst, than through the outworking of staid religious performances from a mindset of duty.

Out of ten, how would you rate your ability to pause and party in the presence of God? Are you discerning the moments that God has ordained to display His glory? Today, bake a bigger cake of generosity to fit the occasion of God's visitation! Learn to throw a party!

top down

Enter into His gates with thanksgiving and into His courts with
praise. Be thankful to Him and bless His name.
Psalm 100:4

Sometimes we may look at a tall building on a steep incline and wonder where the access level is? How do we enter the building? Normally there would be signs to point us in the right direction. If the building occupied a flat site, the ground floor would be the most likely entry point, with a reception area or information desk to direct us from there.

God has given us an *'all-access pass'* into His presence. He wants us to enter into His presence, commune with Him, and enjoy His benefits! The password is not complicated. A heartfelt "thank you" is all that is needed to bring us before His throne of grace. How amazing is that! His word tells us that He has given us who belong to Him a seat in heavenly places to rule and reign alongside Him. Why don't we access this as much as we should?

Perhaps our hearts are not captivated enough with Jesus? Perhaps our minds are too full with earthly concerns, relying on ourselves to solve the issues of life? Maybe we are skimping on our worship and therefore not ascending to sit with Him, high above all worldly concerns and pressure? Worship is a way that we can cut loose the 'sand bags' of life that keep us grounded and faithless in our response. Worship releases us to a greater and more faith-filled perspective. Many people find themselves at ground level, hoping to ascend, but keep looking to themselves for solutions to the issues they are facing. To many, this may appear logical, but as Christians we occupy an 'upside down, inside-out' Kingdom. In other words, we ascend from top down!

In Wellington, the capital city of New Zealand, there is a prominent water feature called the 'bucket fountain'. Some may consider it extremely unattractive, but this fountain has now been operating for fifty years and has captivated much attention from locals and visitors alike! The top bucket, on becoming full, tips into the bucket below, and subsequently, when the second bucket fills, it tips into the third bucket, and so on. The lower buckets wait on the bucket above to overflow.

Viewing this fountain one day, God gave me a very clear picture of worship. Many people are trying to fill the buckets of their life at ground level through their own logic and management. But water does not flow upwards—it can only be pumped in that direction. God longs to fill our heart with the knowledge of the good things He has imparted into our life, the awareness that He is a good, good Father, and every good thing comes from Him.

Every gift God freely gives us is good and perfect, streaming down from the Father of lights.
James 1:17 (TPT)

Our hearts can only be filled from above! Worship fills the top bucket of our life with joy, peace and provision, and from there it overflows, filling and enriching every other area of our life. It's from the 'top down' that we ascend in life and faith!

How's your worship? Are you filling the 'top bucket' of your heart with praise and thanksgiving today? Or are you seeking to ascend in life from ground level, relying only on your natural ability and mechanical means? Today, worship God with a thankful heart and watch Him fill the containers of your life to full and overflowing!

looking for home

How lovely is Your tabernacle, O Lord of hosts! My soul longs,
yes even faints for the courts of the Lord. My heart and my flesh
cry out for the living God. Even the sparrow has found a home,
and the swallow a nest for herself where she may lay her young—
even Your altars, O Lord of hosts, my King and my God. Blessed
are those who dwell in Your house. They will still be praising You.
Psalm 84:1-2

In these verses, the psalmist expresses his deep desire to know God and to *dwell* in His presence. Everyone who has ever lived, or is alive today, has a cry within their heart for home, whether they acknowledge it or not. There is something inherent in the human heart that longs to be connected to others and to belong. We need to resist the temptation to be just a traveller in life, always moving on, passing through but never establishing ourselves. There comes a time when we must choose to settle, stay, abide, unpack, and put our roots down so that a greater and more glorious dwelling may arise. We have 'an appetite for home,' and in particular, for our heavenly home with God, where our heart finds rest, security and acceptance. *God builds the house of our life as we find our home in His heart.*

God has reserved a 'safe space' in His heart for each of us, a place we discover is the 'eternal home' we have been looking for all the time, free of inhibitions, shame and reserve. Let's abide there and enjoy our salvation home full of love, acceptance and forgiveness, which in turn releases us to be all that God has called us to be.

As God's children, we can reflect God's love, creating 'safe spaces' of rest, trust and acceptance for others, that they may feel at home with us. So many people are 'looking for home'! But ultimately, God wants us to be at home (at rest in our soul) with Him.

In Him we live and move and have our being.
Acts 17:28

When we find Jesus, we find home! We find a place of belonging beyond our imagination, a way to express and live out our dreams without inhibition! To date, we may have established what outwardly appears to be a house, but maybe it lacks the spirit of home. There is a difference! Abraham was on a search for such a home.

By an act of faith, Abraham said "yes" to God's call to travel to an unknown place that would become his home. When he left, he had no idea where he was going. By an act of faith, he lived in the country promised him, lived as a stranger camping in tents. Issac and Jacob did the same, living under the same promise. Abraham did it by keeping his eye on an unseen city with real, eternal foundations—the city designed and built by God.
Hebrews 11:8-10 (MSG)

Abraham was looking and waiting for something beyond what he could see in the natural. Abraham was *on a heart-search for a home,* a city that had the mark of God's seal upon it. Other versions of this scripture say that Abraham was "looking forward to the city with foundations, whose architect and builder is God."

Let's discover the city designed and built by God! He wants us to settle in His eternal habitation and build the house of our life there. Let's search out God's dwelling place and find our home in Him today!

*Have you found your home in God's presence? Have you discovered the strong foundation and sincere lines of truth present in God's house? Today, find Jesus, **find home**! As you settle, unpack, and establish yourself, God will build your life according to all He designed from before the beginning of time.*

create space

Arise, O Lord, to Your resting place, You and the ark of Your strength.
Psalm 132:8

Everyone loves space! We need space to breathe, to dream, to relax; we need space for activity, space for solitude, and space for company! In all that we do, we are seeking to create space for our desires. The question is, once we create that space, does it deliver what we were hoping it would?

A television program called *'Amazing Spaces'* shows the ingenuity of people to effectively utilise a small space, allowing everyday functions that would at first not have appeared possible! The ideas about how to use space wisely, and how those ideas are outworked, are truly amazing.

Sincerity is one of the most powerful assets we have to build all that God has shown us, a house that glorifies Jesus! Paul encourages Timothy in his development as a leader of the church to stay with the fundamentals, the doctrine laid down by God, and to build on these with a sincere faith and trust! Sincerity always stands, whereas hypocrisy always falls!

How are we using the space God has given us? Are we utilising it in such a way that God has room to move and function in His fullness? Would the space we create be attractive to God? King David's greatest desire, the longing that fully consumed him, was to build a space for God that was worthy of His presence, a place for His glory to dwell!

God welcomed David's desire and endorsed it with His everlasting commitment to Israel with these words:

> *I, God, chose Zion, the place I wanted, for My shrine; this will always be My home. This is what I want and I'm here for good. I'll shower blessings on the pilgrims who come here, and give supper to those who arrive hungry. I'll dress my priests in salvation clothes; the holy people will sing their hearts out! I'll make the place radiant for David; I'll fill it with light for My anointed. I'll dress his enemies in dirty rags but I'll make his crown sparkle with splendour.*
> Psalm 132:13-18 (MSG)

Our hearts can be a space for God to rest, a place He can occupy from a position of strength and power. Are we, like David, expressing a heart's desire for God to abide fully in our hearts, or are we just extending an invitation to Him as a visitor that we entertain periodically?

God has created a home for us through salvation, and we can reciprocate by creating a home for Him to dwell in our heart. A home of freedom is where everyone functions best. Ideally, home is where the heart can rest. What sort of space are we creating for God to occupy? Let's create a space where God can fully function from a place of rest and freedom in our lives today!

Have you invited God to fully occupy the space of your heart and life? Is there an earnestness within you to know God and His abiding presence in your life? Give thanks that our Almighty God has already chosen you for His habitation! Today, ask God afresh to come and dwell with you. Create a space of freedom for Him to operate from, and welcome Him in so He can fulfil all His promises toward you!

step aside

Have you ever walked on a pavement and had someone approach from either before or behind you at such a speed it has requiring you to *step aside* so they can get past? The same response is needed when an ambulance or police car approaches at top speed from before or behind you with sirens blaring. These vehicles are on an important mission to intervene in a serious accident or misdemeanour, requiring you to get out of the way so they can get to the scene as quickly as possible. In that somewhat heart-stopping moment, a quick decision needs to be made to pull over or manoeuvre safely to the side to create a passage for the speeding vehicle!

Sometimes in life, we need to *step aside* and make room for a new stage of development so we can ultimately gain ground and meet the need of the moment. Perhaps we have adopted heart attitudes, actions or stances that need to *yield to a new system.* We need to move our doubts, fears and anxieties aside, for instance, as they will always stand in the way of God bringing breakthrough in our lives.

As a young Christian, God spoke to me about an attitude of self-protection I had unconsciously wrapped around my life. Being shy by nature, I was afraid of making mistakes and of the exposure that would result from failure. I had a deep-seated fear of embarrassment, which led to an inner striving to please others and to always do things right. This was an ethos that, unbeknown to me, was forefront in my decisions and responses. I could predict discomfort, possible embarrassment and potential shame!

The Holy Spirit spoke lovingly and directly into my heart saying, "If you protect yourself, I can't. You're in the way!" As a child of God, I wanted nothing more than to be protected by God, to be kept safe in Him, but in His kind way, God was telling me that in trying to protect myself, I was preventing Him from doing so. It takes a revelation to *step aside* and allow the Holy Spirit to go before us to help us change habits and intervene on our behalf. Faith is a risk, but it is the most worthwhile risk we could ever take! Faith demands that we let go and *step aside* so God can defend us and work on our behalf. While we remain the guardian of our own dwelling, God's hands are tied from stepping in and protecting us from our enemies!

When feeling challenged or afraid, I learned what it meant to be protected by the grace of God as I took faith steps and trusted God confidently to see me through to the other side. In later years, I have realised that in saying "yes" to God, I didn't only say "yes" to all the great things God wanted to do in and through me, but I also said "yes" to all the apprehension, fear and nervousness that would accompany my steps of faith. This is often part of the package as we step out in faith, but it comes with greater triumph as we break into new territory! I have never regretted saying "yes" to God! He is so much bigger than my weaknesses, my flaws, and my inabilities, and He will always protect me when I respond in faith, causing me to inherit my promised land.

Will I, at times, embarrass myself? *Absolutely!* But the triumphs outweigh any momentary embarrassment. Let's be people who are quick to *step aside*, knowing God has promised to keep us through His power!

Have you been standing in the way of God's promises being fulfilled in your life? In what ways have you been protecting yourself? God can defend and increase you today as you allow your confidence in Him to grow. Know today with full assurance that He will answer your petition when you ask according to His will.

trust doesn't fuss

*Lord, my heart is not proud, nor my eyes haughty; nor do I
involve myself in great matters, or in things too difficult for me.*
Psalm 131:1 (AMP)

Pride and arrogance will prevent us from walking in faith if we allow them to dominate our thinking. Have you ever seen a toddler fuss over something small until it degenerates into a full-on tantrum? Toddlers find it difficult to control their emotions; they struggle with denials or discipline as they don't comprehend the reasoning behind the boundaries. They just know that they want what they want!

Perhaps God views us in the same way when we fuss over situations, decisions and matters that are beyond our understanding. An 'adult fuss' can indicate a lack of trust and perhaps pride in the heart; it could also be an indication that we are well and truly 'out of our depth' and lack the maturity and wisdom to make right responses.

In *The Message*, Psalm 131:1 is expressed this way:

*God, I'm not trying to rule the roost. I don't want to
be King of the mountain. I haven't meddled where I have
no business or fantasised grandiose plans. I've kept my feet on
the ground, I've cultivated a quiet heart. Like a baby content
in its mothers' arms, my soul is a baby content.*

To *'rule the roost'* is a common expression used when someone is dominating and is in full control of people or situations. A roost is a literal place where birds regularly settle or congregate to rest at night. This analogy denotes a pecking order, where the dominant bird (or person!) rules and expects complete subservience and submission from others. Pecking happens from a sense of entitlement and is an attempt to enforce priority. Hopefully we are not guilty of trying to peck God into submission to our plans!

Let's not be guilty of 'meddling'—involving ourselves in matters that God does not want us to concern ourselves with. In Proverbs 26:17 (TPT) we are warned of the danger of meddling, that it would be less risk,

> *. . . to grab a mad dog by its ears than to meddle and interfere in a quarrel that's none of your business.*

The psalmist made a good choice to avoid these behaviours and simply trust in God! Keeping his feet on the ground, he stayed humble in relationship to God and others, dealing with any selfish ambition or lofty thinking in his heart. He cultivated a quiet spirit—he calmed himself, like a contented or well-fed child. By simply trusting that God had his best interest at heart, he eliminated all fuss and whining behaviour.

God has everything in hand! He is not accountable to us for explanations. Let's return to a simple trust in God who loves us completely and believes in us explicitly!

Have you been overly concerned about things beyond your control? Today, recognise any fuss in your spirit, or area where you have become demanding and complaining. Are there situations where you have become dominant and controlling, fearful of losing position or status? Today, let go and release yourself into the arms of Jesus, trusting Him with all your needs.

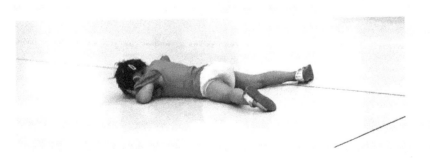

pick it up

*Arise, go to Nineveh, that great city and cry out against it,
for their wickedness has come up before Me.*
Jonah 1:2

In many areas of our life we may be doing really well, but is God asking us to *pick up the pace* in attitude, action and faith in certain other areas? We don't generally just drift into a place of greater faith or better behaviour; someone often needs to prompt us to 'pick it up.'

Parents, for example, have a common continuous cry for children to pick up their toys, pick up their clothes, pick up their books and anything else strewn all over the floor. For us as God's people, the Holy Spirit is continually and lovingly urging us to 'pick it up' and rise to our full potential to be the best person God has called us to be.

Perhaps we have settled for functioning at a level that is well below what God intended for us and He wants us to *pick up the call* on our life more passionately and purposefully. While living in London, the Holy Spirit spoke the challenge into my spirit, to 'pick it up.' He was clearly exhorting me to continue to do the same thing, but *to do the same thing differently.* I needed to operate in my grace-gift at another level, with more faith, more expectation, and more anointing!

At certain junctions of life we may think that God is calling us to do something completely different, when often He is just calling us to do what we are already doing but at another level of operation. Jonah was given a challenge by God which was at odds with his preference. He was a powerful prophet, and when he did finally bring the word to Nineveh, the whole city repented and turned to God. But initially, his attitude was one of resistance. Refusing to pick up the challenge, Jonah headed in the opposite direction from Nineveh, taking a ship toward Joppa instead! Jonah ran because he believed the people of Nineveh, on account of their sinful and wicked ways, did not deserve the goodness and mercy of God. Nineveh was not where Jonah wanted to go, nor the place he wanted his gift to be used! God's command to go to Nineveh cut across Jonah's personal wishes.

We too, may have a sincere desire for God to use us powerfully, but at the same time struggle when God's direction cuts across our preferred location or placement. We need to remember that we are stewards of the gifts of God in our lives, not the owners! God's gifts are given to us to achieve God's purposes under God's direction. Outside God's direction, the gifts are redundant and will never achieve the greater purpose He intended. We can be too selective, too insistent on our own way, too committed to our own choice of placement, willing to go only where we consider our gift will be most effective!

God's call for Bruce and I to go to London to plant a church was certainly not on my preference list, but in coming into alignment with God's directive, I found that His grace came behind me more fully than I could have anticipated. I discovered that the move to London and the blessings that followed were what I really wanted after all! God knew best. We just needed to *'pick it up.'*

 What assignment have you left strewn on the floor that needs to be picked up? How could you do differently (and better) with what you are already in possession of? Where may you have shut down the gift of God in you through resistance? Today 'pick it up' again! Follow through in faith and obedience, and watch God move in power on your behalf.

rearranging space

The Lord is my Shepherd: I shall not want. He makes me to lie down in green pastures; He leads me beside the still waters.
Psalm 23:1-2

Have you ever been in such a large crowd that you feel totally hemmed in and can't find a way through the mass? Crowds can be so much fun to be amongst, especially when there are celebrations, dancing and food, but 'crowding' is another experience altogether—it can become frightening. What if you lose your direction, or become separated from those you came with? There have been some events where hysteria has risen in a crowded space, and as a result, people's lives have been placed at risk and some have even died.

Sometimes our minds get crowded in the same way, especially when there seems to be little room to think, or solve issues, or find a clear path through the muddle. Disorientation is not a brilliant space to find yourself in! At times of crowding, we may need to simply slow down, sort out our thinking, and call on God for wisdom and help so we can move forward again smoothly, peacefully and efficiently.

As a person who highly values peace and harmony, I avoid getting overcrowded or overcomplicated in my mind. A picture I keep in my mind's eye and often use in moments of busyness or full schedules is that I simply need to *rearrange the furniture in my mind!* A lounge room, for instance, that has too much furniture in it, becomes cluttered and difficult to negotiate without falling over or colliding with some object. An easy solution to this problem is to simply *rearrange the furniture,* reposition some objects more effectively and eliminate what is not necessary! Having space in that lounge room just makes one relax immediately and enjoy being there. It's the same with our minds. We need to make space!

Perhaps we need to look at what we are trying to fit into that particular area. Is it cluttering the space and bringing discomfort to our mind and emotions? Are we making things too hard in our thinking, our thoughts too heavy to carry in the outworking of the vision? Perhaps we are allowing panic to rise through emotional 'crowding', sending us into a spin?

My ethos is to firstly say "yes" to Jesus regarding any responsibility He commissions me to carry. The next thing I ask God is, "how?" How would He like me to operate? How should I arrange my thinking to provide a structure for the fresh challenge before me? I am amazed at how the strategies God downloads into my mind and spirit go far beyond what I could have ever thought of. That's how I know it is truly God! Jesus, as our Shepherd, invites us into a wide-open space to reflect, relax, and draw wisdom from Himself today. Let's come into His uncluttered space, a space where we can move freely, order our thoughts, hear Him speak, and enjoy the peace He gives.

Have you become overcrowded in your thinking? What are you making harder to manage because of complex thinking and emotional responses? What could you 'declutter' from your life today? Take some time to 'rearrange the furniture in your mind.' Praise God for clear and creative thinking, trusting Him to download strategy into your mind and heart that will, in turn, bring a new ease to all your operations!

bring it!

When it was evening, His disciples came to Him, saying, "This is a deserted place, and the hour is already late. Send the multitude away that they may go into the villages and buy themselves food." But Jesus said to them, "They do not need to go away. You give them something to eat."
Matthew 14:15-16

Jesus challenges us as He challenged His disciples, who walked with Him on earth, to step into a whole new arena of faith. There is a faith-space that we need to step into, to see God move supernaturally on behalf of ourselves and others. *Faith* is required to change environments!

The disciples' response to the need of the crowd was to send them away, but Jesus instead asked them to feed the multitude. The very thought of this task completely overwhelmed the disciples; this was way too much pressure, especially when they considered that what they had in hand was grossly insufficient to feed five thousand men, plus the women and children with them.

And they said to Him, "We have only five loaves and two fish."
He said, "Bring them here to Me."
Matthew 14:17

Their focus was on the 'only,' the lack in the moment to fulfil the huge task. But Jesus exhorted them to just *bring it*. We too are often consumed and embarrassed by the little we feel we have to offer, knowing it is insufficient in comparison to the size of the need. We wonder if our contribution could bring any sort of change or relief, and in doing so, we underestimate how powerful our 'little' is in the hands of a miracle-working God. God just asks us to *bring it*. Let's hand over our *'only this'* to Him so He can bless and multiply it.

This is exactly what happened when Jesus fed the crowd. He received the small offering, blessed it, broke the bread, and distributed it to the disciples to feed the people. As they stepped into this space the loaves and fish miraculously multiplied in their hands, and not only were the people fed and satisfied, but twelve large baskets of leftovers were collected after the people had eaten! These were not small baskets either, but luggage-size baskets in which Jews would carry both their provisions and their hay to sleep on.

Have you watched talent quests on TV? Contestants on these shows are first asked about the item they intend to perform; then the judges invite them to begin, often using the words, "Bring it!" At the judges' bidding, these contestants then step bravely into that space on stage, believing they have a worthy contribution to make!

Jesus knew the boy's lunch was there in the midst of the crowd and *He called it out!* Jesus knows what is in you and I, and He calls us out of our 'small' and into that faith space. He wants us to *step out and bring it!* In His hands, our little will multiply into much. It just needs to be released and brought to Jesus!

Are you undermining what you have, viewing it as small and insufficient? Are you overwhelmed by the needs before you and seeking to send the pressure away? Today, get ready for some miracles as you hand over to Jesus what you have in your hand! Today, just bring it! God is so ready to receive your offering and multiply it to meet the need!

resign from management

Then the word of the Lord came to me, saying, "O house of Israel, can I not do with you as this potter?" says the Lord. "Look, as the clay is in the potter's hand, so are you in My hand, O house of Israel."
Jeremiah 18:5-6

Like a potter, God is shaping our lives as a vessel that will bring honour and glory to His name, a vessel that will honourably bear His label as His hands gently mould us into the original design that He outlined for us before the beginning of time. How faithful is God to work with us, invest in us, take time with us and lovingly guide us! God sees the end from the beginning. He sees our life's purpose, joy and effectiveness, and He shapes us accordingly to fit the call and direction He has carved out for our lives. God has the very best for us in store!

This scripture from the book of Jeremiah challenged me many years ago when we were looking to purchase a new property with the intention of relocating from the suburbs right into central Auckland. I found a slight hesitation within, preferring to locate a home we would love to purchase, before selling our existing one. I guess I was looking for a guarantee that the new house would equal or better the one we had! What I needed in that moment was to simply let God lead us and shape the future for us. That is faith! *We will never be able to take hold of a new and progressive promise until we fully release the known and familiar!*

Similarly, when the call to relocate to London appeared on the doorstep of our lives, faith needed to be activated to welcome it. To leave our country and grown family at that time was a far bigger step and more heart wrenching for me than previous smaller faith steps! In my inner contemplation, I wondered if God could potentially find someone else to fill the need in London. But God again spoke very clearly into my spirit, instructing me to *"resign from management."*

In essence, God was saying that I needed to take my hands off His plans, to stop trying to manage what He was instigating, to not change His call into a shape I would prefer or thought I could cope with better. Instead, an unconditional faith response was required, along with trust in God and a willing heart. When we try to manage and shape what God has directed, we forfeit internal peace! I am so glad that I listened to God and yielded to His hand as He shaped my life. In so doing, I found the grace to not only relocate to London, but to see churches planted and leaders released, going well beyond what Bruce and I could have hoped, dreamed or imagined! The journey was both challenging and rewarding as we discovered God's greater plan.

Maybe God is calling you to take steps of faith, but an element of management has found its way into your heart. God is simply asking you to yield to Him, to allow Him to shape your future as He has foreseen. If we seek to change the shape of God's design, we will also forfeit the exponential blessing that God will be faithful to outwork through our lives as we take steps of faith and obedience. He is the Potter and we are the clay!

What has God spoken to you regarding your future? Are you resisting the shape He planned for you? Today, repent of placing your hands on God's master plan, and yield to Him afresh. Let Him mould you as you yield to Him. You will be amazed as you experience God's best for your life!

fear-free

Then Saul said to him, "Why have you conspired against me,
you and the son of Jesse in that you have given him bread and a
sword, and have inquired of God for him, that he should
rise against me, to lie in wait, as it is this day?"
1 Samuel 22:13

Saul had a bad case of paranoia, being highly suspicious and wary of David, even though Saul was the one hunting David down! Saul was obsessed with the younger man, fearful of losing his position to him even though prophecies had confirmed David as Israel's next king. Saul's thinking was completely muddled and deluded. *Paranoia* is an extreme level of fear, characterised by a severe persecution complex and unwarranted jealousy. Because Saul had no conviction regarding his anger and jealousy toward David, his outbursts and reactions were out of control.

Saul lacked faith in God for his future. After a good start, Saul had failed miserably in his responsibility as king over Israel, losing his position to rule. If Saul had been humble and repentant, God would have granted him a new and fulfilling future! Saul was not able, however, to step aside from the paranoid fear that gripped his heart. *Role had become more important to him than relationship!*

Saul's suspicion of David was completely unwarranted. He was just projecting what was in his own heart upon David.

Keep your heart with all diligence, for out of it springs the issues of life.
Proverbs 4:23

What are you thinking? Are you a suspicious-minded person who deems others untrustworthy, constantly suspecting people of conspiring against you, believing that others are seeking to take something from you that rightfully belongs to you? *Paranoia* seeks to discredit others, sowing suspicion through innuendos about people they are threatened by.

Then Saul said to his servants who stood about him,
'Hear now, you Benjamites! Will the son of Jesse (David)
give every one of you fields and vineyards, and make you all
captains of thousands and captains of hundreds? All of you
have conspired against me, and there is not one of you who
reveals to me that my son (Jonathan) has stirred up my
servant against me, to lie in wait, as it is this day.'
1 Samuel 22:7-8 (parentheses mine)

Conspiracy is the formation of secret plans made jointly by people to commit an unlawful or harmful act. Because Saul was conspiring to end David's life, he automatically presumed that David had the same intent. His paranoia was built from his faulty thinking.

As a man thinks in his heart, so is he.
Proverbs 23:7

Faulty thinking could be likened to a faulty electrical system that houses the potential to short circuit the flow of the current. In Saul's case, his faulty thinking short-circuited the grace of God, resulting in negative energy and misdirected output. His paranoia, which Saul had failed to control, now placed him outside the flow of God's grace and favour—he had become a danger and a threat to David's life.

We can live *fear free* when we choose to credit others with good intentions, and if that is not the case, then we can look to God for His protection and intervention!

What fear or suspicion of others have you yielded to? What are you projecting from your own heart onto others? Credit others with good intentions and be free from obsessive fear! Today, allow God to deliver you from fear so you can possess your future!

prophetic prayer

*Now faith is the substance of things hoped for, the evidence of
things not seen . . . But without faith it is impossible to please
Him, for he who comes to God must believe that He is, and that
He is a rewarder of those who diligently seek Him.*
Hebrews 11:1, 6

Faith is the key in touching the heart of God to move on our behalf. God loves to hear us pray by faith in accordance with His will and what He has promised, expressing our belief in His faithfulness to make good His Word! We just need to open our ears and our spirit to hear what He is saying in any particular situation.

In my early years of ministry, I began to realise my faith wasn't as strong as I had believed it to be. Though I believed, my faith was somewhat anchored in the positiveness and determination I possessed as part of my nature. These strong attributes, though God-given, were inferior and inadequate to alter spiritual atmospheres and win spiritual battles! This scripture spoke to me on my journey of developing a stronger spirit of faith:

Finally, my brethren, be strong in the Lord and in the strength of His might.
Ephesians 6:10

Through this scripture quickened to my heart, I realised there was a strength available to me as God's child that to that point, I knew nothing about. Just as muscles weaken, losing the ability to flex if they are not exercised, so our faith-muscle can fail to develop when it is not challenged on a regular basis. My faith-muscle definitely needed developing, and I was on a quest to learn how this could happen.

The answer came to me through revelation regarding the power of *prophetic prayer*—not just praying hopeful, wishful prayers from my own mind, but searching out *the prophetic answer* to a need, problem or situation. I began asking God what was on *His* heart regarding a situation and then sending His word out prophetically to accomplish and meet that need. *Prophetic praying* always builds faith in our hearts!

*So shall My word be that goes forth from My mouth. It shall not
return to Me void, but it shall accomplish what I please.*
Isaiah 55:11

This exercise involved listening to the Holy Spirit and searching out the Word of God, so that faith could be born in my heart. It is our faith that overcomes the world and deals with any contradictions of belief. My confidence, discernment and prophetic insight grew, which in turn built my faith, not in what I could do or be, but purely in the word God had spoken into the situation. As a result, I found much joy in answered prayer!

Faith comes to our heart when God speaks, but *faith needs to be sent forth*. When we speak and declare what He has said, praying according to His plan and purpose, God's word will always hit the mark, either detonating enemy forces or bringing forth 'from nothing' God's revealed desires. What a great source of confidence and strength this exercise gave me as I grew my faith muscle and my ability to hear and believe God! God is so willing to share with us, but are we willing to seek Him out so our faith can grow?

How strong is your faith? Is your faith based on the Word of God and what God says, or does it rest in your own ability? Develop your faith muscle today! Search out God's prophetic word and allow faith to be birthed in your heart as you hear it. Faith always hits the mark!

this is the one

*Thus Jesse made seven of his sons pass before Samuel. And Samuel said to Jesse, "The Lord has not chosen these." And Samuel said to Jesse, "Are all the young men here?" Then he said, "There remains yet the youngest, and there he is keeping the sheep." And Samuel said to Jesse, "Send and bring him. For we will not sit down till he comes here." So he sent and brought him in. Now he was ruddy, with bright eyes, and good looking. And the Lord said, "Arise, anoint him, for **this is the one**."*
1 Samuel 16:10-12

We are all faced with choices in life. Many decisions are just small 'everyday decisions' that God expects us to handle well and in a mature manner. Other decisions, relating to future direction and our spiritual welfare, require us to seek God's confirmation.

Samuel had been commissioned to find and anoint a king for Israel, an important assignment, and one which would determine the ongoing welfare of the nation. Many options for a future monarchy were paraded before Samuel, namely Jesse's sons, some of whom looked like they could be 'the right fit' for the role. But Samuel's spirit did not bear witness that any of these young men were God's choice for the position of king of Israel, although in the natural, Eliab the eldest, stood out as seriously impressive!

God instructed Samuel in 1 Samuel 16:7, "Do not look at his appearance or at his physical stature, because I have refused him. For the Lord does not see as man sees; for man looks at the outward appearance, but the Lord looks at the heart." That's when Samuel knew that the task of finding the next king, although there were many worthy candidates, was incomplete. So he enquired further of Jesse whether there were any other living sons? When David entered, God immediately affirmed to Samuel that this was His choice!

Sometimes in our life-decisions, we know intuitively in our spirit that the answer still lies somewhere beyond what we immediately see. The temptation can be to press ahead regardless, to *'force the fit'* by taking a lesser option, only to find that God's blessing and exponential favour is not on this choice. When we force things to fit in any area of life, breakage can result from the pressure and strain. Though there may be many reasonable and promising options before you — even some that appear to 'fit the bill' — choose to follow that 'inner voice' and wait instead until you are confident that God has endorsed and approved your choice!

Peter saw beyond the natural and into the realm of the spirit, and Jesus affirmed him for His insight, for seeing and declaring who Jesus really was. In Matthew 16:17 we hear His words, "Blessed are you, Simon Bar-Jonah for flesh and blood has not revealed this to you but My Father who is in heaven."

God chooses to guide us in our decisions, saying,

> *I will instruct you and teach you in the way you should go;*
> *I will counsel you with my loving eye on you. Do not be like*
> *the horse or the mule, which have no understanding but*
> *must be controlled by bit and bridle . . .*
> *Psalm 32:8-9 (NIV)*

What choices do you need to make today? Have you simply settled for what is immediately before you? Are you 'forcing a fit' that God has not ordained? Today listen for God's, "This is the one!" or "This is it!" — the witness of the Holy Spirit, endorsing your choice! Don't be hasty in your important decisions, but be patient today, relying on God for His approval and favour.

line up

*Oh, that My people would listen to Me, that Israel would
walk in My ways! I would soon subdue their enemies,
and turn My hand against their adversaries.*
Psalm 81:13-14

Can you remember when you *'lined up'* as children at school to enter your
class room or get on a bus for an excursion, or even before venturing onto
the field for sport? The teacher would give the cue either by blowing a
whistle or shouting *"line up!"* to which you dutifully paid attention. When
we grow into adulthood, we discover, that 'lining up' continues to be a
way of life, whether it is at the checkout in the supermarket, queuing at
the ATM, or waiting at a box office to purchase tickets to a show!

There are many accounts in the Bible of Israel's failure to line up with
God's ways, of their non-attention to the boundary lines He had laid
down in His love for their safety and protection. Israel did not want to
conform—they chose not to listen but instead to 'jump the queue,' shifting
God's boundary lines to suit their own selfish pleasures, and demanding
to manage their own lives their own way! In doing so, they missed out
on receiving God's best and witnessing His mighty hand protecting them
from their enemies. In Psalm 81:16, God says,

*He would have fed them also with the finest of wheat; and with
honey from the rock I would have satisfied you.*

Israel missed out because they would not comply with God's instructions nor wait for His very best. There is an old saying that *"good things come to those who wait,"* but how often has impatience played a part in squandering the very best God has planned for us? What events can we recall where God required us to wait, even cautioning us to do so, but we 'broke line' and rushed ahead anyway, refusing to stand behind a delay or even the person God had positioned us before? Perhaps it is only now that we are realising what our impatience cost us!

God longs to lead us and reveal His mighty power to us. He desires to feed us with His very best and longs for us to inherit His promises. Are we 'lining up' in faith and expectation to receive from Him? One way to *line up* is to hear His instructions and stay within the boundary lines He has set for our lives. In Psalm 16: 7-6 (NIV) David wrote,

> *Lord, You alone are my portion and my cup; you make my lot secure.* **The boundary lines have fallen for me in pleasant places;** *Surely I have a delightful inheritance.*

The Psalmist knew the delights and benefits of God's choices for his life and chose to *fall into line* with God's best.

Let's resist pushing ahead and demanding our own way. Let's refuse to short-circuit God's blessings, choosing to not rush ahead, but to stay within His boundary lines. Let's wait upon Him, believing He will provide and release His blessings at the right time.

In Psalm 81:10 God says, "Open your mouth wide and I will fill it." God will satisfy us with answers, fill us with faith, and direct our steps towards His very best for our lives as we bring our hearts into submission to Him, coming before Him with an expectation to receive. As we *fall into line* with God's best, God will subdue our enemies and give us a clear passage forward!

🍃 *Have you been acting impulsively and impatiently instead of waiting for the blessings of God? Begin today by 'lining up your spirit' before God in prayer, expressing a desire to comprehend His pleasant boundary lines for your life. Decide today not to miss out on God's best!*

say the word

*Lord, do not trouble yourself, for I am not worthy that
You should enter under my roof. . . Therefore I did not even
think myself worthy to come to You. But* **say the word**
and my servant will be healed.
Luke 7:6-7

In Luke 7:1-10 we read of a centurion who had a sick servant. He sent his elders (those with authority) to plead with Jesus to come and heal his servant. This passage tells us they begged Jesus earnestly, stressing how deserving this centurion was! But as Jesus was journeying to the house, the centurion sent friends to Jesus with the words, "I did not think myself worthy to come to You, but *say the word* and my servant will be healed."

This centurion teaches us some important lessons about faith.

Faith seeks Jesus. In our everyday lives, we need faith like this centurion to seek Jesus about our circumstances, personal doubts, ill health, relational difficulties, financial stress, and general issues of life! We need to hear God speak into these situations! Our prayer to God should be, *"Say the word! I am listening for Your word of faith, wisdom, healing, affirmation, and direction!"*

God loves to speak into our lives! I have found that hearing a quickened and current word from Jesus settles me and releases assurance into my heart that God will be faithful to fulfil that very word. When I was praying for a very sick woman who was attributed only a one percent chance of survival, God spoke a direct word into my spirit, "She is already healed." So, every time I visited her in hospital, and although every organ of her body was on life support, I positioned her by faith and prayer on the other side of the cross, just as Jesus had spoken into my spirit.

To the glory of God, this woman survived and is a living miracle of the healing power of God.

Faith places you under His roof. Our tendency can be to want Jesus to 'come under our roof,' to answer our need according to our preference or pre-determined mindset. But in doing so, we reduce God and His fullness to the level of our limitations, weakness, biases and beliefs. The more powerful response is to place ourselves *under His roof*, to come under His authority and to hear what He says. That is where we will access greater revelation, and find our faith awakened to move mountains, heal diseases and access supernatural provision.

Faith attracts the attention of Jesus.

> *When Jesus heard these things, He marvelled at him,*
> *and turned around and said to the crowd that followed Him,*
> *"I say to you, I have not found such great faith, not even in*
> *Israel!" And those who were sent, returning to the*
> *house found the servant well who had been sick.*
> *Luke 7:9-10*

One quickened, current word from God can change a destination, a diagnosis, a mistaken belief . . . and a generation!

Is your faith strong enough that Jesus would 'turn around' and move in power on your behalf? Seek Jesus out today and ask Him to say the word over your circumstances. Place yourself under His authority, knowing that difficulty and distance is no issue to God. Let Him speak healing and release into your situation today!

hear me out

Then Peter answered and said to Jesus, "Lord, it is good for us to be here; if You wish, let us make here three tabernacles one for You, one for Moses, and one for Elijah." While he was still speaking, behold, a bright cloud overshadowed them; and suddenly a voice came out of the cloud, saying, "This is My beloved Son, in whom I am well pleased, hear him."
Matthew 17:4-5

I don't know what your immediate family is like, but our family has a really bad habit of not taking turns when it comes to speaking, of talking over the top of each other, not waiting for someone to finish speaking before another begins! We don't always *hear one another out*! This is usually due to being overly enthusiastic as opposed to rude. It's just too hard to wait your turn, especially if you feel you have something important to contribute to the discussion! I wonder if God wishes we would slow down and not talk over the top of Him either? We often interrupt before He's finished speaking, darting off at top speed before He has had the chance to give us the full picture or instructions.

Many of us are like this when it comes to assembling 'flat pack' furniture—we prefer to rush straight into the project, not giving time to reading the instruction manual first. Are you guilty of that?! On the mount of transfiguration, Jesus was seen by the disciples in His eternal glory. "His face shone like the sun, and His clothes became as white as the light" (Matthew 17:2). Moses and Elijah appeared there too, speaking with Jesus. This was too much for Peter! In his enthusiasm, he interrupted the moment with what he thought was a great idea—and he received a direct answer from heaven! In essence, God was instructing Peter that there was much more to be gained by listening rather than speaking too quickly. God was advising Peter to *hear Him out'*—not to rush ahead and thereby fail to grasp the full significance of the moment.

Have you ever offered a suggestion and had it refused? It is hard to handle at the best of times, but imagine getting a 'push back' from God Himself! Peter and John fell flat on their faces in fear . . . only to be lifted to their feet again by Jesus.

Over the years I have learned to let God interrupt me, to let Him have His say in my life. What God has said to me is largely the essence of this book—the result of listening when God has cut across my thinking, and lifted me to a higher level of understanding, believing and living!

Could there be more God wants to say to us, but we have not been giving Him the time or the opportunity? How many more specific instructions does He want to reveal or secrets does He want to share with us? He is often more willing than we are to wait around! Are we cutting God short in His conversation with us, opting to do all the speaking rather than the listening?

Let's apply this principle to the other people in our world. In our marriage, for example, are we hearing one another out? Are we giving each other the chance to speak and be heard? Without hearing, there can be no understanding and no validation of thoughts and feelings. With our children—are we hearing them and listening to what is important to them? If we are constantly interrupting or not expressing value in their thoughts and feelings, we are in danger of 'shutting down their spirit'! Let's be careful to *hear one another out*, understand each other better, and therefore become more relatable!

How could you become a better listener to the people in your world? Is there someone you are not hearing? Lean in today and really listen! Do you need to slow it down and hear God out? Make it your habit to meditate on God's Word today. Tune in, and hear all the amazing things God wants to reveal to you!

make a comeback

*For we all stumble in many things. If anyone does not stumble in
word, he is a perfect man, able also to bridle the whole body.*
Ruth 3:2

In the journey of life, we all stumble and we need to get up again. Sometimes
we need to return to the place we vacated or left empty because prevailing
doubt and fear caused us to fall. We need to make a 'comeback' against
the persuasion of the enemy, against wasted time and lost opportunities!

'Making a comeback' is often used in reference to clothes, fashion, careers, or
sporting records. It highlights the return of popularity and visibility after a
time of inactivity. Likewise in the spiritual, there are times we need to 'make
a comeback' from where we have been. Perhaps we have been struggling in
our faith, or living in the wrong location? We need to 'come back' if we are
to live victoriously and inherit the abundant life God has promised.

The book of Ruth tells the story of Elimelech, Naomi and their two sons,
Mahlon and Chilion. The family moved away from Bethlehem Judah
because of a famine in the land, relocating to the country of Moab. In
that place, disaster struck. Elimelech died, along with Naomi's two sons,
leaving her with only Ruth and Orpah, her two Moabite daughters-in-law.
Naomi was desperate; she found herself bereft and at the end of herself;
she knew she was in the wrong place and that life had turned against
them. After seeking God's direction, we read that Naomi "arose with her
daughters-in-law to *return* from the country of Moab, for she had heard .
.. that the Lord had visited His people by giving them bread" (Ruth 1:6).

Naomi set her direction to return home. She *stumbled* back to Bethlehem, condemned, grief-stricken and bitter! In her own eyes, Naomi felt worthless, having missed the mark in terms of the call of God on her life. Feeling like she had nothing to offer, she tried to dissuade Ruth, her daughter-in-law from accompanying her. But in returning, Naomi fell forward into the hands of God! She *stumbled onto her destiny*, and discovered that God could use even a once-bitter woman for His glory!

> *Now the two of them went until they came to Bethlehem.* **And it** **happened**, *when they had come to Bethlehem, that all the city was excited because of them; and the women said, "Is this Naomi?"*
> Ruth 1:19

God's grace welcomed her home! Although Naomi had the conviction to return, her heart feared the possible rejection or judgment that might have been directed toward her. Instead, Naomi and Ruth were received with warmth, celebration, and open arms.

In returning she recovered! God had already gone before Naomi as she purposed to return to her rightful inheritance, setting her and Ruth up to play an important part in history in the lineage of Jesus!

Are you in the place God has appointed for you, or are you in a foreign 'spiritual land'? Have you vacated your place because of pressure and are now suffering because of that decision? Make a decision to arise from doubt and fear, and return home. 'Make a comeback' today into the full purposes of God!

part ten:

courage

conviction

Now look, God Himself is with us as our head, and His priests
with sounding trumpets to sound the alarm against you. O
children of Israel, do not fight against the Lord God of your
fathers, for you shall not prosper!
2 Chronicles 13:12

As God's people, we should not be bound in condemnation, but be compelled by courageous *conviction*. Conviction is a firmly held belief or opinion. Perhaps you are aware of the saying, *"Have the courage of your convictions."* If we are strongly convinced of something, we should have the courage to act accordingly!

Abijah was a man who had strong convictions and acted on them. In 2 Chronicles 13:12, he appealed to Jeroboam, his opponent, to not engage in the battle he had pitched against him. In essence, Abijah was stating to Jeroboam, "You can't fight against God and expect to win." Abijah was thoroughly *convinced* that God was with him and had assured him of victory, even though the odds in the natural were not in his favour! Abijah was simply confident of victory because God was with him and *God cannot be defeated.*

We too need strong convictions to win in the battles of life, and especially in the battles that come against our faith. It is in the secret place with God that we develop our character and our strength to overcome temptation, anger or fear! Many people think that somehow, on the day a battle breaks out in their lives, they will become strong and brave, that they will 'have it all together,' but in the meantime they neglect to do the work of preparation internally. Those who win on the battlefield of life are the ones who have firstly engaged in defeating giants in their own lives and who have developed godly character! Those who procrastinate in their private training arena will often be the ones defeated by their own shortcomings on the battlefield of life! Deficiencies have a way of showing up under times of pressure and strife. Who we are when no one is looking won't be hidden, but will be exposed on the battlefield and in the challenges we face. God cannot back any discrepancy in our lives!

In 2 Chronicles 13:5-9, we see that Abijah told his opponent the reasons why he couldn't possibly win the battle. Rebellion, inciting rebellion and idolatry, he explained, were the factors that would contribute to certain defeat—even though, in the natural, he had the numbers!

Abijah displayed good character and *confidence through conviction* by warning Jeroboam that the battle would result in his demise if he continued. Instead of desiring his enemy's destruction, Abijah actually cautioned Jeroboam to retreat! Abijah's actions attest to the truth of the saying, "A man of character in peace is a man of courage in war."

Let's work on our character in times of peace, before the real battles emerge, so that our courage will not falter due to a lack of character! Let's cultivate attitudes that will enable us to engage in the skirmishes of life with a pure heart, concerned not only for our own wellbeing but displaying courage and concern for the opposition. When we know God endorses our heart preparation, we can have *strong conviction* that we will win against seemingly huge odds.

What conviction do you need to get a grip on? What confidence do you already possess as a result of deep conviction? Are there character traits you need to challenge in your own life to ensure you are equipped for life's battles? How might you 'do the inner preparation required' so you can engage in clean warfare? Today, rise up with confidence that God is with you, to help you overcome in the battle you face!

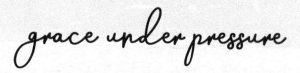

grace under pressure

But Jeroboam caused an ambush to go around behind them; so
they were in front of Judah, and the ambush was behind them.
And when Judah looked around, to their surprise the battle line
was at both front and rear; and they cried out to the Lord,
and the priests sounded the trumpets.
2 Chronicles 13:13-14

Courage has been described as *'grace under pressure.'* King Abijah gives us a great example of this. He knew he was anointed for war and that success was guaranteed. Even so, his *grace came under pressure*—completely surrounded by Jeroboam and his army, his enemy had taken him by surprise. As much as Abijah was gifted for war and graced with godly leadership, this was an unexpected situation, and one that appeared beyond his capacity. Finding himself in such difficulty, he needed a miraculous intervention by God!

Sometimes our grace comes up against a wall; surrounded by pressures and impossibilities, we too stand in need of God's supernatural intervention. We are not surprised when pressures challenge us in areas we are undeveloped in, but when pressure hits us in an area we have been graced for, this is harder to deal with. It can be disconcerting, especially if our confidence lies more in the grace and ability we inherently possess than we realised!

I reconcile this dilemma by reminding myself that when I cry out to God in my weakness, He lovingly helps me; when I am under pressure *in my grace zone*, God is at work, redeeming my gift, 'buying it back' with His blood, redeeming it for eternal purposes. If we rely on our grace and our gifting alone, we may find ourselves lacking in power because God's anointing is not on it. For example, there may be two singers, equally talented, but one displays a greater anointing. Why? Because the Holy Spirit is bearing witness that this person is not only graced, but has met the Giver of the gift, and has sanctified their gift for Kingdom purposes.

Abijah led the people by faith, depending on God for a miracle as they entered the land of the naturally impossible!

> *Then the men of Judah gave a* **shout***;*
> *and as the men of Judah* **shouted,** *it happened that God struck*
> *Jeroboam and all Israel before Abijah and Judah.*
> *2 Chronicles 13:15*

God moved in and took charge in this seemingly hopeless situation! We are all graced by God and empowered by Him, but at certain points we come under pressure, so as to shift our reliance from our own abilities to a stronger dependency on His power. Their miraculous breakthrough involved a *shout of faith!*

In Mark's gospel we read that the disciples, in obedience to Jesus, were crossing over to the other side of the lake when something big came up—a storm that they were unable to handle! I love the fact that Jesus came to them in response to seeing them 'straining at the oars!' Yes, they were in His will. Yes, they were doing what they were called to do. Yes, they were experienced in handling storms—but this one was too much for them, and when they cried out to Jesus, He figuratively placed His hands on theirs, releasing the strain and calming the storm. Mark 6:51 says, "They were greatly amazed beyond measure." This miracle went well beyond what the disciples were graced to do. It demonstrated *grace without measure,* through the release of Jesus' supernatural power.

In what areas are you under pressure, feeling puzzled or confused? What is your 'grace gift' that God is redeeming? Submit your gift to Him today. Let God place His 'super' on your 'natural', causing miraculous interventions. Today, meet the Giver of your gift afresh; allow God to take the **strain** *from your life as you cry out to Him. Expect the miraculous as you operate in your grace today!*

concentrate on the basics

Whoever can be trusted with very little can also be trusted
with much, and whoever is dishonest with very little
will also be dishonest with much.
Luke 16:10 (NIV)

How often do we want to rush ahead, to acquire 'all the extras' we think we might like? Perhaps it's accessories to go with an outfit, or technical gear to enhance the devices we already have? Sometimes we just need to decide, at least for the moment, to *stay with the basics*. Otherwise we can find ourselves in tricky situations, having run too far ahead of ourselves, creating a dilemma we then need to redeem.

In Luke 16, we read a parable about an 'unjust steward' who knew he was in danger of losing his stewardship. After contemplating how he could restore favour with his boss and his debtors, and thinking about what to do next, he decided to *do what he could do*—he would *employ his gift* to get him out of the sticky situation he found himself in. This man was obviously a gifted networker and a great salesman, so rather than look outside himself, he began to work what was already within. What a lesson for us!

What is your gift? What are you good at? Let's not take the gift we possess for granted, viewing it as ordinary and thus underestimating its effectiveness. From our viewpoint, our gifts may not appear that spectacular, but they are the very key to releasing us out of difficult situations and into the 'much more' of God!

What difficult situation do you find yourself in right now? Simply *use the gift* that God has bestowed upon your life by faith. I have received the gift of mercy, and when I employ it in prayer, in loving those in my world and in setting environments of faith, it just works!

In Luke 17, the apostles were questioning themselves and their ability to function. When they asked the Lord to increase their faith, He replied, "If you have the faith as a mustard seed, you can say to this mulberry tree, 'Be pulled up by the roots and be planted in the sea,' and it would obey you" (Luke 17:5-6). The disciples thought they needed more faith, but in essence, Jesus told them that working even the little faith they thought they had would produce great results. They didn't need more faith—they just needed to *exercise more* the faith they already had!

Bruce and I have found in our life together that it is the concentration and consistent use of the gifts and grace given us that has moved and changed things in our world, both naturally and spiritually! Success springs from what you do well. Doing the same thing consistently and faithfully 'over and over again' is what propels us forward into greater heights and larger spheres of influence.

When we concentrate on what we are good at and express faith in the gift that we already have, God can cause supernatural results to spring from it! Let's not 'overshoot' in our projections, going *beyond basics* before we have exercised them well, as we could well end up defeated and discouraged! Let's not look to other people's gifts, wishing they were our own. It has been said that *we are content until we compare!* Instead, let's give our attention to the 'bare essentials'—being happy with the person God has made us to be, and choosing to be content with the gifts and skills God has graced our lives with.

Consider the 'bare essentials'—relationships, friendships, marriage, family and community. Are you being loving, patient and unselfish? Are you spending time building your relationship with Jesus, praying, reading your Bible and exercising your faith? What about the stewardship of your possessions and responsibilities? Would you be happy to allow another to view your work ethic, or the cleanliness of your home? What about how you handle your finances?

Where are you 'overshooting'? Is there an area where you are concentrating on the bigger picture but failing in the 'here and now'? Appreciate the gift God has given you and use it well! Today, concentrate on the bare essentials and live, really live!

freedom fighters

*Be sober, be vigilant; because your adversary the devil walks
about like a roaring lion, seeking whom he may devour.*
1 Peter 5:8

Bravery and the display of courage in the face of danger are attributes we all greatly admire, especially when people risk their own lives to fight for freedom for others! I have been greatly inspired by the story of Nancy Wake, who fought on behalf of others in the Second World War. Born in Wellington, New Zealand but raised in Australia, Nancy moved to France as a journalist in her early twenties. As a result of the atrocities she witnessed as enemy forces rolled into France, Nancy made a decision to engage in warfare, resolving *'right then and there'* to do everything within her power to resist evil forces and destroy the right of the enemy to prevail. As an operative in the resistance movement, Nancy transported wounded soldiers in an old truck she had converted into an ambulance, evacuating many British soldiers as well as creating safe houses and safe pathways across the mountains into Spain, from where they could safely return to Britain. Nancy's reputation for bravery became well known; her effectiveness was even acknowledged in the enemy's headquarters, where she was dubbed the 'white mouse'—the one they sought but could never catch! For her service to humanity, Nancy became the most decorated woman in the Second World War!

As God's people, we too, are *freedom fighters*, called to stop the tide of evil and save as many people from destruction as we can. We need to identify threats, including subtle, destructive threads of unbelief, then intercept and push back potential attacks of the enemy. We need to create safe passageways along the road of our spiritual journey, not only for ourselves but others, just as Nancy Wake did for the soldiers who needed to be evacuated and rescued from the line of fire!

We also need to watch out for the landmines that the enemy has planted to harm and maim us. Proverbs 4:26 says, "Ponder the path of your feet, and let all your ways be established." Panic and despair are some of the landmines the enemy may have planted, intending for them to blow up in our face, but we have the power and authority to defuse them and render them powerless! Staying calm in the battle is imperative. Panic has killed more pilots than bad weather, simply because panic clouded their ability to think clearly. That's why we need to *have our wits about us,* possessing a God-given ability to think and act clearly in times of threats and pressure. Let's not be those who are 'scared out of their wits,' bewildered, confused, and subject to enemy domination.

Paul exhorted God's people not to be ignorant of how the enemy operates when he wrote,

> *. . . in order that Satan might not outwit us.*
> *For we are not unaware of his schemes.*
> *2 Corinthians 2:11 (NIV)*

No enemy force can outwit the Holy Spirit! He will give us the 'in' on the enemy's plans, so we can deny him any opportunity. We need to be *in* the Word of God and prayer in order to be a commando in God's army, sometimes 'rolling with the punches,' but coming up triumphant every time! Today, let's establish ourselves as *freedom fighters* that others can depend on!

What landmines might you need to defuse before they destroy you and people in your world? Today, create safe places and paths for yourself and others, places of equipping, mending and training in the truth of God's Word. Be ready to counteract any scheme of the enemy. Acknowledge and be thankful that Jesus, the greatest freedom fighter of all times, won the victory for you on the cross so you could live in freedom!

spiritual equipment

And He said to them, "Go into all the world and preach the gospel to every creature. He who believes, and is baptised will be saved; but he does not believe will be condemned. And these signs will follow those who believe. In my name they will cast out demons; they will speak with new tongues; they will take up serpents and if they drink anything deadly, it will by no means hurt them; they will lay hands on the sick and they will recover."
Mark 16:15-18

Every war requires equipment to fight with! Nancy Wake knew she needed to equip herself to fight in the French Resistance Army in the forests of France. She prepared herself for the warfare by learning *hand to hand combat* so she would be physically able to resist and overpower an attacker. She also learned parachuting, enabling her to enter the French forest undetected. During a brief spell of training in England, she learned *Morse Code* so she could communicate with personnel in Britain regarding supplies for the troops in the forest, and she learned how to *handle explosives,* which equipped her to blow out bridges before the enemy.

When the army's radio was confiscated in a raid, Nancy knew the location of another one involved a round trip of approximately four hundred kilometres over mountainous terrain! Nancy volunteered to fetch the radio, which many thought was too much for her physical capabilities, but they agreed, knowing a woman would look less suspicious at the checkpoints. Nancy completed the entire journey on a bicycle in seventy-two hours; when she returned, she was in great pain as all the skin had rubbed away from the inside of her thighs. What courage she displayed, but what dedication she had demonstrated in order to train and be equipped in warfare for this great cause!

As God's children, we have the greatest cause before us. We are in the midst of warfare to see evil defeated and the Kingdom of God advance as lives are being saved! Are we doing what is required by availing ourselves of the equipment Jesus has already made provision for us to use? It starts with a commission we need to respond to "go into all the world and preach the Gospel" (Mark 16:15).

This is no small task, but it is possible through the authority God has entrusted to us as He sends us forth to minister. We just need faith similar to the apostle Paul who, when shipwrecked on the island of Malta, simply shook off a deadly viper into the fire, showing no alarm, and amazing the inhabitants who watched on expecting him to die! Paul knew his authority and was not afraid for his life, and we read in Acts 28 that when the leading citizen's father got sick, Paul simply went and prayed, laying hands on him, and the man was instantly healed.

We need to demonstrate the same courage in the face of danger. I personally love this aspect of warfare, taking back from the enemy what he seeks to steal, and witnessing healings and deliverance instead! One of my great desires is to see the power of God at work! God has infused a godly courage into my soul over the years to fight spiritually with His anointing. I avail myself to be fully equipped and empowered by Him to rise to this task!

If we were planning to climb a mountain or deep-sea dive, it would be wise to prepare thoroughly, ensuring we have the right equipment to keep us safe. Let's ensure that we are also well equipped to fight spiritual battles on behalf of others.

Have you responded to the great commission to "go in Jesus' name"? What is the fear that stops you? Identify the equipping that needs to take place to release courage and confidence into your spirit today. Know that you have been given authority in Jesus' name to defeat all the enemy's plans. Today, rise in power to take territory, arming yourself with spiritual equipment so the battle can be won!

resolutions

*Now it came to pass, when the time had come for Him to be
received up, that He steadfastly set His face to go to Jerusalem.*
Luke 9:51

Resolve is the quality of being *resolute*, of having a great determination to win, not shrinking back or vacillating. Jesus was resolute—He steadfastly *set His face* to go to Jerusalem!

A *resolution* is the solution to a doubt, problem or question. We often make resolutions at the beginning of a year in response to areas we desire to see changed or improved. Perhaps we resolve to read a certain number of books, or get our weight to a certain point, or exercise a certain number of times each week. Some resolutions are fulfilled, while others simply lay around waiting!

The parable of the unjust steward tells the story of a man who was in a sticky position. Having been accused of wasting his master's goods, he was now being called to account for his stewardship! This unjust steward asked himself,

> *. . . What shall I do? For my master is taking the stewardship
> away from me. I cannot dig; I am ashamed to beg.*
> Luke 16:3

Then he comes up with an answer, a cunning plan, a *resolution* to combat his previous laziness, carelessness, and dishonesty. He decided to get on the right side of his debtors, doing them a favour by letting them pay only what they could afford toward their outstanding debt. In that way, he hoped they would reciprocate the favour when he was in need.

Surprisingly, his master commends him for his efforts. In Luke 16, Jesus exhorts us to be smart in the same way, but for what is right; to look out for ourselves by making wise decisions and implementing wise resolutions, to make changes so we can overcome current setbacks and continue to advance!

Change comes firstly through a decision. Decisions create a place of stability, while procrastination never solves anything! This man's world was rocked, but he came up with a solution. Yes, it was cunning, but it was also creative! How much more creative should we be as God's children, to solve dilemmas and implement change? People's worlds often implode, simply because they don't have a solution or a resolution that will bring about a change of prospect.

Are you going through some sort of collapse emotionally, physically, or relationally? Has the 'boat' of your life overturned in the midst of the storm? God's anchor of hope, when thrown out, can give you stability to turn and face the tide with solutions!

Let's use our adversities to stimulate us to creative survival. Any challenge we face can be resolved in God! Let's stop wasting our time and energy bailing water from our boat, and instead find the solution that 'puts the bung back in' so we can move forward without any fear of sinking. Let's call on the *creative solutions* of God to answer the dilemmas we face today!

Where are you procrastinating or losing energy by bailing water out of your sinking boat? Ask God to stimulate a resolve for survival! Seek Him today for creative solutions in the face of your storm.

the same spirit

But if the same Spirit who raised Jesus from the dead dwells in
you, He who raised Jesus from the dead will also give life to your
mortal bodies through His Spirit who dwells in you.
Romans 8:11

How wonderful it is to be 'Spirit-filled'! The Bible tells us that when we are Spirit-filled we are full of the *same Spirit* that raised Jesus from the dead—we have supernatural power to overcome what is naturally impossible!

There are times in our journey when we may feel afraid and intimidated; often we are sabotaged by our own thoughts, doubts and fears as we view the enormity of the task before us. A certain rise of nervousness in our mind forfeits the courage that we wished we had or know we should have as God's child and favoured one! Feelings of inadequacy overwhelm us at times and can cripple us, causing us to feel imprisoned and incapable emotionally and physically of responding to the challenge before us.

Romans 8:11 helped me significantly, even in its simplicity. This scripture testifies of God's great power in raising Christ from the dead. I have learned over the years to trust in the *resurrection power of God* for breakthrough in the supernatural realm, which in turn greatly empowers my natural responses.

Subconsciously we can adopt a certain way of thinking that dictates what needs to happen and in what order so that adverse situations can be overcome. Perhaps we say, "When certain conditions are met and my emotions are calm, then I will find the courage to proceed with whatever God is asking of me as a child of faith." God, however, has a different order, wanting us to first rise by faith, even when our feelings may pull us in the opposite direction.

Let's realise that conditions weren't perfect when Jesus rose again. He was bound in cloth and sealed in a tomb! No one came to release Him; no one rolled the stone away so He could reappear alive. Jesus just broke right on through that tomb, nullifying any physical law that declared it impossible.

Nothing we are seemingly bound to, imprisoned by, or physically restricted from is too difficult for the resurrection power of Christ that indwells us to overcome! Jesus did not require the situation to be perfect before He rose, and neither do we. When we understand that the *same spirit* that raised Christ from the dead also dwells in us, we can respond to any challenge. As we draw on God's resurrection power within, we can break through every fear and reserve! God's order is *'faith first, evidence second.'* The stone of the tomb was later rolled away as evidence that Jesus had risen—it was impossible to hold Him down!

What can we learn from this? We don't need our circumstances or our emotions to be perfectly in order before we rise in faith and obedience! We just need the Holy Spirit's power to give life to our mortal bodies, releasing conviction and confidence within, and overshadowing our fears. It's time to *break through* in situations and see God move supernaturally though our lives!

Is something causing you to cower or to live smaller than God intended? Is there any order in your thinking and believing that you need to release to Jesus? Today, choose to break free from fear and timidity by acknowledging that you have the same spirit within you that raised Christ from the dead. It's time to rise, to break through, to see God move by His Spirt on your behalf. Faith first, evidence second!

resurrecting hope

*And behold one of the rulers of the synagogue came, Jairus by name.
And when he saw Him, he fell at His feet and begged him earnestly,
saying, "My little daughter lies at the point of death. Come and lay
hands on her, that she may be healed, and she will live."*
Mark 5:22-23

Have we pronounced certain aspects of our life 'dead' when in fact they are only sleeping, awaiting an awakening? Perhaps past dreams, relationships, health or finances haven't gone well, and as a result we may have considered them dead, nailing them down under the lid of hopelessness and removing the casket from our sight. For many areas we have dismissed, we may just need to use the *'crowbar of faith'* to release those nails and *call forth* buried dreams, desires and visions! Maybe we have let things die because of condemnation, failure, disappointment or unbelief? Today, God wants us to *call them forth!* We just need to cooperate with the Holy Spirit.

The account in Mark 5 looked like one of those *'too late'* moments:

*While he was still speaking, some came from the ruler of the
synagogue's house who said, "Your daughter is dead. Why
trouble the teacher any further?"*
Mark 5:35

We can think, mistakenly, that for ourselves and certain aspects of our life, it's 'too late, the expiry date has passed, the cause is hopeless.' Perhaps we have *called time* on the possibility of those dreams and desires ever living or thriving. Let's speak *to* the situation instead! Jesus spoke to the crowd who were mourning at Jairus' house, saying, "Why make this commotion and weep? The child is not dead, but sleeping" (Mark 5:39). Then He spoke to Tabitha, the little girl, taking her by the hand, and she arose to life.

What do we need to speak to? What do we need to take by the hand, saying, *"Rise up in the name of Jesus"*? Have we closed down some part of our soul and are now living with a resigned hopelessness, our faith having become redundant and inactive? Proverbs 13:12 says, "Hope deferred makes the heart sick, but when the desire comes, it is a tree of life."

As humans we cannot live without *hope*; a projection of a good and desired future. Sorrow and grief have a way of inviting death into our lives! 2 Corinthians 7:10 puts it this way: "For godly sorrow produces repentance leading to salvation, not to be regretted: but the sorrow of the world produces death."

Medical science advocates that an incredibly high percentage of sicknesses are psychosomatic, caused by a deep internal sorrow! As the curtain is drawn on hope, dreams and desires get buried, and a spirit of death begins to work its way from the inside out, eventually affecting the wellbeing of a person's mind and body. As Christians, we have the opportunity to turn away from this and to renounce any associated hopelessness or unbelief that seeks to settle in our spirit! A strong hope in Jesus keeps us alive and well and able to navigate life in a healthy manner, even through a time of sorrow!

Let's *call time* on sorrow, bitterness, disappointment, judgment and unbelief. Let's stop resuscitating those attitudes which need to die, make peace with them, and let them go! Let's stop giving breath to things that need to cease to be! Lost dreams and desires are waiting to be resurrected; they need fresh faith and hope so they will spring to life again. Let's call them forth!

Have you adopted the sorrow of the world and allowed a spirit of hopelessness to come upon you? What do you need to call forth that you have prematurely pronounced dead? What 'casket lids' need to be released in your life? Today, call time on attitudes of death and hopelessness! Believe today that you will see the resurrection power of God at work bringing to life those hopes that were 'only sleeping'!

the bravest

Therefore do not cast away your confidence, which has great
reward. For you have need of endurance, so that after you have
done the will of God, you may receive the promise.
Hebrews 10:35-36

We can easily assume that *the bravest* ones are those who look the strongest, have the biggest muscles or talk the fastest, but this is not always the reality. Those who look strong and sound strong in the natural are not always the bravest when it comes to a battle for what is right! Take David, for example. He was simply a shepherd-boy, possibly the youngest person on the battle field when Israel faced Goliath, but he was able to defeat the giant who had absolutely terrorised the men of war in Israel!

Every year in Australia and New Zealand, we celebrate ANZAC Day, commemorating the brave soldiers who both stood or fell in battle, in the war for freedom for our nation and the nations of the world. The Greek historian, Thucydides, wrote these famous and inspiring words regarding bravery:

> *"The bravest are surely those who have the clearest vision of what*
> *is before them, glory and danger alike, and yet go out to meet it."*

Courage has clear vision. It may not have the best resources, the best training, or the strongest army, but courage has the clearest vision of what needs to be done and what it will take to overcome the odds!

In 2 Chronicles 13:1-3 we read about Abijah, a man with clear vision in battle:

> *In the eighteenth year of King Jeroboam, Abijah became*
> *king over Judah. He reigned three years in Jerusalem . . . and*
> *there was war between Abijah and Jeroboam. Abijah set the battle*
> *in order with an army of valiant warriors, 400,000 choice men.*
> *Jeroboam also drew up in battle formation against him with*
> *800,000 choice men, mighty men of valour.*

With the odds against him two to one, Abijah could have been intimidated. His army didn't look the strongest of the two armies, his troops numbering merely half of Jeroboam's. But Abijah had a clear vision to defend what God had entrusted to him.

Clear vision gives us the *courage* to change what we need to change! Clear vision also works in our favour when it comes to overcoming the odds. Whatever looms large before us or threatens to come against us, the odds cannot defeat us when we know what God has promised! Yes, we could get hurt in stepping out to defend what God has entrusted to us, but *the bravest* go anyway, not unaware of the danger, but meeting the challenge head on with courage in our heart.

Abijah knew the danger but he still lined up to fight because of the *clear vision* he had in his heart. 2 Chronicles 13:16-18 says,

> *And the children of Israel fled before Judah, and*
> *God delivered them into their hand. Then Abijah and*
> *his people struck them with a great slaughter; so 500,000*
> *choice men of Israel fell slain. Thus the children of Israel were*
> *subdued at that time; and the children of Judah prevailed,*
> *because they relied on the Lord God of their fathers.*

They relied on God and He granted them the victory! There's the key to bravery right there! Bravery is the ability to stay present, stay confident and not shrink back, but to *keep lining up in the battle of faith!*

🍃 *Has something caused you to shrink back and lose your confidence? Are you underestimating your strength because the odds don't look that great? Today, express a reliance on God, thankful that He is on your side and will fight on your behalf! Step onto the battle ground with* **clear vision***, and God will impart courage into your heart.*

stand up spirit man 1

Watch and pray, lest you enter into temptation.
The spirit indeed is willing, but the flesh is weak.
Matthew 26:41

Our *spirit man* within needs to *stand up*, to withstand battles that rise against us and to subdue the wars that rage internally, competing for our affection! If we fail to *stand up* in our spirit, we may find ourselves being knocked down by the appetites of our flesh, or our soul. As Christians, we are exhorted to live *from the inside out*; from our *spirit man,* the part of us that comes alive in Christ through salvation.

Our conscience, intuition and communion with God make up our *spirit,* whilst our mind, will and emotions make up our *soul,* and our sight, smell, touch, taste and hearing constitute our *flesh.* Our *spirit* needs to be the control centre of our life, from where all decisions and responses are made. If our *spirit man* is not in charge, our soul and our flesh will sabotage our reach, limiting us to only what is possible physically, mentally or emotionally, and we will fall short of apprehending the larger, more expansive life God has planned for us.

The Bible encourages us to walk in the spirit; then we won't fulfil the lust of the flesh! It describes the struggle as an internal 'tug of war'!

For the flesh lusts against the Spirit,
and the Spirit against the flesh; and these are contrary
to one another, so you do not do the things you wish.
Galatians 5:17

Our *spirit man* needs to stand up, to guard our God-given conviction so our flesh doesn't override our commitment. *"Stand up, spirit man"* was a statement God gave me personally, an exhortation to resist yielding to any fleshly desire that sought to compete internally or persuade me toward another direction. It was a call to the *control centre* of my life, to my *spirit man,* to stand up and to rule over fleshly, selfish responses.

We need our *spirit man* to stand up against the temptation of the flesh! David was described as "a man after God's own heart." He was a shepherd, a worshipper, a warrior, a leader and a king, yet we witness him responding wrongly on several occasions in his life. In the scriptures we read that David made a response from the *flesh.* Viewing a beautiful woman caused lust to dominate his thinking and reasoning. On that occasion, his 'spirit man' did not stand up. He yielded to his flesh, committing adultery with Bathsheba, Uriah's wife. 2 Samuel 11:2-4 says,

> *Then it happened one evening that David arose from his bed and . . . from the roof, he saw a woman bathing. And the woman was very beautiful to behold. . . then David sent messengers, and took her . . . and he lay with her.*

How did this happen to a person such as David, whose heart was fully God's? It happened because he became careless. He *disengaged from the battle*—from his critical call to lead Israel into victory. David stayed home while his troops fought on the field! In the moment, on sighting Bathsheba, he was weak-willed, and yielded to the voice of his flesh.

When our flesh is in control, it produces lust, a desire to get rather than give. The emphasis shifts to *self*, which says, "fill me, feed me, satisfy me, entertain me." David allowed his sensual drive to override his spirit conviction! His sin had serious consequences—he sinned against a brother, took something that didn't belong to him, robbed a man of his life, and brought reproach on Israel. The outcome was barrenness within and trouble without.

Today, ask yourself what is at the control centre of your life? From what aspect of your being are your decisions being formed? What temptations are you falling prey to? Is something continuously knocking you down? Today, call your spirit man to stand up and take control! Get back on the battlefield — it's the safest place to be!

stand up spirit man 2

Now David had said, "Surely in vain I have protected all that this fellow has in the wilderness, so that nothing was missed of all that belongs to him. And he has repaid me evil for good. May God do so and more also to the enemies of David, if I leave one male of all who belong to him by morning light."
1 Samuel 25:21

Did you know that even when we are right, it's possible to be sincerely wrong? Our conviction may be right, but our response to people and situations that oppose our conviction, may be wrong! There are times we simply need our 'spirit man' to *stand up* and respond with an attitude of humility, trusting God for His vindication, rather than responding from a natural and carnal mindset.

David would have come completely unstuck if he had followed his own instincts in response to the 'withholding spirit' of Nabal. If it had not been for the intervention of Abigail, who appealed to David not to take matters into his own hands, David would have succumbed to the temptation and forfeited his position as future king over Israel. David had been *right* in his request to Nabal, as it was customary in that culture to seek an offering for a favour shown; but David was *wrong* in his response when denied! David's response was from his soul, one of anger and planned revenge! His desire was to punish Nabal for being unwilling to repay the favour and help David's men in their time of need.

In that moment, David was on the wrong battlefield — thus, he responded out of anger. When your soul is in control, it produces *ungodly ambition*, a temptation to prove yourself right, to win over another, to engage in an unhelpful battle that potentially endangers and hurts others. We've all heard it said, "Two wrongs don't make a right."

Defensiveness is a soul-ish response, an unhealthy spirit of competition that raises its head in an ugly manner, seeking to win at any cost! Even when we are right, if we respond out of ambition in the soul, we are wrong.

In 1 Corinthians 3:1-4, Paul asks,

For where there are envy, strife and divisions among you, are you not carnal and behaving like 'mere men'? When one says "I am of Paul" and another "I am of Apollos," are you not carnal?

Carnal responses force others to pick sides, causing wedges to come between people. However, when we are led by the Spirit we can step into the gap as Abigail did, to deflect and discourage foolish responses. There is an alternative—we can remain angry at someone for their actions, or we can 'stand in the gap' and pray for them.

"Stand up, spirit man" and back down when you need to! Back down from being competitive, judgmental and opinionated. Back down from the need to win every argument because it appeals to the vanity of the mind. This will not result in a win, but invariably a loss, damaging and defeating relationships and morale.

When we respond with revenge and judgment from the ambition of the soul, the Spirit of God within is grieved. A bigger person internally will forgive, letting go of offences and wrongdoing. Jesus did just that when He said, "Father, forgive them for they know not what they do" (Luke 23:34). We can do the same. Today, let's tell our spirit man to *stand up*. Let's surrender our right to retaliate, humiliate and take revenge on another. Let's resign from all competition and trust God to act on our behalf. James 4:5 reminds us that, "the Spirit who dwells in us yearns jealousy." The Holy Spirit is our fierce defender and He will take action, vindicating us when we are wronged. He jealously desires to lead us in His everlasting ways!

Are you responding wrongly from your soul or from a position of ambition? Is there a space within that needs to always be right or to always prove itself? Does your anger turn ugly, lacking humility and the grace of God? Stand up, spirit man, and respond to any provocation today with humility, prayer and faith!

stand up spirit man 3

Every commandment which I command you today you must be
careful to observe, that you may live and multiply, and go in
and possess the land of which the Lord swore to your fathers.
Deuteronomy 8:1

"Stand up, spirit man" with courage and conviction to take hold of all God has placed in your spirit to possess, to be that person who influences and inspires others to also possess their future in Christ! Why does our spirit man need to stand up? So we can live above temptation and reach further than we ever could in the natural, possessing our God-given inheritance, and dispossessing anything that seeks to lay claim to our lot!

God has a mandate for each one of us to live out, a revelation both individually and corporately with our name on it! 1 Kings 19 caught my attention one day, causing me to wonder if Elisha was surprised when Elijah threw his mantle on him, or not? Did it come like a 'bolt out of the blue,' or was he prepared? We read,

. . . so he departed from there, and found Elisha
the son of Shaphat, who was ploughing with twelve yoke
of oxen before him, and he was with the twelfth. Then Elijah
passed by him and threw his mantle on him. And he left the oxen
and ran after Elijah, and said, "Please let me kiss my father and
my mother, and then I will follow you."
1 Kings 19:19-20

Elisha was not surprised! There had already been a preparation of heart during years of service assisting the prophet Elijah. Although Elisha had fulfilled many menial tasks as a servant, Elisha had already *'been there in the Spirit'* —he was 'at the ready,' poised to step up into the greater call of God at the appropriate time. When the Spirit is in control, it produces vision! There is a knowledge of the will of God and direction ahead.

When God spoke into our spirits what He had purposed for Bruce and I, they were things well beyond our qualifications and ability, yet there was *a knowing in our spirit* of the accuracy of these things in God. This spirit-comprehension of the mission He had placed within included travelling to other countries to minister! In response to this call, I coined the phrase, "I am amazed but not surprised!" I was amazed that God would call two unqualified people from a small rural town to serve on platforms around the world, but equally, I was not surprised as we had already *been there in the Spirit!*

We need to allow ourselves to *go there*, to *dream in the spirit*, to allow God to reveal things to us that we couldn't possibly see with our natural eyes! We can choose either to stay grounded in the realm of our soul, limited by our mind and reason, or we can soar as we venture into the realm of the spirit.

Today, *"stand up spirit man"* by opening your eyes to what God wants to show you; release your spirit to dream about your godly purpose, His kingdom, and His mission! When responding to the dreams of the Holy Spirit, resist the temptation to censor them, edit them, scale them back or dismiss them! Submit them to God so He can form the right environment to produce the results, and share them with others who are over you and responsible for you! *"Stand up spirit man,"* and witness the revelation of God come to pass!

Have you released your spirit to dream in God? What dream are you holding close and trusting God to bring about? Today, keep dreaming! 'Go there' in prayer and vision, allowing God to show you in your spirit the greater plan He has for you.

simply worship

Job . . . was blameless and upright,
and one who feared God and shunned evil.
Job 1:1

When testing comes our way, worship may be the last thing we feel like engaging in, but *worship is the key* that unlocks the door to freedom in spite of the trials and tribulations that may surround us! Job is a man who is often referenced when people go through tough times, as he had some heavy-duty situations to deal with in his lifetime!

Why was Job tested so hard when he was such a good man? It hardly seems fair that all these devastating troubles would descend upon such a good man's life. The enemy taunted God, claiming that Job only served God for what he would receive in return. In other words, the enemy was asking if Job would still worship God, if his life wasn't so good? In response, God allowed Job to be tested. We read,

" . . . does Job fear God for nothing? Have You not made a hedge
around him, around his household and around all that he has
on every side? You have blessed the work of his hands, and his
possessions have increased in the land, but now, stretch out Your
hand and touch all that he has and he will surely curse You to
Your face!" And the Lord said to Satan, "Behold all that he has is
in your power, only do not lay a hand on his person." So Satan
went out from the presence of the Lord.
Job 1:10-12

God, confident in the sincerity of Job's heart and his ability to endure and withstand any pressure to denounce Him, gave Satan permission to test Job. The enemy is on a quest to buffet God's people. In Job 2:2 we read of Satan pacing up and down the earth in a frantic manner, wanting to afflict people so they will falter in their faith. Job's response to this time of hardship was not what the enemy expected at all. Job's first instinct was to respond Godward with *worship*! He says,

> *Naked, I came from my mother's womb and naked*
> *shall I return there. The Lord gave and the Lord has*
> *taken away; Blessed be the name of the Lord.*
> *Job 1:21*

Job knew that Satan didn't have any power over him unless God had first allowed it. That this was not an equal battle, as God is in no way subject to demonic forces! *Worship* was a lifestyle for Job, and even in severe testing, the most natural response for Job was to *worship*!

Is worship our default setting when times get tough or when we are tested in some way? Is our first response to honour God in a time of need as well as in a time of blessing? Job did not falter in who he was, but remained steadfast in *worship* and in *faith*! The Bible tells us that "in all this, Job did not sin nor charge God with wrong" (Job 1:22). He remained confident, knowing and understanding the nature and heart of God. Although he was in a period of pain and suffering, Job knew he would emerge stronger on the other side! In Job 23:10 we read his words, "But He knows the way that I take; when He has tested me, I shall come forth as gold."

What an example Job has set for us all! Gold is formed in the fire—likewise our faith and character are formed in the heat of testing. Something strong, beautiful and valuable comes forth in our lives when we remain in *worship*—something solid, enduring and inspiring! How will we emerge from the flames of testing? Let's learn from the life of Job to maintain faith and worship in the fire of affliction. Job remained constant and God restored Job's losses, releasing to Job twice as much as he had before!

What is your 'constant' in the furnace of affliction? Is it worry or worship? Do we give God the same honour in affliction as in times of blessing? Today, attribute to God His magnificent power over any scheme of the enemy. Steady yourself to face any testing today with faith and worship!

simply trust

I have heard of You by the hearing of the ear, but now my eyes see
You. Therefore I abhor myself and repent in dust and ashes.
Job 42:5-6

In the fire of testing, we discover who we are. Job went through a devastating time of affliction in his life. He was human, just like you and I, with very real emotions and responses. He was not superhuman, and he suffered deeply, devastated by the calamities that suddenly came his way. In the face of these trials, Job chose courageously to trust God even though questions arose in his heart as to why God would allow these events to take place. *We have an adversary!* Satan's plan was to overwhelm Job with a rapid succession of calamities, giving him no opportunity to recover from one disaster before another devastating report would reach his ears. We can probably all identify with this feeling of deep despair—when not just one problem, but many, seek us out all at once. Often, we hear people ask, "Why me?" This is where our trust and faith in God is tested.

What Job didn't know was that Satan had asked God if he could test him; his goal was to completely overwhelm Job in the hope that his faith in God would falter. God had every confidence in Job that he would remain strong and steadfast! But we witness Job suffering on many fronts; his peaceful existence no longer existed, his income was destroyed, his stock was plundered and consumed, his health deteriorated and, in a final blow, his family was eliminated by a great wind which brought a building down upon them. At this point, Job arose and tore his robe. In brokenness and grief, he "shaved his head and he fell to the ground and worshipped" (Job 1:20). Job still chose to worship *and trust* although he had no answers to the questions plaguing his heart and mind. God's silence in the situation was also unbearable—no explanation from God was forthcoming! To *trust* is to believe firmly that something or someone is strong enough to hold you when things don't appear to be that steadfast!

We would never board a ship or plane that did not have the capacity to carry us safely to our destination. In life, we make informed choices regarding who or what we are going to trust; we decide what or who is competent to sustain and protect us. Many people express distrust regarding others because their confidence has been destroyed through testing times, and sadly, they opt not to trust again. In response to Job's trust, God reached out to him, seeking to capture his attention and reveal more of His strength and power! God did this, not by answering Job's questions, but by inviting him instead for a walk through creation. Issuing Job a challenge to 'man up,' God sought to question *him* instead. In Job 38:3 we hear His words, "Now prepare yourself like a man; I will question you and you shall answer Me."

As God revealed to Job the wonder of creation and how everything has a pattern and purpose and flows together with ease, Job was totally overwhelmed. God's power and glory on display caused Job to repent, admitting that he had uttered things he did not understand, things far beyond his ability to comprehend. God led Job into a greater level of trust in His faithfulness and commitment to Him, not only in his successes, but also under life's pressures. In our trials, we may be tempted to call God to account, cross examining Him with our attitudes and accusations. We need to realise that the enemy is seeking to overwhelm us, to make us feel out of our depth and beyond our ability to cope or survive. We need to know when to battle and take authority in adverse situations, and when we need to *simply trust*, knowing He has it completely in control! Let's emerge with a fuller understanding of who God is by allowing Him to show us the bigger picture and His glory amongst it all!

Do you feel overwhelmed by circumstances? Are you trusting or struggling in your trials? Today, let God show you the bigger picture. Let Him take you for a walk around His garden and open your eyes to His greatness! Affirm your simple trust in God today!

getting up again

Now the Lord said to Samuel, "How long will you mourn for
Saul, seeing I have rejected him from reigning over Israel?"
1 Samuel 16:1

Under God's guidance and in response to the people's request, Samuel commissioned and anointed Saul as the first king of Israel, yet the appointment failed miserably. Saul had a problem following instructions, and God made a choice to terminate his reign over the nation.

Samuel took Saul's demotion really hard. He was disappointed by Saul's disobedience and inability to rise to the challenge of kingship. Perhaps Samuel allowed some of Saul's failure to deflect upon himself. God said to Samuel that it was time to move on! Enough time had lapsed in mourning Saul's failure, and Israel was still in need of a godly leader. It was time for Samuel to *get up again*!

Is disappointment or rejection lingering in your heart over things that didn't quite work out or didn't produce what you had expected? Maybe you are rightfully mourning the loss of someone very dear to you—such a painful process to work through!

To everything there is season, a time for every purpose under
heaven . . . a time to weep, and a time to laugh;
A time to mourn and a time to dance.
Ecclesiastes 3:1,4

The seasons of life can cause different emotions to surface that sometimes surprise us, even though they may be legitimate expressions in the situation. This scripture illustrates, however, that there is a *'grace period'* for certain seasons, and to prolong the season beyond its appointed time will leave us weakened, vulnerable and exposed! God has put a 'time frame' on seasons, alerting to us when *time is up* or *time has expired.* God was saying to Samuel that it was time to move on. A new season awaited! God reassured Samuel of success in his quest to find a new king. He said,

> *. . . Fill your horn with oil, and go; I am sending you to Jesse the Bethlehemite, for I have provided myself a king among his sons.*
> 1 Samuel 16:1b

Do we need to *fill our horn with oil* again? Prolonged loss and disappointment have the potential to drain us and leave us feeling empty and bereft, concentrating on the lack we feel. But God Himself promises to fill us again and again with 'fresh oil' so we can resume our position of strength and anointing, and outwork God's purposes through our life. We just need to ask to be filled! On being filled with the Holy Spirit once again, Samuel was encouraged to go in response to God's sending, to complete the mission appointed to him!

What have we left undone because of a lingering season of grief and loss? There is joy in rising, in waking up to a new season and moving forward with renewed faith and expectation. Psalm 30:5 assures us that, "weeping may endure for a night, but joy comes in the morning."

Are you stuck in a season? Have you 'overstayed' in a certain mindset or emotion? It's time to get up and go again! Today, ask for renewed strength to move on through the empowerment of the Holy Spirit. Go where God directs, knowing that in that place, answers await you! Begin afresh today. As you enter the new season God has for you, expect significant God encounters

on the back of

*"Many a time they have afflicted me from my youth; yet they
have not prevailed against me. The plowers plowed on my back;
they made their furrows long." The Lord is righteous;
He has cut in pieces the cords of the wicked.
Psalm 129:2-4 (MSG)*

In times of trials, it is so important to choose the right responses so we can make it through safely to the other side. Although trials may be confusing and painful in the moment, we can know with certainty that *God has our back!* The psalm include many accounts of people's afflictions, but they also tell of triumphant victories over the enemy by God. These afflictions are not described merely as scratches on the surface of the skin that resulted in a small show of blood, but as furrows, large indentations in the flesh incurred from the strength and sharpness of a plough. In *The Message,* the experience is translated,

*. . . they have hurt us more than can be expressed,
ripping us to shreds.*

This paints a picture of the intensity of pain inflicted and damage done, but the psalmist also expresses strong faith in the prevailing power of God to deal with the enemy on Israel's behalf.

We may feel like large ridges or furrows have been ploughed on our back because of pain and affliction we have endured or untoward circumstances we have been subjected to that have indelibly marked our lives. But just as the farmer chooses what he will plant in the furrows of his field, we get to choose what will grow in the furrows of pain in our lives—bitterness and hatred will constantly fester and expose the wound, causing more pain, while seeds of faith and forgiveness will yield a harvest well beyond their natural potential! What can be seen in our lives? Is it a scar that disfigures, or a plentiful harvest as a result of trusting God and His ability to make all things good?

On the back of trials, testing and pain can come great victories and beauty, and on the back of mistreatment and criticism can come love and mercy toward others! Joseph was able to love his brothers even though they had caused him severe pain, because he had chosen to trust God to fulfil His purposes in his life. In Genesis 50:20 we read Joseph's words, "But as for you, you meant evil against me, but God meant it for good, in order to bring it about as it is this day, to save many people alive."

As we trust God through the trials and persecution that come our way, choosing faith instead of fury, God wages warfare on our behalf against those who have 'run roughshod' with disdain and anger over us.

> *But He was wounded for our transgressions,*
> *He was bruised for our iniquities; The chastisement for*
> *our peace was upon Him, and by His stripes we are healed.*
> *Isaiah 53:5*

On the back of the betrayal of Jesus and His timely death on the cross came salvation, forgiveness, and redemption for all mankind, for whoever chooses Jesus as their Lord and Saviour. Let's view the furrows on our backs in a new way! The seeds of faith we sow into our furrows will in time reap a beautiful harvest!

Today, acknowledge the pain of the past, or even the pain of the present. What can you plant by faith on the back of an incident that has hurt you deeply? Choose to forgive today! Acknowledge God's faithfulness to triumph in the situation, to bring forth good on the back of your trials and testing!

thank you, fear

In everything give thanks; for this is the will
of God in Christ Jesus for you.
1 Thessalonians 5:18

Did your parents ever make you say *"thank you"* when you didn't really want to? When I was in primary school, I was mortified to receive a Christmas card from a boy in my year group. In those days a gesture like this indicated that the young man had feelings for you that he wanted to convey. In this instance, I wanted to totally ignore this gesture, only to find out that my parents insisted I thank him personally! To my young ten-year-old self, this wasn't a gift I cherished or was thankful for!

We are generally quick to be thankful for situations that bless us, delight us or prosper us, but how about those things that are hard to handle and have even been potentially damaging? Fear is an example. Can we find the courage in our hearts to 'thank the fear' that has buffeted us—sometimes relentlessly—over the years?

Can we thank the fear that we tried to avoid at all cost, or the fear that prompted us to run and hide? What about the fear that caused us embarrassment and shame, that confirmed our self-doubts and decimated our self-worth?

As we discover Christ, we discover that the fear itself may have been the very agent that pushed us firmly into God's presence and into His Word. This positive outcome is possibly fear's 'worst nightmare'! Instead of being immobilised by fear, we have exercised courage! We have used the fear to motivate us to find God!

"Thank you, fear!" If it hadn't been for you, I would not have discovered:

- God's perfect love that casts out all fear

- God as my Safe Refuge to whom I can continually resort

- God as my Designer from before time began, the One by whom I am fearfully and wonderfully made (Psalm 139:14)

- God as my Gift-Giver, the One who has wired me a specific way to accomplish His powerful purposes

- God as my Vinedresser, who has chosen me to bear much fruit and for that fruit to remain

- God as the Anointed One who has also anointed me with fresh oil and the power of the Holy Spirit

- God as my Conqueror who has imparted the *same Spirit* in me to overcome the enemy

- God as my Source of knowledge and revelation

- God as my constant Companion, the One who is with me eternally

Paul testified similarly to God's grace discovered through trials. In 2 Corinthians 12:9-10 (TPT) he says,

I will celebrate my weaknesses, for when I'm weak
I sense more deeply the mighty power of Christ living in me.
So I'm not defeated by my weakness, but delighted! For when
I feel my weakness and endure mistreatments—when I am
surrounded with trouble on every side and face persecution
because of my love for Christ, I am made yet stronger.
For my weakness becomes a portal to God's power.

So thank you, fear! Hats off to you! I have become who I am through the pressure you brought against my mind, my heart, my life. I have discovered a treasure in Jesus!

Today, make a list of all you have discovered about God and yourself in the face of fear, and thank God!

perspective

*The Philistines stood on a mountain on one side and Israel stood
on a mountain on the other side with a valley between them.*
1 Samuel 17:3

Perspective is the lens through which we view a particular object or situation; it often stems from an attitude or experience that has affected our belief system either negatively or positively!

Have you ever stood on a mountain and taken in the amazing view? Everyone appreciates mountaintop experiences and the perspective afforded from an elevated position! We can have the mindset that life should simply be lived from one mountaintop experience to another, but often the biggest victories come from engaging in the battle in the valley!

We may view the valley with a fearful perspective, that in descending to face the enemies that intimidate us, our lives will be in danger. This fear has the potential to overwhelm and defeat us. Before we have even begun the challenges and the odds may appear far too big.

In scripture, Goliath the Philistine looked impressive; not only did he have a reputation of being a champion in battle, he also possessed intimidating height and strength, plus some serious fighting gear! Goliath was also very loud and boastful in his challenge to the army of Israel. In 1 Samuel 17:10 we hear his words:

And the Philistine said, "I defy the armies of Israel this day; give me a man that we may fight together."

Goliath was self-assured and confident that he would win over any Israelite who came out to fight. His perspective was that he had the advantage over any Israel soldier due to his size! We hear the term *advantage* being used in games such as tennis. When a player or team get to the position of *advantage*, they are poised to take the opponent down and win the game!

For forty days, morning and evening, Goliath presented a challenge to the army of Israel, but no one volunteered to step forward and meet him in the valley. Their *perspective* was one of being disadvantaged, hopeless, and easily defeated. Except for David. His *hearing* was different—he heard Goliath's taunts as being directly against the Lord God of Israel. David heard a defiant, proud, 'loud mouth' pitching himself against the Almighty God. So David volunteered to fight Goliath that day—in the valley!

Then David said to Saul, "Let no man's heart fail because of him; your servant will go out and fight with the Philistine."
1 Samuel 17:32

Let's not be like the army of Israel who shrank back because of the spirit of intimidation that presented itself through Goliath's threats. They felt seriously 'disadvantaged,' small in their own sight, and unable to overcome the enemy. Let's respond instead like David, destroying every force that seeks to reduce us and tower over us with lies and intimidation.

David's *perspective* came from the confidence he had gained in God when he had defeated a lion and a bear while protecting his father's sheep. His confidence to fight Goliath rose when he heard the audacity of the claims of this giant. David knew he had the *advantage* because God was on his side. Let's change our perspective and engage in the battle before us! Let's step into the valley and destroy the power of the enemy, with all his threats and intimidation, once and for all!

Are you confident that with God on your side, you have the advantage over every enemy force? Today, let God infuse you with His courage! You are assured of victory through Jesus!

part eleven:

provision

god's supply

*And my God **shall supply** all your need according
to His riches in glory by Christ Jesus.*
Philippians 4:19

When we think about *supply*, we think about having enough of all we need, not just to survive, but enough to stretch into the future so we can thrive and prosper in life. Before setting about our day or going on a hike or playing sport, we usually ensure we have enough water with us, or that water will be readily available to keep ourselves hydrated. Otherwise, our energy will drain and dehydration or exhaustion could be a real possibility. Water is one of our primary needs. Without water we wouldn't survive very long, and our thirst would not be quenched.

Just as we need natural water to satisfy our natural thirst, our souls are also thirsty to find meaning and satisfaction in life. Jesus met a woman at a well who was relationally and emotionally bankrupt. He spoke about the water *He could supply*—water that would fully satisfy her inner thirst and her severe spiritual and social dehydration!

> *Jesus answered and said to her, "Whoever drinks of this water will
> thirst again, but whoever drinks of the water that I shall give him
> will never thirst. But the water that I shall give him, will become
> in him a fountain of water springing up into everlasting life."*
> John 4:13-14

The water Jesus was offering her was the security of connection with Himself, a source which would not only satisfy the deepest longings of her soul, but would overflow from her life into others! When the Samaritan woman gratefully received what Jesus offered, it became in her, *"a fountain of water springing up into everlasting life"* just as He said. The woman who had been despised and alienated by her community because of her past activities now had become a *resource, a supply* that others gathered around!

> *And many of the Samaritans of that city believed in Him because
> of the word of the woman who testified,
> "He told me all that I ever did."*
> John 4:39

The desire to belong is a huge thirst in every human heart. We crave being acknowledged, loved and celebrated. Our souls thirst for care, community and connection, and we tend to experience problems in whatever area of life these thirsts have not been met. Only Christ can fully meet this internal thirst! We need to connect with Jesus who satisfies our inner thirst entirely, and *supplies* all we need for our future through His riches in glory.

The *water supply* for a city is made functional by the connection of enormous pipes through which huge volumes of water flow. For vitality and fullness of life to flow, we need to be firstly connected to Jesus and then to others. Life just flows better and more powerfully in connection! *Disconnection* will cause a dehydration of spirit rendering us dry, barren and lacking. Let's find *God's supply* for our thirsty souls!

How connected are you to Jesus? How connected are you to others? Today, deal with any isolation or disconnection in your life, and recover your vitality! Draw from Jesus' supply and find true satisfaction and fullness within.

even champions need water

*Then he became very **thirsty**; so he cried out to the Lord
and said, "You have given this great deliverance by the hand
of Your servant, and now shall I die of **thirst** and fall
into the hand of the uncircumcised?"*
Judges 15:18-20

Strength is admirable. We can't help but stand in awe at the achievements of athletes, scientists, inventors, weight lifters and the like. We also admire people who have defied the odds and survived tough times intact and with a healthy and happy spirit. These champions possessed an inner strength that allowed them to persevere in the struggle and which subsequently pushed them over the line of success! We can look at these strong characters and think they need little, that somehow life is just easier for them. But *even champions need water*!

Samson was a champion in the Bible who successfully and singlehandedly defeated the Philistines, winning a spectacular victory against them with the jawbone of a donkey. Talk about supply! *The supply of the Spirit of the Lord* came mightily upon him! However, the conquest was not enough in and of itself, to sustain him. Samson returned to thirst.

Samson was in danger of being weakened and his life was threatened, even after a significant victory. But God in His grace provided—He opened a rock, out of which water poured to sustain and strengthen Samson. We can achieve and amass many significant victories in our lives only to find ourselves always returning to thirst, both in the spiritual as well as the natural. The victory is not enough in itself; only Jesus can fully satisfy!

Elijah was another champion who accomplished many spectacular feats but found himself, after significant victories, in a place of great lack. In 1 Kings 19:4 we read, "But he himself went a day's journey into the wilderness, and came and sat down under a broom tree. And he prayed that he might die and said, 'It is enough! Now, Lord take my life, for I am no better than my fathers.'"

A great hopelessness entered Elijah. Instead of taking on the enemy, as was his usual custom, he ran from the enemy! Lacking in connection, feeling isolated, and believing he was the only man left standing, Elijah begun to despair of life itself. His cry of faith for God to release supply was lacking—he resorted to complaining instead! In essence, Elijah was just exhausted, hungry and thirsty, and therefore vulnerable to the enemy.

A number of years ago, Mexico City experienced a phenomenon that became known as the 'Sinkhole Syndrome.' The city was originally built on a large underground lake with small underground rivulets feeding into it. However, due to over-extraction of water from the area's subsoil, an unexpected problem occurred. As the rivulets dried up, the ground began to open under the pressure and weight of the city, causing big buildings to collapse like a pack of cards!

Sometimes we can have the mentality that when we reach certain milestones or pinnacles, life will become easier and our needs will not be as great. We are surrounded by people who have reached great heights in their careers and are using their gifts in society, yet they still struggle within because the thirst of their soul is not satisfied. Sadly, many famous movies stars and singers, despite winning accolades and awards, have had their lives shortened because on the inside they remained miserable, empty and unfulfilled. Jesus is our Champion, the One who is able to satisfy our inner thirst. Whatever feats we accomplish, let's not forget to tap the provision we have in Him to be refreshed, renewed and continually refilled with His Holy Spirit.

Today, acknowledge Jesus as your Source, the one who grants you strength and success. Acknowledge that you will never surpass your need for Him, that victories alone will not sustain you. Draw on Jesus today for your supply!

rent-free

But I want you to know, brethren, that the things which happened to me have actually turned out for the furtherance of the gospel, so that it has become evident to the whole palace guard, and to all the rest, that my chains are in Christ; and most of the brethren in the Lord, having become more confident by my chains, are much more bold to speak the word without fear.
Philippians 1:12-14

How confident are we in the ability of our God to provide? Hopefully we all have wonderful testimonies of God intervening in our lives, providing for us, releasing us, and delivering us from situations that were intended to bind and imprison us. Paul, one of Jesus' 'greats,' had the utmost confidence in God's provision in every situation he faced, even while in prison!

Situations in life can bring confinement at times to our external world, but we can learn to live in a larger space *internally* because our trust is firmly established in God! Over our lifetime we will all experience our 'Joseph' prison, where the external environment tests the internal strength of our conviction. In that place of restriction and maybe even false accusations, we have important choices to make; will we get bigger and better, or smaller and bitter? External restrictions have a way of testing internal resolve. Why would God allow this? At times He permits delays or restraints so we can develop internal capacity to handle what He wants to fully release! Proverbs 24:10 tells us that "if we faint in the day of adversity, our strength is small."

Paul had absolute trust in God's provision and faithfulness even when imprisoned for his faith. He knew that *while he was serving time, time was serving him* opportunities to glorify God! Paul was never diverted, never dissuaded from his purpose—therefore he never wasted opportunities even in times of restriction. His faith gave him favour with Felix, the governing authority and through him, God made provision for Paul to be granted accommodation *rent free!*

> *So he commanded the centurion to keep Paul and to let him have liberty, and told him not to forbid any of his friends to provide or visit him . . . Then Paul dwelt two whole years in his own rented house and received all who came to him, preaching the kingdom of God and teaching the things which concerned the Lord Jesus Christ with all confidence, no one forbidding him.*
> Acts 24:23; 28:30-31

From this *rented space*, Paul was able to touch and persuade countless people regarding the truth of Jesus, as well as write many letters to the existing churches, which we benefit from reading today!

Man cannot restrain what God chooses to release! Don't despair if you find yourself in a time of confinement due to circumstances beyond your control. God can make good out of this season. Let's re-evaluate our lives, rewrite our prayers, and revamp our expectation with a greater faith in God who makes everything work out for good! Perhaps it is in this sphere that we have an opportunity to gain a new appreciation of what was already there, to see what was available to us all along—provision within our reach that we may have failed to recognise! When we find ourselves in a space we had not planned or a place of restriction, we can be sure that God has *rented space* in the spirit for us to remain fruitful—to perhaps even produce some of our very best work! *God is not restricted by the boundary lines and times of man!*

Are you finding life and situations restrictive in any way at this time? Have you allowed 'bars of confinement' to reduce your faith? Today, realise that God has made provision for you. He has granted you a 'rent-free space' in the spirit, enabling you to be more productive than ever before. Thank God today for His accommodation in every situation and the bountiful supply of His Spirit!

sit down

Oh, taste and see that the Lord is good;
Blessed is the man who trusts in Him.
Psalm 34:8

Have you ever entertained guests, but as much as you invited them to sit down, they remained standing? Somehow this impacted on the whole environment, not creating the relaxed atmosphere you had imagined and hoped for? Your goal for the occasion had been to take weight from people, to give them a reprieve from the daily pressures of life by creating a pleasant surrounding and serving great food. Somewhere in the depth of your heart you just wished they would *'sit down!'*

I am sure Jesus longs for us at times to *sit down*, not in apathy or laziness but in a mode of expectation to receive and be filled with the finest He has to offer. Some years ago, on a very busy day, with much to accomplish, I heard the Holy Spirit whisper into my spirit that He wanted to host me that day. He wanted me to *sit down*, even in my busyness, and let Him serve me. My heart responded with gratitude to the invitation!

Some of us may struggle with this. We feel a sincere urgency to fulfil God's call to host His presence, to host a pending move of God, and we busy ourselves with associated tasks! However, even in our sincerest desire to be productive in God's work, or to be successful in our careers, our families, our sports or our other endeavours, we sometimes miss the invitation from God Himself to pause and be refreshed by Him. How much more effective would we be as God's hosts here on earth if we allowed ourselves to be personally hosted by the Spirit of God, receiving His provision—to *taste and see* all the goodness He has spread before us?

As I worked that day, I sensed and acknowledged the Holy Spirit hosting me, serving me, waiting on me—and my spirit delighted and fed on God's portion set before me! When we have enjoyed a great meal out, we are inclined to freely talk to others about the experience, recommending the chef, the menu and the restaurant. How much more, when God feeds us with the finest of His love, truth and revelation, will we want to share our experience of His goodness!

Have you missed the invitation to '*sit down*'? Have you simply tossed the invitation into the 'later tray' of your mind, being more consumed or anxious about the immediate tasks that demand your time and attention? Could you be allowing the urgent to rob you of the important? Are you settling for something less than the best portion from Jesus? Maybe you sincerely intend to sit down but you succumb instead to the pressure of the 'to do' list, and let the moment of opportunity pass?

Tasting takes time. Life-changing moments happen as Jesus encounters us. Feasting on all He has set before us causes our spirit to be revived and renewed in His presence. A relaxed approach is necessary to savour, digest and fully enjoy His presence and provision. When we sit at God's table, let's absorb His fare! Let's allow Him to delight our hearts and open our eyes wider and wider to the goodness He has stored up for all those who love Him!

Have you accepted God's invitation to 'taste and see' how good He is? Have you taken time to sit down and be hosted by His gracious Holy Spirit? Today, let God take some weight off you as He feeds you with His finest of fares! Talk about the provision of His goodness to others!

tap the source

*Give ear, O Lord to my prayer, and attend to the voice
of my supplication. In the day of my trouble I will
call upon You for You will answer me.
Psalm 86:6-7*

Thirst is demanding and draining. When we are thirsty, we can think of nothing but our need for water to quench the thirst within and revive us. Unmet thirst destroys. In New Zealand, tragically, we have one of the highest rates of youth suicide in the developed world. We live in such a beautiful country, yet even this is not enough to satisfy the inner thirst for love, belonging and a vibrant hope for a better future. This thirst is a craving for authenticity, value and meaning in life. We need a spiritual awakening in our nation and in the nations of the world to fully meet this cry; such thirst needs the prayers of men and women, boys and girls, to intervene in prayer and counteract every lie the enemy uses to destroy and prematurely end life.

Samson understood the demand of thirst. He knew that he was unable do what he was called to do without God's help, that his supply, not only to perform supernatural acts, but for his very existence, came directly from God. At the beginning of his ministry, Samson's thirst reminded him of his own humanity and vulnerability!

> *You have given this great deliverance by the hand of*
> *Your servant and now shall I die of **thirst** and fall*
> *into the hand of the uncircumcised?*
> *Judges 15:18*

God responded to Samson's cry for help! He intervened with supernatural provision.

In Judges 15:19 we read,

> *So God split the hollow place that is in*
> *Lehi, and water came out, and he drank; and his*
> *spirit returned and he revived. Therefore, he called*
> *its name En Hakkore which is in Lehi to this day.*

En Hakkore means, "the spring of the caller." The provision of God was released when Samson called! Samson drank, and his spirit to fight and push back oppression returned. How good are we at calling on God to provide our needs and refresh our supply when needed? Another name for *En Hakkore* is, "the well of him who cried." It is the supplication well! Supplication is the action of asking or begging for something earnestly or humbly.

Let's *tap the source* for our needed supply! God leans in to hear our cry, to intervene supernaturally on our behalf and provide, but we need to cry out to Him! In Psalm 3:4, David wrote, "I cried to the Lord with my voice, and He heard me from His holy hill." God can supply all our needs!

Is your spirit thirsty today? What is your heart's cry? Is there a seemingly impossible 'hard rock' before you that needs to split open today so supply can come forth? What is the supply you need? It could be as simple as 'perseverance' or 'patience.' Cry out to God today and release a spring that satisfies both yourself and others!

cover me

He shall cover you with His feathers, and under His wings you shall take refuge; His truth shall be your shield and buckler.
Psalm 91:4

Have you ever asked someone to *cover for you*, maybe at work or at home, while you attended to some situation that arose unexpectedly, a need that was urgent, out of the ordinary, and out of your control? More than likely you would have made a phone call to a friend or colleague, asking them to cover your responsibility or commitment. Being a reliable person, you wouldn't allow things to just drop through the gaps—you would make arrangements for someone to cover you, right?!

In our Christian walk we sometimes become more aware of areas in our life that need our attention, responsibilities that demand more time. Our 'spirit man' requires more energy to accomplish the task before us! God wants us to grow *internally*, so we can extend ourselves *externally!* We so desperately need His covering and protection while we stretch!

Ruth was well aware of her vulnerability. She needed the covering of her nearest kinsman to fulfil the mission that had engaged her heart.

And after Boaz had eaten and drunk, and his heart was cheerful,
he went to lie down at the end of the heap of grain; and Ruth
came softly, uncovered his feet, and lay down. Now it happened at
midnight that the man was startled, and turned himself; and there,
a woman was lying at his feet. And he said, "Who are you?"
So she answered, "I am Ruth. Take your maidservant
under your wing, for you are a close relative."
Ruth 3:7-9

Ruth was asking Boaz, her nearest relative, to *spread the corner of his garment over her*, to *cover* her, redeeming her from a life of poverty and uncertainty. This became my personal prayer as I realised that what I had been 'wearing' up to that point was inadequate for where I was going in the future. In the natural, it was like a garment I had outgrown. I could try and force it to fit, but the truth was, parts of my body would become exposed and visible! In other words, I would not be fully covered! Rather than constantly tugging at the 'old garment' hoping it would oblige, I needed *a larger-size garment in the spiritual* to cover the growth and development of my life.

As I stretched in response to the ongoing call of God in my life and the greater responsibilities accompanying that call, I was very conscious of needing more of His covering! Knowing I needed His mantle to cover me as I entered another season of demand and effectiveness, I began to sing, *"Cover me. Extend the border of your mantle over me,"* and I kept singing those words over the next year! God is so willing to cover us when we ask!

As Christians, we acknowledge Jesus as our Saviour. He is the only One who can cover us from the power of sin and death, through His amazing blood shed for us on the cross. However, we need the *continual covering* of Jesus as we enter into spiritual territory and exercise Kingdom authority. Like Ruth, we need to ask Him to *cover for us*, rather than attempt to take on spiritual challenges in our own strength. Failing to do this leaves us exposed and vulnerable to opposing principalities and powers. God is our nearest Kinsman, our Redeemer, and He wants to protect us!

Do you have a desire for 'covering,' for God's mantle to fully cover you? Are you attempting to take on spiritual challenges without being fully covered? Where are you exposed to the attack of the enemy and in need of God's covering? Today, acknowledge Jesus as your nearest Kinsman, and allow Him to redeem and cover you.

as far as the east is from the west

Bless the Lord O my soul, and all that is within me, bless His holy name! Bless the Lord, O my soul, and forget not all His benefits. Who forgives all your iniquities, who heals all your diseases, who redeems your life from destruction, who crowns you with loving kindness and tender mercies, who satisfies your mouth with good things so that your youth is renewed like the eagle's.
Psalm 103:1-5

Have you ever worried or been anxious about who you may meet up with again one day, maybe someone from your past who bullied you or ridiculed you, or took advantage of you? Or maybe you are anxious about what may come head on to meet you, past failures or mistakes that you assume hide around every corner, poised to jump out and expose you? Perhaps you worry that circumstances from the past may reappear in the future in the form of poverty, neglect or shame?

Psalm 103 tells us that God has *covered it all!* There is nothing and no-one outside His reach! God has freed us from all shame and condemnation by dealing with every penalty that was due us because of our mistakes and failures. In Psalm 103:11-12 we read,

> *As the heavens are high above the earth, so great is His*
> *mercy toward those who fear Him. As the east is the from*
> *the west, so far has He removed our transgressions from us.*

When we sincerely repent before God and receive His forgiveness, God removes our transgressions from us *as far as the east is from the west!* In reality the east and the west are never going to meet; that's how far he has distanced our mistakes from us! Jesus made provision for our transgressions. He paid the penalty for our sin once and for all, through the shedding of His own precious blood on the cross! In Christ, we don't have to keep meeting up with our failures, revisiting regrets, or fearing shame will turn up unexpectedly and unannounced, 'hand-in-hand' with condemnation. We can learn from past failures, but we don't have to dwell with them! What good news it is to know we are pardoned—that God has made complete provision for all our shortcomings. He has paid it all in full!

> *If we confess our sins, He is faithful and just*
> *to forgive us our sins and to cleanse us*
> *from all unrighteousness.*
> *1 John 1:9*

Could there be areas in our life yet to be accounted for? In our everyday affairs, when we reconcile our bank statements with our current finances, the aim is to make them balance. We do this by taking into account *any unpaid expense* yet to be shown on the statement, revealing whether we are in credit or debit! It's the same in the spirit. We need to keep short accounts and seek God's provision of forgiveness to wipe out every debt of sin. Sin is a costly item that, apart from Jesus' intervention, leaves us in debt and despair. Today, let's receive His forgiveness for whatever issues may still remain outstanding!

Today, itemise the 'expenses' in your life, things yet to be accounted for. Has anything gone under the radar that needs to be repented from? Today, thank God that when you repent, He forgives all your sins and removes them as far as the east is from the west. You don't have to meet up with them ever again!

our greatest weapon

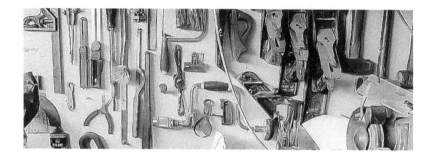

*When he came to Lehi, the Philistines came shouting
against him. Then the Spirit of the Lord came mightily upon
him; and the ropes that were on his arms became like flax that is
burned with fire, and his bonds broke loose from his hands. He
found a fresh jawbone of a donkey, reached out his hand
and took it, and killed a thousand men with it.*
Judges 15:14-16

Samson engaged in an unusual warfare against the Philistines! Other judges in the Old Testament, like Deborah, deployed armies to defeat the enemy, but Samson was just a 'one man army' standing against the Philistines! What were the odds of him overcoming them?

God supplied Samson with a really unique weapon—the jawbone of an ass! It was the thing Samson could put his hand on in the moment that God used to defeat the enemy. This was a most bizarre weapon, but it was totally effective in slaying a thousand Philistines. How incredible! But ultimately, it was God's supply and anointing upon Samson that brought about the real victory.

We too are engaged in warfare; we have a very real enemy who wants to strip us of our power and authority in God. God has supplied us with the greatest weapon of all time—the Gospel that frees us, delivers us, strengthen us, equips and empowers us! When we come against spiritual powers, too many people stop short of using the greatest weapon ever supplied because of unbelief, preferring to elevate their own intellect or employ their natural skill. But all these will fall short of gaining true victory against spiritual forces. We cannot win apart from the Gospel of Jesus Christ!

The apostle Paul wrote,

*And my speech and my preaching were not with
persuasive words of human wisdom, but in demonstration
of the Spirit and of power, that your faith should not be
in the wisdom of men but in the power of God.*
1 Corinthians 2:4-5

God's power is released when we activate the Gospel, share the Gospel, and claim the victory of the Gospel which was won by the 'unique warfare' of Jesus, who lay down His life for us so that we may live eternally. This may sound foolish to our carnal way of thinking, but it is "the power of God unto salvation" (1 Corinthians 1:18).

Our warfare is unique to each of us. Some battles we fight with others, and some battles we fight alone, but the common denominator is the Gospel of Jesus. The message of salvation and the testimony of God's power and forgiveness in our lives remains the best weapon to change society and reverse the negative statistics in our nations. We can win wars by winning hearts!

🍃 *Thank Jesus for your salvation and for the Gospel, the greatest weapon of all time. Remind yourself today of the power of the Gospel to win the battle for the souls of mankind, and rise up with courage knowing that you are empowered and anointed to share the good news of Jesus Christ with others. Start with your testimony! Reach out today to someone, and win them to Jesus with your greatest weapon.*

part twelve:

prayer

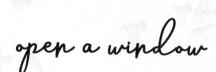

open a window

*Now the flood was on the earth forty days. The waters
increased and lifted up the ark, and it rose high above the
earth. The waters prevailed and greatly increased on the earth,
and the ark moved about on the surface of the waters.*
Genesis 7:17-18

Sometimes we may feel tired, only to realise that there is not enough fresh air circulating in the environment for us to breathe freely. Perhaps the room has become stuffy and conducive to sleepiness. Sometimes all we need to maintain energy and momentum is for fresh air to invade our environment! In the natural, this can be as simple as opening a window! Rooms that have been closed for too long produce stale air which can become slightly overwhelming to our senses! Just think of teenage boys' rooms, spilt milk in the car, or a musty smell from a prevailing dampness and you will get the idea! As in the natural, so it is in the spirit. If we hang out in these environments too long, the stale air of hopelessness, poverty-thinking and unbelief can begin to exude from the pores of our lives. We need to throw open the window to a fresh revelation of Jesus!

In the Bible, we read about God's plan to destroy mankind. When sin on the earth became overwhelming in His sight, God commissioned Noah to build an ark in which to house his family and the animals of the earth, carrying them to safety. Noah was a man of faith—he followed God's instructions in building the ark, trusting God for the safety of all on board and believing for a positive outcome on the other side of the flood. There are no reports of Noah feeling overwhelmed, but we can assume there were moments when he found being shipbound claustrophobic and stuffy. The smell of the animals alone would have invaded the environment! Even the quandary of *'how long?'* would have been a question that 'hung around' in the atmosphere! Yet in all this, Noah maintained faith! Then, there came a moment when Noah sensed the time of confinement was coming to an end. Seeking confirmation, Noah opened a window to test the waters. Genesis 8:6-9 says,

*Noah opened the window. . . then he sent out a raven, which kept
going to and fro until the waters had dried up from the earth. He
also sent out from himself a dove, to see if the waters had receded
from the face of the ground. But the dove found no resting place
for the sole of her foot, and she returned into the ark to him, for
the waters were on the face of the whole earth.*

Noah firstly sent a *raven* to test the waters, but it never returned. Next, he sent a dove. The raven, an unclean bird, was inclined to put its feet down into the mud, eat from carcasses, and settle for 'second best.' In contrast, the *dove* was a clean bird; it came from Noah and returned to Noah, possessing discernment and accountability! The dove is symbolic of the Holy Spirit, God's true witness! We can rely on a pure report when we *open a window* for the Holy Spirit to search out truth for us.

> *And he waited yet another seven days, and again he sent the dove*
> *out from the ark. Then the dove came to him in the evening, and*
> *behold, a freshly plucked olive lead was in her mouth; and*
> *Noah knew that the waters had receded from the earth.*
> *Genesis 8:10-11*

353

Like the dove, the Holy Spirit will return a pure witness into our hearts, bringing us the discernment of the season and the direction needed! Noah knew the promise but not the timing of their release. Don't be hasty! We need to *handle our landing* by complying with God's appointed time.

What is pervading the space in your spirit, causing a stuffiness and lack of air? Do you need to 'open the window' of your soul to the freshness of the Holy Spirit? Who are you listening to or relying on in a change of season? Today, choose to release the Holy Spirit! He will return to your heart with wisdom and discernment so you can exit one season and enter the next victoriously!

directives

And it came to pass . . . that He sent two of His disciples, saying,
"Go into the village opposite you, where as you enter you will find
a colt tied, on which no one has ever sat. Loose it and bring it here.
And if anyone asks you, 'Why are you loosing it?' thus you shall
say to him, 'Because the Lord has need of it.'" So those who were
sent, went their way and found it just as He had said to them.
Luke 19:30-32

When we set our heart on God to seek Him and to serve Him with all of our being, He releases *specific directives* into our spirit. Jesus' triumphal entry into Jerusalem, in fulfilment of the prophecy spoken by the prophet Isaiah relating to that precise moment in history, was preceded by preparations.

Tell the daughter of Zion, "Behold your King is coming to you,
lowly and sitting on a donkey, a colt, the foal of a donkey."
Matthew 21:5

Jesus gave His disciples some *specific directives* as he sent them! When we prepare in prayer, God makes the way clear with specific instructions. When we know God has given a prophetic directive, we know in faith that we will arrive at the right place at the right time for God to deliver what He has promised!

In our life and ministry, the Holy Spirit has always directed Bruce and myself as we have looked to Him for guidance. It's not about singing from a karaoke 'song sheet' or producing a 'paint by numbers' art piece that brings results, but by *prophetic directives* spoken into our spirit. We all need the voice of God to guide us in areas of our life and responsibility. I see a directive from God as being simply the *next step* I need to take in my journey of faith. Do you know what your next step in God is?

When I was involved in leading kids' ministry for several years, God was very faithful in giving progressive *directives* as I sought Him. We need to be faithful with the first directive God releases—outworking it, implementing it, living in it fully by faith so we will be positioned well for the promise to become a reality! We may be tempted to project our own ideas and vision, but specific *directives* give us that edge of faith and confidence because they carry the exponential weight that God wants to release, the power that comes with Holy Spirit-breathed initiatives.

We can be confident that God's directives just *work*. The disciples found, when they went looking for the donkey that was to carry Jesus into Jerusalem, that it was "just as He said." The ground was prepared for the release of the donkey, which in turn facilitated Jesus' triumphant entry into the Holy City. Don't you just love that?!

We need to pray into God's directives as we step out and witness them become a reality. As they become visible, they are establishing a 'new normal' that lifts us into another level of believing and receiving! In commencing the London church, God gave Bruce a prophetic directive regarding hospitality being a key to releasing growth and unlocking the purposes of God through the church:

> *Lady Wisdom has built and furnished her home; it's supported*
> *by seven hewn timbers. The banquet meal is ready to be served:*
> *lamb roasted, wine poured out, table set with silver and flowers.*
> Proverbs 9:1 (MSG)

Because God gave the direction, it fully worked! Jesus is *precise* and willing to share His *directives* with us!

🍃 *Today, acknowledge God and seek Him for a word in season to lead and guide you. Tune your ears to hear what He is saying to you specifically. God is into details when we choose to enquire! Be confident in the directive you receive, expecting it to happen just as He says!*

too much noise!

*And when you come before God, don't turn that
into a theatrical production either. All these people
making a regular show out of their prayers, hoping
for stardom! Do you think God sits in a box seat?*
Matthew 6:5 (MSG)

It's part of being human to want to be noticed, to be affirmed, to be celebrated! The One who does this the best is Jesus. He notices us, loves us, affirms us, and blesses us richly in our walk of faith. We need to be careful in our Christian living that we don't turn the volume up on our own self-righteousness, becoming self-seeking of approval, attention and admiration from others.

An amusing incident occurred while Bruce and I were travelling many years ago. We were on a substantial car trip with our three young grandchildren. The two little girls had been talking incessantly—until the male toddler on the journey shouted, "Quiet!" He had simply had enough of too much talk, too much noise!

The Bible warns us about making too much noise and drawing too much attention to ourselves on our journey of faith. We read some fairly explicit instructions in the Bible on how we should conduct ourselves. We are told how we can cut down the noise of self, and centre more on Jesus. In Matthew 6:1-2 (MSG) we read,

*The world is not a stage! Be especially careful when you are
trying to be good, so that you don't make a performance out of
it. It might be good theatre, but the God who made you won't be
applauding. When you do something for someone else, don't call
attention to yourself.*

Likewise, Matthew 6:16-18 (MSG) says,

*When you practice some appetite-denying discipline to better
concentrate on God, don't make a production out of it. It might
turn you into a small-time celebrity but it won't make you a
saint. If you 'go into training' inwardly, 'act normal' outwardly.*

We are called to pray with simplicity, and fast without platforming! 1 Corinthians 4:20 says, "For the kingdom of God is not in word, but in power." Do our prayers carry weight and not just sound? We are advised by Jesus that prayers directed solely for the attention of an earthly audience, will never activate Kingdom power. We are mistaken if we think that more words equal more power.

> *And when you pray, do not use vain repetitions as the heathen*
> *do, for they think that they will be heard for their many words.*
> *Therefore, do not be like them, for your Father knows the things*
> *you have need of before you ask Him.*
> *Matthew 6:7-8*

We live in a world where celebrity culture is encouraged and applauded, creating a self-centred approach that subtly seeks to draw others to participate also. Could it be that we are making too much noise about our own spiritual development and discipline, unintentionally drawing attention to ourselves rather than Christ? In our world, active self-promotion has become the 'norm,' but God chooses to be seen, known and highlighted through our sincerity and simplicity of faith in Him.

Have you been making a big deal out of that which is supposed to be just a natural progression of spiritual growth? Have you become a performer on your own stage, seeking the attention of the crowd? Today, review your motivation and eliminate any unnecessary noise and performance. God promises He won't overlook what you are doing. He will reward you well!

take it up

*O my dove, in the clefts of the rock, in the secret places
of the cliff, let me see your face, let me hear your voice;
for your voice is sweet, and your face is lovely.*
Song of Solomon 2:14

Have your ever tried to have an in-depth conversation with someone who never turned their face to look at you? The value of the interaction is lost and a moment of exchange missed. We have all experienced this, I am sure, and have probably been guilty of doing the same thing, absorbed in a screen or busy about another activity? God is keen to see our face and hear our voice!

Prayer is conversing with God, communicating with Him, resting in Him and enjoying His presence. But prayer is also stretching into the dimension of the spirit by faith, activating God's power to touch earth and change lives and environments for good! We can talk about needs and complain about lack, or we can *take it up* another level, praying and investing in a higher realm in the spirit.

Hosea is a book in the Bible with an unusual storyline. The prophet is instructed to marry a woman called Gomer, but their domestic life is hardly harmonious, as he deals with his wife's wanderings and unfaithfulness. The account of Hosea's marriage is an accurate depiction of Israel's disloyalty in their relationship with God, yet it is also a beautiful illustration of God's loyal love to pursue her.

We all have unusual stories of how God has pursued us—and maybe unusual places where God has met us! For Bruce, it was in the cow shed. One morning as he pushed the button to activate the milking machine, God flooded his heart and he began to speak in other tongues for the very first time.

"It shall come to pass in that day (betrothal) that I will answer,"
says the Lord. "I will answer the heavens, and they shall answer
the earth. The earth shall answer with grain, with new wine,
and with oil; They shall answer Jezreel."
Hosea 2:21-22

There is a flow of activation here—different areas answering each other! Let's look at what this means and how can we apply this to our prayers. These verses indicate that in our relationship with God, we share our heart's longings for His safe keeping and intervention. As we fill the heavens with our requests, God answers the heavens, which in turn, refresh the earth, and the earth reciprocates with produce and blessings!

Could it be that we are expecting so much from our relationship with God, yet not fulfilling our part? The best relationships are two-sided. We need to invest! God is looking for His people to engage and invest in seeing His Kingdom come on earth, activating it through our prayer and petition!

There was a time when our son, Sam, was critically ill and hospitalised for forty-two days; this was time to invest, to call on our close relationship with God so as to activate power in the spiritual realm to heal his body! The picture I received in prayer was of all the requests prayed for Sam stacked in a huge pile in heaven; there was an assurance in my spirit that it would only be a matter of time before the answer would simply 'swoosh' down to earth, and Sam would be healed. The pile of petitions was so big that it was impossible for God to ignore! And so it happened. With a spike in temperature and an emergency operation, a miracle took place, and the former prognosis was reversed.

What are we 'stacking up' in the spiritual realm that God cannot possibly ignore? Are we stacking up prayers, or are we stacking up complaints which have no power to overcome or change anything? We need to *take it up* into a higher level today in relationship with God and prayer.

How is your relationship with God? Can He see your face and hear your voice? How are your words? Are they forming prayer and expressing confidence in God's ability? Today, let's take it up, activating miracles as we touch heaven!

look alike

Be anxious for nothing, but in everything by prayer and supplication,
with thanksgiving, let your requests be made known to God.
Philippians 4:6

Note that this scripture, says 'in everything.' God is interested in *everything* that concerns us; we have the freedom to bring every petition and need before Him, confident that He will pay full attention to our request. We may hear parents tell children to stop bothering them, but it's different with God—He can be bothered! He encourages us to come to Him with anything, no matter how small it may seem and no matter how often! He's never going to tire of our voice. We just need to ask for what we need!

Therefore humble yourselves under the mighty hand of God,
that He may exalt you in due time, casting all your care
upon Him, for He cares for you.
1 Peter 5:6-7

Does God not know about all our bothers and issues without us telling Him? Yes, He does, but He wants to hear us *voice our faith*. Faith has a voice and it needs to be heard; faith needs to be spoken and directed to a God who has every answer and provision that is needed.

Praying out loud, even when alone, builds our faith as we *give voice* to the requests of our heart. Not only does God hear us, but *we hear ourselves* as the Holy Spirit helps us articulate our prayers. As we begin to voice our prayers, there are moments we will hear God's voice in ours, moments when God gives a prophetic expression to our prayer. This Holy Spirit-inspired prayer has the "yes and amen" of God all over it! I love this experience! We have all probably heard the expression, "Words create worlds." This is so true—both negatively and positively! When we engage in the Spirit and in

prayers of faith, our world is shaped for good. I look at certain people and I can tell what they have prayed because they *look like their prayers*, they have *'become what they prayed.'* Prayer has a way of moulding us into the shape we have been inspired by the Holy Spirit to pray.

> *But we all with unveiled face, beholding as in a mirror, the glory of*
> *the Lord, are being transformed from glory to*
> *glory, just as by the Spirit of the Lord.*
> 2 Corinthians 3:18

In the early days of the Auckland Church, we prayed the same prayer consistently, week in, week, out from the Book of Isaiah:

> *In an acceptable time I have heard You, and in the day of*
> *salvation I have helped You; I will preserve You and give you as*
> *a covenant to the people, to restore the earth, to cause them to*
> *inherit the desolate heritages; that you may say to the prisoners,*
> *"Go forth," and to those who are in darkness, "Show yourselves."*
> Isaiah 49:8-9a

As our church prayed, believing God had given us as a gift to the city, we begin to 'look like our prayers.' People were getting saved, delivered and set free from some very dark places. We *became what we prayed.*

If people were to observe us personally, or as a group of believers, would they be able to tell what we had been praying because of what or who we have become in the process? That's a challenge for us all, but something worth considering. Our prayers shouldn't just be 'one-off wonders,' but consistent 'work-outs' that shape us to look like our prayers!

Do you have an attitude that you don't want to bother God? Today, God invites you to come and 'cast all your cares' onto Him. Turn your cares into prayers, and find God's voice in yours. What 'look-alike' prayer do you want to see become a reality in your own life.

go a little farther

> Then Jesus came with them to a place called Gethsemane, and said to the disciples, "Sit here while I go and pray over there." And He took with Him Peter and the two sons of Zebedee, and He began to be sorrowful and distressed. Then He said to them, "My soul is exceedingly sorrowful, even to death. Stay here and watch with me" . . . Then He came to the disciples and found them sleeping, and said to Peter, "What? Could you not watch with me one hour? Watch and pray, lest you enter into temptation. The spirit indeed is willing but the flesh is weak."
> Matthew 26:36-38, 41

This is an account of the last hours before Jesus was arrested in the garden of Gethsemane, subsequently condemned, and later crucified. His heart was sorrowful and his soul distressed! Jesus sought comfort in communication with His heavenly Father and in the support of His disciples. We too, need to pray at all times and in all seasons, going further in our engagement and intensity in prayer. As I view this passage, I see three aspects of prayer.

1. SIT HERE WHILE I PRAY Jesus instructed His disciples to just sit while He prayed. There are moments in our life when we need to follow that same, simple directive. Jesus knows that some difficulties are beyond our capacity to carry. Perhaps it is the sheer weight of the problem or just that we are not yet mature enough to handle it ourselves—either way, Jesus asks us to simply trust Him and wait in faith as He carries our request in prayer. Hebrews 7:25 puts it like this: "He is also able to save to the uttermost those who come to God through Him, since He always lives to make intercession for them."

2. STAY HERE AND WATCH WITH ME This statement of Jesus reminds me of supportive prayer—being together and strengthening one another as we pray and seek God's comfort and intervention in tough situations. Jesus was requesting support as He faced the biggest battle of all time, a yielding of His will to die voluntarily on behalf of all mankind. He needed support from his mates to *win the war internally* so He could proceed externally, just as Moses needed support to stay steady at his post of prayer.

And so it was, when Moses held up his hands, that Israel prevailed;
and when he let down his hands, Amalek prevailed. But Moses'
hands became heavy; so they took a stone and put it under him,
and he sat on it. And Aaron and Hur supported his hands . . .
and his hands were steady until the going down of the sun.
Exodus 17:11-12

Victories are won in prayer together!

3. WATCH AND PRAY Jesus strongly encouraged the disciples to stay awake, to be active and engaged in the battle for territory in the spirit as the hour of His arrest approached. He requested the supportive warfare of His disciples in the garden to counteract demonic forces. There is no time to sleep when a serious battle rages, but a certain persistence and perseverance is needed to push back any advances by the enemy! Though Jesus agonised in prayer, He triumphed over every attack He faced on the path to victory over sin and death for you and I.

How's our prayer life? Where do we need to go farther in prayer? *Jesus went a little farther and fell on His face in prayer.* Where do we need to win it for ourselves and others? Let's go that little bit farther in prayer, into the territory of spiritual warfare, taking authority over the enemy and winning the battle!

Do you know how to release your petitions in prayer, how to give them over? Do you know how to watch in the spirit, praying and supporting others for breakthrough in their struggles? Do you know how to engage in warfare, denying the enemy territory by exercising your God-given authority? Today, know that as you go further in prayer, God will release His strength and power to win amazing victories!

knit one, purl one

Eye has not seen, nor ear heard, nor have entered into the heart of man the things which God has prepared for those who love Him.
1 Corinthians 2:9

I never persevered at knitting, and consequently haven't produced any amazing homemade garments! Some people are just so skilled with their knitting needles! We know that when threads are woven together they are capable, through the interlocking of each strand, of making a beautiful garment or tapestry, a beautiful depiction of love! God has woven a beautiful picture for all our lives, a story that comes together with essential strands of His love, wonder, faith and power so we can reach our full potential.

Bruce and I have experienced God 'pulling threads' together over many years, bringing more fullness to the tapestry He has designed for our lives. God *links and loops* us with people who He has planned, before time even began, to be part of our future. Even while we are sleeping, He continues working. In my words, "God knits behind our back," pulling threads, connecting and linking us with likeminded people!

Prophetic words are the threads, and as we work under His direction, He connects these threads with people and places in amazing ways. What may appear initially like a random dot can prove to be very significant in the bigger plan of God as He joins the dots together.

Bruce and I can testify to countless 'divine linking' that we have experienced as a result of prophetic words spoken over our lives. In 1989, I received a 'random' burden for Germany while praying in my bedroom, just prior to the Berlin Wall coming down! This wasn't anything I had been thinking about or praying for, but a burden landed heavily on my heart for this great country to experience salvation and freedom in Jesus. This was one of those 'dots,' random in nature, and 'out of the blue,' but definitely God-given! This huge dot in my heart set my prayer life in a direction of regular intercession for Germany. It was only a matter of time before Bruce was 'randomly' approached by a young German pastor asking if he would mentor him. When this young man heard Bruce speak at a Bible College in Denmark, his spirit witnessed with Bruce's, and the rest is history! God *divinely knit* us with Juergen and Miriam Eisen, who we have been closely associated with for many years now, and we have witnessed their amazing leadership in churches in Germany, particularly in Celle and Berlin. God joined the dots then 'pulled the thread' on something more amazing than we could have imagined. He had this in mind from the beginning of time.

In 2002, we saw the fulfilment of a prophecy given years earlier regarding Bruce and my transfer to London:

> *"As I begin to work, there are others that I will begin to release . . . there is another house in Europe, in Switzerland, and that too will quickly come to you," says the Lord. ". . . I have a man, a young man waiting, waiting for you to come, and he shall be as a son in the Lord . . . you will train him as a son in the Lord, and he too shall father a great house."*

God was already linking us with Dan Zeltner, a young man who had come to London to learn English. Not long after his arrival, he began serving under Bruce's leadership, fulfilling many roles in the beginnings of this new church! It was only years later, when we remembered that prophecy, that we stood amazed again at God's ability to pull threads together! Today, Dan and his wife, Oana, lead *Equippers Zurich*. These are just two of the many stories of God 'knitting behind our back' in relationship, linking us with significant others to bring about Kingdom purpose!

God has designed an amazing tapestry of your life which testifies to His goodness and grace. Today, look at what you think are 'random' dots or connections in your life. Rediscover what God has already said or revealed—you may be amazed that words spoken over you have already been fulfilled! Know that today, many threads are being pulled and linked together in the greater purpose God has for you!

overturn the tables

Then Jesus went into the temple of God and drove out all those who bought and sold in the temple and overturned the tables of the money changers and the seats of those who sold doves. And He said to them, "It is written, 'My house shall be called a house of prayer,' but you have made it a den of thieves."
Matthew 21:12-13

Prayer is our open expression of communication with God, but at times other expressions try to cut across our lines of communication, distracting us from the main purpose of prayer. Jesus, on entering the temple, took action against the deviations He observed, the disturbances that cut across the flow of purposeful prayer and communication with God.

Jesus wants to *overturn* anything in our life that spoils the purity of prayer, anything that disturbs the open channel between Him and ourselves, rendering us prayer-less and powerless. Jesus wasn't passive when He addressed the problem but responded in a way seldom seen in His time on earth. My husband, Bruce, would ask, "What gave Jesus the authority to do what He did?" — the answer being that *Jesus knew what His Father's house should look like.* What He saw grieved His heart! People were in the temple peddling their wares and looking out merely for their own interests!

I remember Jesus *overturning* my prayer life one day. Although I was diligent, I had become a little too predictable in my devotional life. He chose to come and *mess up* my routine. He revealed to me that I had lost power as I had become quieter, more meditational in my expression, rather than using the roar of faith I had possessed previously. Somehow, without realising it, I had *stepped back* from the assertiveness in prayer which is needed to stand against spiritual forces and powers! God wanted me to *step it up* again if I wanted to see tables of sickness, poverty and oppression overturned.

There are things God calls for us to *overturn in the spirit*. Let's not get too passive in our prayers, turning the volume so low that we can't be heard in the heavenly realm. Instead, let's amplify our voice so as to exercise force and power against demonic realms and see God's Kingdom come and His will done here on earth. Forces are seeking to rule and empty God's people of Spirit-led prayer which is effective in warfare! Authority is not quiet but is strong and commanding. It is not necessarily about volume, but it's about strength in verbalising our thoughts and feelings!

Jesus gave expression to His feelings. His accusations were strong toward the merchants who had turned the temple into something other than what it was designed for. God's house was to be called, "a house of prayer for all nations" and they had reduced it to a "den of thieves." Here's a thought: Is the function for what we are called, recognisable by our actions?

> *Then the blind and the lame came to Him*
> *in the temple; and He healed them.*
> Matthew 21:14

Jesus' actions made way for healing, deliverance and salvation. When we allow our 'temple' to be cluttered with noise, we hinder the power of God from moving in our lives and situations. As we shift every distraction that competes for attention out of the way, God's power will operate freely!

367

What is distracting you or competing for your attention? What noise is taking you away from the true purpose of God? What has caused you to turn the volume down in prayer? Are there tables that need to be overturned in your life today? 'Turn the table' on every ploy of the enemy and fill your life with fervent powerful prayer today! Step it up!

serving and giving

keep your apron on

Nothing is better for a man than that he should eat and drink and that his soul should enjoy good in his labour. This, also, I saw, was from the hand of God.
Ecclesiastes 2:24

How do we view work? Do we see it as a chore, or a blessing? Are we thankful if we have an occupation that rewards us for our efforts? Some people have an aversion to the concept of work, viewing it is as something to be endured or avoided at all costs, a bind they want to be released from. However, when we think in this manner, we can end up depriving ourselves of the very activity God designed to bring us satisfaction. Work brings purpose into our lives as well as a sense of achievement!

In our everyday work, there are times we need to metaphorically *keep our apron on*, and also times to enjoy the fruit of our labour! Much joy and satisfaction come from generating supplies and being productive, resulting in an ability to bless our households and others. It's about choosing our attitude toward work. Ecclesiastes 9:10 urges us, "Whatever your hand finds to do, do it with your might."

When it comes to the Kingdom of God, we never 'take our apron off'! When Jesus was on earth, He instructed us to work while it is still day, in order to see His Kingdom come and Jesus glorified. Luke 12:35-38 (MSG) reads,

Keep your shirts on; keep the lights on! Be like house servants waiting for their master to come back from his honeymoon, awake and ready to open the door when he arrives and knocks. Lucky the servants whom the master finds on watch! He will put on an apron, sit them at the table, and serve them a meal, sharing his wedding feast with them. It doesn't matter what time of the night he arrives; they're awake—and so blessed.

Don't lose heart! Your labour has a great reward. In certain seasons, you may feel like there is no let-up, that it is 'all work and no play,' and like Cinderella, you wonder when it will be your turn to go to the ball! Maybe you are looking at snapshots of people relaxing, perhaps cruising the Mediterranean, but you fail to see the snapshots of the same people scrubbing floors, tending to others and working hard behind the scenes. This can leave us resentful, feeling left behind, unnoticed and like we are missing out on the fun because of the daily chores that need to be done. Today, be encouraged that the King of Kings does not take your labour of love lightly. He sees it as Kingdom-work! He notices your diligence and He comes, puts *His apron on,* sits you down and serves you with the best of His wedding food. What an amazing picture—Jesus in His apron for us!

I can testify to the joy of serving Jesus and of experiencing specific seasons where Jesus came and served me, blessing me in special and unexpected ways. There is fruit for our labour, and in Matthew 25:21 we read that there is a joy into which we enter through serving:

His lord said to him, "Well done good and faithful servant; you are faithful over a few things, I will make you ruler over many things. Enter into the joy of the Lord."

Don't have a breakdown because of work, but instead *break through* in your attitude toward your responsibilities! Adjust the load if need be, but choose carefully your frame of mind regarding work. There is joy in serving Jesus! Perhaps Noah learned to sing and praise God even while shovelling the animal dung in the confines of the ark!? Let's *keep our apron* on and be faithful! Let's enter into His joy today!

When you consider your work, are there mindsets that you need to change? Identify your 'apron,' your place of service in the Kingdom, and put it on today! Get ready for God's blessings. As you **keep your apron on**, *He will serve and bless you in unbelievable measure!*

pay it forward

*Now David said, "Is there still anyone who is left of the house of
Saul, that I may show him kindness for Jonathan's sake?"*
2 Samuel 9:1

David remembered his special friendship with Saul's son, Jonathan,
the bond they shared and the companionship they enjoyed. Jonathan
demonstrated huge levels of loyalty toward David, putting his own life
on the line many times so that David could be spared. In a moment of
reflection and deep gratitude, David expressed his desire to repay the
debt of love that he felt he owed, seeking to *pay it forward* with kindness
toward any person left in Saul's household. When David made enquiries,
he discovered one of Jonathan's sons, Mephibosheth, was still alive!

*And Ziba said to the king,
"There is still a son of Jonathan, who is lame in his feet."*
2 Samuel 9:3b

Mephibosheth's response to David's generosity was initially one of fear and
unworthiness, labelling himself a 'dead dog.' But David responded by saying,

*". . . do not fear, for I will surely **show you kindness** for Jonathan
your father's sake, and will **restore to you** all the land of Saul your
grandfather; and you shall eat bread at my table continually."*
2 Samuel 9:7

Paying it forward is a commonly-used expression that relates to showing kindness from a pure heart without compulsion, but from a simple desire to make someone else's life easier, to provide a way forward for them. Has someone *paid it forward* for you? Perhaps someone sacrificed their time, money or skills to help you out? For me, it was an elderly couple called Freddie and Edna Gardiner who opened their home in Otaki, a small town in New Zealand, every Saturday night for young people to gather, learn the Word of God, share food and enjoy wonderful activities like bonfires on the beach and hay-rides on the back of a truck! This was another era altogether, not one that was as 'health and safety' conscious as we are today!

Freddie exemplified a level of commitment, generosity and care toward us which now, at a mature age myself, I appreciate at a whole new level. His smile was like the smile of Jesus, expressing how proud he was of us all. He *paid it forward,* investing into the likes of myself and other young people. Looking back, I wish I had thanked him more—immaturity doesn't always recognise another's sacrifice—but we left this small town as a young family to pursue the call of God on our lives and lost touch in the process.

Bruce's father also invested heavily into his two sons. He would say to them, "You should be better men than I, because you stand on my shoulders!" Let's take the time to remember and recognise people who have helped us, to turn around and say "thank you" to people in our lives for what they have done, the parents who nurture us, teachers who believe in us, leaders that encourage us. Being thankful is a great motivation to *pay it forward* and to invest in others, particularly into another generation. Let's ask how we can show *love* and *kindness* toward another, passing on the same kindness that has been afforded us.

Today, give thanks for those who have invested in you and shown you kindness. Consider who you can pay it forward to, investing into the lives of others in order to see them blessed and prosperous. Any sacrifice, large or small, inspired by God, has the power to impact another! Let's thank Jesus today that He paid it forward for us!

get loud

*And Jesus cried out again with a **loud voice** and yielded up His Spirit. Then behold the veil of the temple was torn in two from top to bottom and the earth quaked and the rocks were split. And the graves were opened and many bodies of the saints who had fallen asleep were raised . . . So when the centurion and those with him, who were guarding Jesus saw the earthquake and the things that had happened, they feared greatly, saying, "Truly this was the Son of God."*
Matthew 27:50-54

The enemy wants to silence the message of the Gospel, but God wants to turn the volume up! He wants the message of the cross to be heard loud and clear! God can amplify His heart through His people as we operate with *generosity*.

Jesus is our greatest example of *giving*. He had a vision for our redemption, and His faith was loud! He paid the ultimate price, dying on the cross for our sins that we might be reconciled to God. Vision causes us to give sacrificially because of the dream within. The enemy hates this message of love, and seeks to oppose and muffle it, but the sound of the good news will eternally be loud! In Matthew 27:50 we read,

And Jesus cried out again with a loud voice and yielded up His Spirit.

When Jesus got loud, heaven got loud too! When He gave up His spirit, heaven resounded! In the natural it is difficult to raise your voice above a certain volume, but when heaven sounds loudly, it commands an attentive reverence! You can't argue with a loud sound!

Giving has a loud sound. As God's children and as His church, we need to *get loud* through our genuine giving—not as a carnal display to impress others, but as a statement of faith in the face of principalities and powers of poverty and withholding spirits. God has called us to speak for those who don't have a voice, who are oppressed and downtrodden in their circumstances, by praying, giving and serving. *God gets loud* as we stand in the gap to meet needs!

People may argue that they cannot afford to give, but we can all give *something*—a smile, our time, kind acts, and financial blessing. The Bible tells us that our tithes alone, which are the minimal requirement of giving as a child of God, open the heavens over our lives for God to *get loud* on our behalf! God promises to reward with abundant blessings those who give sacrificially. Jesus said,

> *Assuredly I say to you, there is no one who has left house or brother or sisters or father or mother or wife or children or lands, for My sake and the gospel's, who shall not receive a hundredfold now in this time—houses and brothers and sisters and mothers and children and lands, with persecutions —and in the age to come, eternal life.*
> Mark 10:29-31

Bruce and I have lifelong testimonies of God's open heaven over our lives as we have chosen to give. God has *gotten loud* on our behalf, constantly and consistently surprising us with His goodness! Jesus was not forced to die on our behalf, but He chose to because of the vision in His heart of redemption for lost humanity. As He released His last breath, Jesus *yielded up* His spirit, conforming to the will of His Father. *Yielding* may have a negative connotation in certain situations, but when it's about yielding to the will of God in our lives, it releases a loud sound of faith and authentic worship!

*How is your giving? Is there a loud sound of faith emanating from your giving today? Do you desire to see heaven sounding loud behind you, as you give in love and faith? Today, yield to God and watch His reversals over natural limitations in your life. He promises to **get loud** on your behalf!*

find your voice

But a generous man devises generous plans,
and by generosity he shall stand.
Isaiah 32:8

Have you noticed that right from the beginning of life, babies have no problem exercising their lungs to express themselves? At first, it is not a mature sound, but over time, their voices grow and develop. Everything in the world around us has a voice. Our lives speak, the way we live speaks, our environments speak—even when words are not used! I believe *giving* also has a voice that develops gradually; it speaks from a heart that is learning to be generous and gracious towards others.

I find that giving makes my soul sing! In directing our giving by faith and under the guidance of the Holy Spirit to God's house, missions, individuals and people groups, it is a joy to know we are the answer to someone's prayer! Our souls find delight in the anticipation of the release our giving will bring to someone's need or to the resourcing of projects. That's probably why the Bible says, "It is more blessed to give than to receive" (Acts 20:35). Being stingy, possessive, and controlling of our time and possessions mutes our voice and limits our expression.

Worldly worries and needs can knock us down and cause anxiety, but choosing to be generous causes us to stand strong and steadfast with joy, peace, security and confidence. When we dream generous plans, fresh delight is awakened in our soul and a brighter sound is heard through our voice—one of excitement, expectation and anticipation!

In Matthew 16:25, Jesus said, "For whoever desires to save his life will lose it, but whoever loses his life for My sake will find it." People are robbed when happiness becomes their ultimate goal. Life becomes very uncertain for them, and grasping for alternative things to bring security and contentment can become a preoccupation.

At the end of our life, a final voice will be heard. A summary of what we have done with what we had will be recounted. Did the fruit of our life, our character, and the influence we exercised, sound like the plan God originally designed for us? Or is the life we lived going to sound futile and wasteful because, in trying to preserve our life, we entrusted our well-being to things that rot, rust and fade? There is nothing we can take to heaven besides people; everything else we may have amassed, remains behind.

> Now the multitude of this who believed, were of one heart and
> one soul, neither did anyone say that anything he possessed was
> his own, but they had all things in common. And with great
> power, the apostle gave witness to the resurrection of the
> Lord Jesus and great grace was upon them all.
> Acts 4:32

The early church *found its voice* though *giving*. Their soul was singing and there was harmony and unity of sound that caught the attention of the multitude who observed them. They bore a message of generosity and were an active demonstration of God's grace.

Jesus *gave voice* to the woman who anointed His feet with oil. The sound of her pure worship still echoes down through the corridors of time. Likewise, the world *gave voice* to Mother Teresa, amplifying the giving of one lady who dedicated her life to bringing comfort and healing to the sick and needy. Let's push through today and release our voice as we give to the needs of others!

Is your soul singing? If you are depressed and muted in expression today, try giving! If you are in financial bondage, give your way out of debt! Today, recognise that it is not in the getting but in the giving that you will find your voice!

more metaphors

And let us not grow weary in doing good, for in due season we shall reap if we do not lose heart.
Galatians 6:9

Are there aspects of life we may have grown beyond, physical activities that we now consider 'off limits' or 'out of range'? Some years back my husband needed two knee replacements. As a result, some past activities he had enjoyed were no longer possible due to the risk of undoing the good work of the surgeons. It would have been very unwise for him, for example, to pursue water-skiing, as his artificial knees would not have withstood the pressure that quick responses at high speed generate. The flexibility was no longer there! God wants us to be flexible in serving and *doing good* in every season of our life, independent of our physical or financial situation. Nothing God asks of us will be out of our range or off-limits. Serving wholeheartedly from our spirit enables us to have an impact well beyond our natural abilities!

At retirement age, I was asked to lead the kids' ministry in our local church. This may have seemed ludicrous to some, especially following many years in church planting and leadership. But at this stage of life, God was requiring me to sow into another season, and into yet another field of ministry. In response to the challenge to 'do good' in this area, I reaped an increased richness of expression. My creative thinking, planning and writing for children took on more metaphors—fuller ways to describe the person and character of Jesus. This added colour and vibrancy to my existing faith, expression and ministry as God constantly 'wowed' me with inspiration and ingenuity!

God wants to *colour* our world. Don't settle for being bland and colourless! Saying "yes" to God unlocks potential and flair within that we may not previously have been aware of. God wants to give us all more metaphors, more relatable and visible ways of expressing our faith, along with an ever-increasing effectiveness. Imagine the greater stories of breakthrough yet to emerge as we respond positively to *the need with our name on it*, not yielding to excuses, but stretching ourselves in service and doing good!

Perhaps we have viewed and declared certain areas of service 'off-limits' for us personally. Could it be that God is calling us to invest in areas we may have previously dismissed? Let's be careful we do not rob ourselves of significant personal growth and breakthrough by our resistance. Let's live larger, more colourful lives today, using *more metaphors* to express our love and devotion to Christ.

God desires to release His amazing creativity in and through all of our lives as believers. An expression of His heavenly glory is revealed as we respond positively to the opportunities presented to us! Let's stay amazed with our Creator and co-operate with the leading of the Holy Spirit. Let's heed Mary's instructions to the servants at the wedding in Cana of Galilee, "Whatever He says to you, do it" (John 2:5). Serving wholeheartedly and in quick obedience releases miracles and God's glory!

Have you become weary in your serving, and need to be refreshed and recharged? Today God wants to encourage you to persevere in doing good. In doing so, you will reap His reward which goes well beyond your wildest dreams!

reinterpreting demands

For what will it profit a man if he gains the whole world,
and loses his own soul?
Mark 8:36

Many people have a mindset which has become a pre-occupation—that if we work hard in the first half of our life, the latter years will somehow just take care of themselves. They think this will ensure a life of ease, freedom from labour, and enjoyment of what they have managed to accumulate. While that may be a legitimate goal in itself, God's perspective on work is twofold—firstly, that we bring increase to our own lives, and then that through our serving and giving we also bring increase to others! Rather than gathering only for our own pleasure, we gather for those around us and also for the generations to come!

What are we looking at to bring 'gain' to our life? Proverbs 23:5 says, "Will you set your eyes on that which is not? For riches certainly make themselves wings; they fly away like an eagle toward heaven." This scripture tells us that there is no profit in self-seeking and self-amassing, that in the end, money and possessions cannot save the soul of those who strove after them! Maybe we need to take a look at the treasures we have set our heart on. Eternal treasures are not always tangible but are invaluable to our wellbeing—genuine love, inner peace and pure joy that Jesus alone can bring. We may be rich in earthly goods but void of the possessions that money cannot buy.

Only Christ can guarantee inner joy and satisfaction both in life and in the work of our hands. Perhaps we need to take another look at how we view work. Do we see it as a means to an end, labouring for earthly riches to guarantee future security? Do we see it as a demand to be avoided wherever possible? Little do we realise that some demands are a blessing in disguise! In Luke 11 we read about a man who had a visitor arrive late at night. Having no bread in his house, he woke his neighbour to ask for help in this situation. Initially, the neighbour replied, "Do not trouble me; the door is now shut, and my children are with me in bed; I cannot rise and give to you" (Luke 11:7). Although the neighbour was a reluctant starter, at the persistence of his friend, he eventually got up and gave him as many loaves as he needed.

This request wasn't the normal behaviour of the man's friend, but an emergency that warranted a knock on his door. Are we refusing requests and potentially closing down what could be a 'God set-up' where His power can be seen and released through us? Personally, I have found that when I have risen to meet a need which initially demanded more of me, something bigger in God issued from my life as a result.

How do we view requests? Do we immediately dismiss them because we see them as extra demands, feeling our own comfort and leisure are more important? Do we issue the same excuse as the neighbour did in the story Jesus told? There are God-ordained moments when we simply need to *get out of bed* and respond to the need before us, to help and bless another! Excuses have a way of wearing us down. We are not going to sleep at all well when conviction remains thumping on the door of our heart. Far better to get up and respond to the need! The man who knocked on the door knew that his friend had the capacity to provide, that within his house he had the means! God knows too, that we have the inner capacity to provide and He will permit needs to come knocking on our door, even at inconvenient times. Let's reinterpret the demands in our life and *get out of bed*, out from under the blankets of self-protection and self-preservation! What miracles could be released through our lives if we would simply rise in God to meet the challenges before us?

What need or opportunity is 'knocking on your door' that God wants you to respond to? Are you restless, 'tossing and turning' because you haven't yet risen to the challenge before you? Today, choose to 'get out of bed,' confident that God's provision is already present within you to release to another!

part fourteen:

gathered

pass it on

384

So I came to Jerusalem and was there three days. Then I arose in
the night, I and a few men with me; I told no-one what God had
put in my heart to do at Jerusalem; nor was there any animal
with me, except the one on which I rode.
Nehemiah 2:11

Have you ever heard a strongly resounding echo, perhaps in a ravine or in a small space? Imagine shouting into the stillness of the Grand Canyon and hearing your words reverberate all around! An echo is a sound that is repeated. Our lives shout about something, and as Christians we trust we are *passing on* the right sound—the sound of faith, sincerity and devotion! Sounds are more caught than taught. A transference of attitude and spirit rebounds between people and repeats over a period of time.

Nehemiah's life had a sound. The burden on his heart shouted *hope* into a canyon of despair, declaring restoration to the broken walls of Jerusalem. Nehemiah desired that others would catch the importance of the mission too. His burden for Jerusalem and its state of vulnerability provoked vision and mission within him to see the protective wall around the city rebuilt. In preparation for the task ahead, Nehemiah took a few men with him to view the devastation of the city and, as they went, something of Nehemiah's burden was transferred to the hearts of his men. Courage was imparted and it *re-echoed* through their commitment and belief that God would enable them to restore the wall.

Then I said to them, "You see the distress that we are in,
how Jerusalem lies waste, and its gate are burned with fire.
Come and let us build the wall of Jerusalem, that we may no
longer be a reproach." And I told them of the hand of my God
which had been good upon me, and also of the king's words that
he had spoken to me. So they said, "Let us rise up and build."
Then they set their hands to this good work.
Nehemiah 2:17-18

These few men that Nehemiah took to view the walls caught the vision, perceived this burden was 'a good work,' and strengthened themselves spiritually and physically to undertake the huge task before them. They *resounded* with the same passion of heart, as Nehemiah invited them into the vision and showed them what they had previously neither seen nor heard. The cry, "Let us rise up and build" would have *echoed* around the city, and the Bible tells us that progress happened because the people had a mind to work (Nehemiah 4:6). How did Nehemiah recruit such great workers? Because the missional sound of his soul was *passed on*.

Let's ask ourselves, *"What is the sound of our life? How strong is our mission ethos? Is it resonating in other people's heart as we speak? Is it being passed on and picked up by another?"* We only need to listen to our children to hear what we have passed on. Maybe we are hearing some of our 'not so great' traits, and the echo is telling—it's like hearing ourselves on surround sound! Would we like these sounds to reverberate through the generations? If not, we need to adjust the sound of our heart. Let's address any negativity we hear in our family lines, and change the tenor. Let's deal with unhelpful traits that have been passed on, and pass on instead the great stories of faith, the ways God has been so good and favourable to us.

Psalm 145:4 says, "One generation shall praise Your works to another, and shall declare Your mighty acts." As a church, let's *shout* about Jesus and see His passion for mission and church-planting *echo* around the world. Today, let's *pass on* our stories of faith!

*What is the sound coming from your life? Would you want the sound of your heart echoed and repeated through your sphere of influence, and generationally? Where may you need to change the **shout** of your heart and life? Today, declare God's goodness, and His constant help as you achieve great things for Him.*

sound gathers

For if the trumpet makes an uncertain sound,
who will prepare for battle?
1 Corinthians 14:8

We all love gatherings. It is part of being human to enjoy connection and celebrations, especially when we come together *en masse*. Numbers add weight to special occasions, reinforcing our togetherness, joint purpose, focus, and delight. Gatherings on a smaller and perhaps more regular basis are also dynamic moments of caring, connecting and encouraging one another. In every setting, either big or small, we gather to a *sound*, to a call or a cry. It would be rare for a person to miss the call for dinner, for example, especially when their stomach is hungry and demanding food! Some calls are very easily heard!

Even as a fugitive, before he was positioned as king over Israel, David had a sound about his life that others gathered to. We read,

> *David therefore departed from there and escaped to the cave of*
> *Adullam. So when his brothers and all his father's house heard it,*
> *they went down there to him. And everyone who was in distress,*
> *everyone who was in debt, and everyone who was discontented*
> ***gathered to him.*** *So he became captain over them. And*
> *there were about four hundred men with him.*
> 1 Samuel 22:1-2

What sound did they hear in David's life that caused these men to join him, even in his time of trouble? The men who gathered to David heard:

The sound of *authenticity*. David was a man of integrity and uprightness!

The sound of *worship*. David had a song in his heart that glorified his God!

The sound of *courage*. David was not afraid to stand up to anything that contradicted the truth of God!

The sound of *strength*. David didn't blame others for his demise but handled his testing from a place of inner strength.

The sound of *purpose*. David served God with all his heart, just as he served his father, Saul, and the nation of Israel.

I believe that as these sounds resonated from David's life, they were heard and applauded by the people who joined him in the cave! David had a sound that appealed to them, causing them to desire his leadership to impart strength and confidence into their lives. David's life and reputation had a sound that exhorted the people out of their discontent, distress and debt, and caused them to seek for answers.

David didn't call these people to himself; *the sound of his life* called them to become all that God had called them to be. Let's make sure our lives, like David's, have a *certain* sound about them! An invitation to gather sounds forth in the final book of the Bible where we read,

> *The Spirit and the bride say, "Come!" And let him who hears*
> *say, "Come!" And let him who thirsts, come. Whoever*
> *desires, let him take the water of life freely.*
> Revelation 22:17

Will we be gathered to that sound?!

What sounds can be heard through your life? What sound in your life may need to change? Is there a certainty about the sound of your life? Is your conviction and commitment heard clearly? Today God wants to gather you to Himself, to clarify the sound of your life that will in turn gather others to Him!

care has a sound

Blessed are the people who know the joyful sound! They walk,
O Lord, in the light of Your countenance.
Psalm 89:15

There is a sound that is heard in the spirit that we want to fall into line with—a sound of joy, love, care and meaningful purpose, that we want to follow! Everything in life has a sound, a reverberation that bounces from every person, purpose or plan. Jesus' sound throughout eternity is one of love and care, and it is heard particularly through His powerful act of dying on the cross.

But God demonstrates His own love toward us,
in that while we were yet sinners, Christ died for us.
Romans 5:8

Jesus paid the price for our freedom and forgiveness of sin, and not only for us, but for every person that has ever existed, does exist and is yet to exist! God's great love is why we gather around Him and follow Him as our personal Lord and Saviour.

Care is a sound that gathers. Everyone wants to be noticed and cared about, even those who may initially object to the notion. When people react negatively to an expression of genuine love, it is often a reflection of suppressed hurt. Perhaps they have experienced a lack of care or concern at some point in their life and as a result, an outer shell has formed in an attempt to protect their heart, blocking the vulnerability associated with gathering to the sound of genuine care. In spite of adverse reactions to love and care however, the truth remains that the innate desire of every human is to be affirmed and valued, to live in connection and community *with joy and without fear!*

The more important question is not about who is caring for us, but about the level of care we can show to others. Does a genuine sound of care for our fellow human reverberate from our heart? Our care and sincerity of love can penetrate the shell of the most damaged heart, causing people to feel safe to share their life with us. The world needs to hear a sound of genuine love from caring communities such as the church that gathers others more fully to Christ's love and care!

Time is one of the most precious gifts we can give another person to show we care. The climate of the day can easily be one of rushing and pressure to be somewhere—or someone! These quests may not be wrong in themselves, but when they step over the genuine needs of others to get where they are going, much less is achieved or celebrated overall! Let's destroy the notion that it is weak to show feelings of care, that it's not 'time-efficient' to attend to the needs of another, or that it is not necessary to listen to a broken heart. Care is not a stage we can skip on our quest to fulfil our destiny!

As Christians we are all called to care, to be ministers of the new covenant, and to pastor people. Pastoring, in essence, is like *being a parent*, caring about the welfare of another and ensuring they receive every help they need along the journey of life. Care and value is seen when we respect one another, acknowledge one another's presence, show an interest in another's world and care about the difficulties they may be experiencing. Care is shown in both attitude and action!

Is the sound of care coming from your heart and life? Do people gather because of the expression of care emanating from your life? Today, consider where may you need to slow down in order to take an interest in the wellbeing of another. Remember the sound of God's love and care toward you, and emulate Him!

god's eyes

The lamp of the body is the eye. If therefore your eye is good,
your whole body will be full of light.
Matthew 6:22

Have you ever looked into the eyes of a person and perceived genuine love and care residing in their soul? Have you ever stopped and considered how *God's eyes* constantly behold us with love and mercy, but on a much more magnified, committed and eternal scale than is ever possible on a human level? This verse in Matthew is often rephrased by psychologists as the common expression, "The eyes are the window to the soul." When Peter failed Jesus by strongly denying he knew Him, Jesus looked at Peter with eyes of *love*!

But Peter said, "Man, I do not know what you are saying!"...
And the Lord turned and looked at Peter. Then Peter remembered
the word of the Lord, how He had said to him, "Before the rooster
crows, you will deny Me three times."
Luke 22:60-61

Jesus was in the most desperate season of His life, but Peter lacked the courage and fortitude to stand with Him and acknowledge that he was a follower of Jesus! When the rooster crowed as predicted and he caught Jesus' eyes, his heart fainted with dismay as he realised he had failed Jesus miserably in His hour of need! Was the look from Jesus one of anger, frustration or disappointment? I believe it was none of these. Rather, it was a look of *great love*, a look of sadness and empathy for Peter, who had been unable to rise to the strong conviction he had previously declared. One *knowing look* from Jesus conveying deep understanding and compassion was enough for Peter to fall apart in sorrow and repentance! When we fail to live up to our own convictions or well-meaning intentions, God continues to look at us with love! Jesus is concerned for us as a person when we let ourselves down, knowing the accompanying burden of guilt and shame. A knowing and loving look from Jesus invites us back into His presence where we can stand up once more even though we may feel cast down.

The Lord opens the eyes of the blind;
the Lord raises those who are bowed down.
Psalm 146:8

Another man who caught the look of love in Jesus' eyes was Zacchaeus. He was living alienated from others because of his conniving disposition. Consumed by greed and power, he had become somewhat of an outcast, an unpopular member in his community. Zacchaeus had heard of Jesus and desired to see Him as He passed by that day. Because he was short of stature and unable to see over the crowd, Zacchaeus opted to run ahead and climb a sycamore tree to gain a vantage point. Luke 19:5 tells us when Jesus came to the place, He *looked up* and said, "Zacchaeus, make haste and come down, for today I must stay at your house."

Jesus chose to look up and let Zacchaeus know that He had seen him! In His eyes was a *look of approval*, not for what Zacchaeus had done, but for him as a person! Zacchaeus had fallen well short in his dealings with others, defrauding and cheating them in the collection of taxes. Zacchaeus assumed that wealth, money and power would compensate for his low self-esteem and give him a sense of value along with the importance and status he craved. Nothing could have been further from the truth! Jesus' eyes told Zacchaeus that it was he, as a person, who *mattered*—so much so, that Jesus invited Himself over to his house! This encounter with Jesus changed this man's life for ever. He was so dramatically delivered from his insecurity, that he repaid all the money he had taken fourfold, and gave half of his goods to the poor!

Have you positioned yourself to see Jesus? Do you need to 'run ahead' of all your shortcomings, excuses and misgivings to encounter Jesus and experience Him face to face? Look into His eyes today and see how much He loves and values you, no matter what! Be gathered by His grace, and transformed by His look of love!

keep showing up

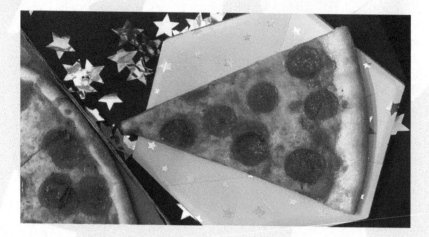

*Let us consider one another in order to stir up love and good
works, not forsaking the assembling of ourselves together.*
Hebrews 10:24

We probably all know what it is like to organise an event only to have people
we expected to be there not show up, sometimes with no explanation.
As a host, this can be really disappointing! We always vow never to be
that person who discourages others by not turning up! It is important to
develop the habit of *showing up* no matter what, unless circumstances are
completely contrary and unavoidable! We need to know how to gather, to
turn up, *show up* and participate in corporate events. Sometimes it is hard
to fulfil all our obligations, but if we have accepted an invitation, we need
to support the host, honouring them with our attendance. I have found that
when I have willed myself to attend an event, even when I have felt tired or
unwell, God has honoured my commitment and these occasions have often
turned out to be significant moments in my life.

Our prayer and devotional life is an invitation from Jesus to meet Him
'one-on-one,' and it is vital that we honour Him by *showing up*. I often
wonder if Jesus is disappointed when we don't show? The disciples knew
how to *show up;* following the directions Jesus left on His departure, they
arrived in the exact place they were instructed to be—gathering, as Jesus
had instructed them, in the upper room. Acts 1:12-14 says,

And when they had entered, they went up into the upper room . . .
(and) continued with one accord in prayer and supplication, with
the women and Mary the mother of Jesus, and with his brothers.

The disciples *showed up* in obedience to Jesus' command to be together, pray, worship, and wait with expectant hearts for the promise of the Father. They actively waited in the upper room until, after many days, the Holy Spirit *showed up* in power, touching them all. From that point on, the disciples would never be the same again! They received far more than they would have ever thought possible.

When the day of Pentecost had fully come,
they were all with one accord in one place. And
suddenly there came a sound from heaven, as of a rushing
mighty wind and it filled the whole house where they were
sitting. Then there appeared to them, divided tongues, as of
fire, and one sat upon each of them. And they were all filled
with the Holy Spirit and began to speak with other
tongues as the Spirit gave them utterance.
Acts 2:1-4

What an experience! Just think what we potentially miss! When we don't show, we may forfeit a significant touch from God, a release of His supernatural power enabling us to reach our world more effectively!

Let's *show up* in other areas of life also — in our marriage, our parenting, our workplace. Let's not be an absent spouse, employee or parent, dishonouring others and letting people down. For the health and wellbeing of ourselves and our loved ones, we need to learn to *show up*, to be present no matter what, and to fully receive the blessings of relationship. Let's not miss out on all God wants to bless us with!

Where in life do you need to improve your attendance? Are you 'showing up' in your relationship with Jesus, your prayer life and your church attendance? Do you have a bad habit of not showing up, thus disappointing God and others? What is causing you to make excuses and rob your availability? Today, commit yourself to keep showing up, positioning yourself before God for His supernatural impartation and blessing.

helen monk

about the author

Born in Wellington, New Zealand, I was raised in the small town of Otaki. My two wonderful parents, Eddie and Dulcie Jorey, ensured that their three girls experienced a fun and adventurous childhood. Our needs were totally taken care of and life growing up was carefree!

In my teens, I fell in love with a handsome young farmer, Bruce; we married in 1970 and together raised a family of four—our beautiful daughter, Rebecca, and our three wonderful sons, Hamish, Samuel and James. We are so grateful for our adult children, our three delightful daughters-in-law and our twelve amazing grandchildren. We are a blessed couple indeed!

Responding to the call of God on our lives, we left our farm in 1977 to take on the leadership of a local church. Over subsequent years we pastored several churches in New Zealand before pioneering and pastoring a church in London, England. God has been so faithful to His call on our lives. With the subsequent planting of many other churches and the raising up of multiple leaders, we have witnessed God multiplying our endeavours well beyond our expectation!

My middle name is Joy, and I have lived with so much joy, even when I have had to process change and difficult seasons! It has been in these times that I have found the whisper of the Holy Spirit and His empowerment, bringing strength to my soul, His revelation guiding me along His path of life and peace. The joy of the Lord is truly my strength and I am grateful for His work in my life. As I have received freely, it is my deep desire to give freely!

To you, dear Reader, I pray that you will be inspired by the many entries in this book, and greatly encouraged to make the necessary shifts and changes in your heart so that you may be better positioned to receive the 'much more' of God's love, power and purpose for your life.

Lightning Source UK Ltd.
Milton Keynes UK
UKHW020209220821
389264UK00003B/7